Limerick Post Office

Memories of Forgotten Times

Frank O'Connor

LIMERICK POST OFFICE

MEMORIES of FORGOTTEN TIMES

Written and Published by Frank O'Connor.

137 Ballinacurra Gardens, Ballinacurra, Limerick, Ireland.

Email: Ballinacurra@eircom.net

Dedicated to the Memory of my Father

Proinsias O'Conchubhair
1922—1974

Irish Defence Force 1939/46, P&T 1946/61, RTE 1961/74

CONTENTS

Abbreviations

AD = Allowance Delivery / Allowance Deliverer.

AGM = Annual General Meeting.

AIPOC = Auxiliary Post Office Clerk.

AIB = Allied Irish Bank.

AIF = Australian Imperial Force.

BO = Branch Office.

BST = British Standard Time.

CBS = Christian Brothers School.

CO = Clerical Officer.

CS = Civil Service.

CWU = Communications Workers' Union.

DOB = Date of Birth.

DPD = Dublin Postal District.

GMT = Greenwich Mean Time.

GPO = General Post Office.

GSWR = Great Southern & Western Railway.

GWR = Great Western Railway.

HO = Head Office.

HPM = Head Post Master

HQ = Head Quarters.

LC = Letter Carrier.

LFO = Letter Forward Office.

LPYMA = Limerick Protestants Young Mens Association.

MO = Medical Officer.

M O = Money Order.

M O O. = Money Order Office.

NAI = National Archives of Ireland.

NDA = Night Duty Allowance.

NE = National Executive.

OPW = Office of Public Works.

PM = Postmaster

PMG = Post Master General.

PO = Post Office.

POC = Post Office Clerk.

POWU = Post Office Workers Union.

PTTI = Postal Telegraph and Telephone International.

P&T = Post and Telegraph.

RIC = Royal Irish Constabulary.

RLB = Return Letter Branch.

RO = Receiving Office.

RTE = Radio Telefis Éireann.

SB = Savings Bank.

SBO = Station Branch Office / Salaried Branch Office.

S CLK = Sorting Clerk.

SC&T = Sorting Clerk and Telegraphist.

SDS = Special Distribution Service.

SE = Saorstát Éireann.

TMO's = Telegram Money Orders

TPO = Travelling Post Office.

TSO = Town Sub Office.

RSO = Railway Sub Office. An RSO was not necessarily on a railway line - e.g. Valencia (island) was a RSO at the turn of the 20th century.

Introduction

For many years I have thought about publishing a book of the history of the Post Office in Limerick and surrounding areas. In this publication I researched as far back as possible; mail delivery in Ireland dates back to 1638.

I started with photographs in mind but that would be only half the story, I would also have to include a little history of how the Post Office was established, especially in Limerick. Nothing really has been documented about the Post Office in this area; the earliest reference I came across was recorded in1653. The first Post Office was established in Limerick near the Widows' Alms Houses in the Nicholas Street area.

With the introduction of mail coaches in 1789, mail deliveries in Britain and Ireland were usually carried by 'post boys' who provided their own horses. Mail was very expensive and had to be collected after a conveyance fee was paid at the post office by the addressee. In 1840 Rowland Hill reformed the postal service by introducing postage stamps so that the sender paid for the postage. He maintained that more people could be encouraged to exchange letters; thereby postal charges could be greatly reduced. From 1855 to 1994, mail was mainly transported by rail on special mail carriages Travelling Post Office (TPO), where postal staff sorted the mail as the train travelled through the night, stopping at stations across the country to collect and deliver mail. In a major modernisation project in 1994, Letter Post shifted to the more flexible road transport system.

This book is a simple but important record of the people who worked in the Limerick Postal area down through the years. We all have some memories, good and bad, some great stories of our colleagues who went before us. I have tried to capture some of these memories in photographs and by publishing this book some of these memories won't be forgotten or lost to the new generation of postal workers in Limerick.

The people I contacted during my research were most helpful, both within An Post, retired members, deceased members' families and members of the public.

My first memory of life in the Post Office is when I received a telegram on Friday 18th July 1975, to report for duty as a postman on Monday morning at 6 am. I got the shock of my life "Who goes to work in the middle of the night"?, Little did I know that I would be a member of the staff for the next 31 years.

With the birth of An Post in January 1984 and especially more recently with the introduction of new computerised mail sorting, Limerick was down graded from being a Letter Forward Office (LFO) to a Delivery Office.

This book would have not been possible without the help of my colleagues at An Post, Limerick and my friends through out the Country, and especially my wife, Breda, my daughter Maryse and her husband Derek Mackessy, my son Tadhg and my grandson Brandon. I would also like to thank my Mother Maura O'Connor, my brothers Raymond, Thomas and Gearoid, my sisters Mary Casey, Kathleen O'Sullivan and Nuala Lowe and my cousin Kathleen Keating.

A special word of thanks to my proof readers, Colm O'Connor, Patrick McNamara, Military Historian, Roseleen Casey and to my sponsors, Permanent TSB Limerick, An Post, G.P.O. Dublin, Communications Workers Union Limerick & Communications Workers Union Dublin, Postal Workers Sport & Recreation Club Limerick Post Office.

Frank O'Connor

Acknowledgements

Jimmy O'Connor. Author of *Aspects of Galway Postal History 1638-1984*.
Stephen Ferguson. GPO Dublin. Limerick Leader. Limerick Chronicle.
Limerick City Library. Limerick County Library. Celine Marsh.
Harry from Georgian House. Joe O'Sullivan, Bresndan Fennell, Joe Collopy.
Christy Bromell & Donal Hayes, CWU Limerick. Tony Cassidy, Ennis.
Chris Cody Paris. Jan O'Sullivan. T.D. Mayor Joe Leddin, Brian Warren, Dublin.
Royal Mail, Heritage Centre London. Stephen Connelly, Galway.
Tony Browne, RLO Radio. Seamus Lawlor, Bennetsbridge, Co. Kilkenny.
GPO Limerick Sorting Office Diary, courtesy Jimmy Harrold. Jim Conway.
Liam Hanley Manager, Letter Office Limerick. Pat Delaney Manager, Galway PO.
Bernard O'Hara, Galway and Mayo Institute of Technology. Kieran Hoare.
National University of Ireland, Galway. John Lennon, Dublin.
Tom Keogh and Larry Walsh Limerick Museum. N.A.I. Dublin.
John Fitzpatrick, OPW Limerick. Sean Real. Ken Kiely. Colm O'Connor.
Paddy Bennis, Margaret O'Shaughnessy, Foynes Flying Boat Museum.
Valerie Ingram, OPW Dublin. Norma O'Connor. Mr. & Mrs. Pat Quilty, Bruff.
Tess Gloster. Mike Hackett, *Postnews*. Mary and Bill Jennings, Newport.
Marie Ryan, Killaloe Post Office. Joan O'Neill, Regional Hospital Limerick.
Philip White. Mrs. Peggy Moloney and Dermot Moloney. Paddy Hayes,
Paddy Mitchell, Dermot O'Brien, Alfie Nolan, Joe Spearin, Finbar Power.
Catherine Ryan. Joe Mangan. John Cotter Tom O'Neill, Manager, Waterford PO.
Patrick and Ann Murphy, Knockaderry Post Office. Bart Cleary,
Elizabeth M. Kirwan. National Library of Ireland. Paddy Carroll.
P.M. Gerry O'Brien, Tom McElligott, Mary Rodgers, Catherine Bourke Area
Office Limerick. Tom Donovan, *Ballybrown Journal*. Mrs. Nuala Quinn.
Mrs. Kathy Bennis. Mr. Fred Hourigan. Joe McGrath Kilmallock.
Paddy Gubbins, Kilmallock. Noreen Lynch, Manager Kilmallock P O.
Mr. & Mrs. Daniel Kelly. Tom McNamara. Gus Corker, New St.
Steve Fitzpatrick, CWU Dublin. Michael Cunningham, Manager GPO Cecil St,
Limerick. Billy Whyte. Imelda Wall, Monica Hempenstall, CWU Dublin.
Pat & Martha Mackessy. Patrick McNamara. Roseleen Casey.
Mrs. Margret Henn. Teresa Kelly, HR Manager RTE Dublin. Des Ryan.
John Quinlivan, Ger Imbusch, Martin Griffin, Tom Williams,
St. John's Cemetery, Limerick.

FOREWORD

Limerick is an Ancient City that was first granted its Charter by King John, back in 1197. It is a City that has a rich and wonderful story to tell because of the many factories, organisations, and local people who contributed over the years to it's history.

One such organisation, which played a very important role in the City's continued development, was the Post Office. At a time when the means of communication between people was considerably less advanced than today, post office telegram boys, were common place on Limerick streets.

During very difficult periods in our City's history when Limerick people were forced to emigrate in search of work, the 'Parcels from America' were a standard feature in the sorting rooms in Limerick.

This is a very informative book detailing the great history of the Post Office in our city. Many Limerick people worked either as telegram boys, postmen, or sorters. Unlike any other organisation in this country, the Post Office has chartered the history of our State through the publication of commemorative stamps.

On a personal level, I am particularly pleased to write this foreword. The Leddin family starting with my grandfather, Jack Leddin, has a long and distinguished record of service with the Post Office, which continues to the present day.

The publication of this book will give people a unique insight into the great stories told by dedicated workers, who were fully committed to the job they did, and to the organisation they served.

Joe Leddin

Major of Limerick

Delivery Office Staff

Post Persons

J Spearin	J Hartigan	John Conway
C Morrissey	W Jackson	E Cussen
G Brien	A Gleeson	J Barron
L Gleeson	A McNamara	P O'Hanrahan
Joe Kiely	K McDonagh	M Tierney
Pat O'Connor	J Mc Elligott	C Tuite
I McNamara	S Real	J Dennehy
K. McNamara	J O'Dwyer	L Hayes
G Clancy	K Horrigan	E Madigan
L O'Donoghue	N Cosgrave	E Hannon
J Hackett	M Long	S Ryan
H Ryan	W O'Connor	J Hayes
B Farragher	E Lowe	Jim Conway
L Hayes	E McMahon	M Kiely
A Murphy	M Tobin	I Guerrini
J Hannon	L Sheehan	P Ryan
G O'Sullivan	M Moore	R O'Flynn
G Cunneen	G Lowe	M Cantillon
N Whyte	P Crean	G Spearin
P Dwane	G O'Connor	E O'Flynn
C Purcell	B Madigan	K Wynne
N Supple	R O' Brien	C O'Connor
E O'Neill	B Meaney	M O'Connor
P Comer	S Meaney	F Barry
P Bennis	K Mc Carthy	D Cosgrave
C Daly	Ger Kiely	P McNamara
ST Griffin	SZ Griffin	L O'Connor
P Barry	D McNally	C Hickey

N Walsh

T Keane

M Harvey

A Curtin

D Hayes

A Kennedy

C Nolan

P McCarthy

D Henn

M O'Leary

G O'Riordan

J Cotter

M Reddan

J Kelly

M Folan

D Crean

S Barry

M Tracy

K Kiely

C. Morrissey

J O'Connell

J. Moloney

M. Tierney

M. O'Connor-Mackessy

R Spearin

H Fleming

D O'Mara

G Cross

C Collopy

M Cadogan

L Butler

A Bennis

G Hanrahan

J O' Byrne

J Ryan

C Cleary

M Mullane

M Neville

C Mc Nally

W O'Brien

B Quilty

P Moran

A Hickey

A. Gleeson

A. O'Connor

D. Blake

H. Ryan

N Kinsella

P Browne

J Madden

N McGowan

K O'Connell

D Leeman

D Kelly

C Stokes

P Vaughan

M Thompson

S Cahill

K O'Dwyer

T O'Brien

C McNamara

M Collins

J Mulcair

D Parker

M Hayes

J O'Neill

J. O'Dwyer

B. Madden

N. Kendall

E. Hannon

Liam Hanley Manager Limerick.

Superintendents	Inspectors	Cleaners
S O'Neill	M Blake	T Kirby
J Harrold	J Dillon	V Kennedy
D. Barry	J Cahillane	J Costello
	P White	N Sheehan

Clerks Letter Office Limerick

Dermot Small - *Manager*

John O'Brien   Paddy Browne

Billy Reeves   Maurice Downey

J.J. Hurley   Christy Bromell

Stan Rogers

Postal Sorters

Sean O'Brien	Brendan Fennell	Noel Ryan
John Manning	Gabriel Hunt	Ray Neville
Martin Sheridan	Adrian Lipper	Cormac Ryan
David Reeves	Dermot Leddin	Anthony Cronin
Michael Murphy	Tom O'Connor	Neil Tobin
Denis O'Flynn	Derek O'Connor	

G.P.O Cecil Street Staff

Michael Cunningham - *Branch Manager*
John Connellan - *Support Manager*
Patrick Rowan - *Support Manager*

Counter Clerks

Pat O'Donoghue   Aidan Curtin
Oliver Naughton   Jim Jackman
Miriam Kerin   Joan O'Flanagan
Roger McMahon   Margaret Conway
John Devine   Tom Murphy
Jonathan Byrne   Patricia Cassidy
Pat O'Brien   Brenda Leslie
Bernadette Leonard   Barry O'Connor
Margaret McCoy   Triona Bresnihan

Area office

Jack Dempsey - *Area Manager*
Mike Reilly - *Operations Manager*
Michael Collins - *Manager*
Adrian Gordon - *Customer Manager*
Tony Corr - *Human Resources Manager*
M. Burke - *Transport Manager*
Tom McElligott - *Change Manager*

Mr. A. Brown   Mr. E. Lenihan
Mr. J. Crowe   Mr. P. Howard
Ms. C. Lenihan   Mr. K. McCarthy
Mr. R. O'Leary   Mrs. M. Rogers
Mrs. C. Treacy   Ms. C. Bourke
Mrs. C. Cunningham   Mr. L. O'Brien
Mr. J. O'Sullivan   Mrs. P. Nealon
Mr. B. Malone   Mr. G. O'Brien
Mr. G. O'Coileain   Mr. S. O'Geoighe

Deputy Postmaster

DUTIES.

THE duty of a deputy postmaster is to receive and dispatch the general and bye mails at their proper hours, and in a secure and safe state ; to check and enter the exact amounts received and forwarded daily ; to furnish to the proper officers in Dublin, monthly returns of his respective accounts of the postage sent to and received by him, the correctness of which he must vouch by affidavit.

He must keep his office in a convenient and central part of the town, and have a place set apart in his house for the letters, &c. to which only he, or his sworn assistant, can have access : and in which he must have a receiver or letter-box for the public, and a proper alphabet for their correspondence. His office must remain open for the receipt and delivery of all letters from eight o'clock A.M. to eleven o'clock P.M. except when he is receiving and dispatching the mails, and then his office is closed merely for the time necessary to enable him to perform this duty with accuracy and dispatch.

He must remit periodically the amount of postage with which he is charged, to the secretary, and find two solvent sureties for the due performance of all duties and trust confided to him or attached to his situation as deputy postmaster.

By Command,

26th July 1823

Edwd S. Lees

TO ALL POSTMASTERS.

GENERAL POST OFFICE,
7th May, 1840.

REFERRING to the Circular of last Month, transmitting Specimens of the Penny and Twopenny Stamped Covers and Envelopes, and of the Penny Adhesive Labels, I now enclose *two Specimens of the Twopenny Adhesive Labels,* which you will preserve with the Specimens already sent to you, for the purpose of comparison with any doubtful Postage Stamps passing through your hands. I also enclose, for your information, two Specimens of the Label Stamp bearing the Letters V. R. at the upper corners, which are to be applied to the correspondence of Public Departments, and other Persons formerly enjoying the privilege of Official Franking. This latter Specimen of the Label Stamp is merely sent to prevent, when it may come into use, any misapprehension arising from the Letters V. R. which are intended to denote that the Stamp is employed for Official Correspondence.

I embrace this opportunity also of stating, it is at present understood that Postmasters and Letter Receivers will be required to sell *the Adhesive Label Stamps,* and the *Stamped Covers,* (but not the Envelopes) under Licence from the Commissioners of Stamps; upon this subject, however, you will receive full Instructions when the issue of Postage Stamps is extended to other Places than London.

By Command,

W. L. MABERLY
SECRETARY.

THE EARLY DAYS

France may perhaps, be considered as being the first nation' that established a regular and systematic method of transferring letters; England, of course, quickly adopted so obviously important an advantage.

The King's letters to his subjects are known to have been carried by relays of couriers as long ago as the 15th century. In 1510, Sir Brian Tuke was appointed as "Master of the King's Post". In 1609 it was decreed that letters could only be carried and delivered by persons authorized by the Postmaster General.

The regular use of the words "Post" and "Litir" in 15th century Irish manuscripts, suggests that by that time a postal system was already in existence here.

Edward VI. (1547-1553) prescribed a certain rate per mile to be charged; for post horses, one penny post was established between London and Edinburgh and also between Chester and Dublin, by way of Holyhead.

In 1635, Thomas Withering, a wealthy London merchant, was appointed Postmaster of England and Foreign parts. He reformed the English system, establishing posts along five main roads from London, served by postboys. For this service he charged a fixed rate of 2d. for a single letter, sent to a destination within 80 miles; 4d. to a destination between 80 and 140 miles; 6d. between 140 miles and the Scottish border; 8d. beyond and 9d. to Ireland. A single letter was a single sheet on which the letter was written, folded on itself with the address on the outside.

Withering was asked to establish a similar system in Ireland. In 1638, he sent Evan Vaughan, a soldier and Royalist, as Deputy Postmaster of Foreign Parts'. By 1653, post stages were established from Dublin to Belfast, Coleraine, Derry, Sligo, Galway, Limerick and Cork. Cromwell, with the aid of Parliament put the management into the hands of government, at this time packets sailed between Dublin and Parkgate or Chester, and between Milford and Waterford.

In June 1657, a Bill was passed "for settling the postage of England, Scotland and Ireland". It established "one General Post Office" for the three countries and fixed more reasonable charges. 1660 saw the establishment of the General Letter Office, this would later become the General Post Office (GPO).

The first director of the Post-office, appointed by government, was John Manley, who was obliged to make uniform charges for the conveyance of letters, at the rate of two pence for 80 miles. A Postmaster General for the British Dominions was appointed in 1711 and a separate establishment opened in Ireland, under the direction of two Postmasters General, in 1784. From this date, the facility of communication through the kingdom has rapidly increased and the number of post towns in Ireland, at which this office advertises to deliver letters, amounts to above 400.

The next feature of importance is the establishment of mail-coaches, a measure fraught with much advantage to the general interests of Ireland. Mail-coaches were first established in England in 1784, in Ireland in 1790. John Anderson, a Scottish immigrant, who set up business in Cork bought part of the Fermoy Estate where he had settled, laid out the town in its present form and was first contracted to run a coach, carrying the mail-bags between Dublin and Cork. He also laid the first five principal roads in the country to carry his coaches and Mr. Grier, between Dublin and Newry. Mail in Britain and Ireland was usually carried by 'post boys' who walked 16 to 18 miles a day, or went on horseback. They provided their own horses. Mail was expensive and had to be collected after a conveyance fee was paid at the post office by the addressee.

The first stone of the G.P.O. O'Connell Street, Dublin, was laid on 12 August 1814. It was the first Irish building specifically designed as a post office. The foundation-stone of this magnificent edifice, which is built after a design of Francis Johnston, Esq., was laid by his Excellency Charles, Earl Whitworth on August 12, 1814, and the structure was completed in the short space of three years, for the moderate sum of £50,000.

The General Post-office was at first in a small building on the site of the Commercial Building, and was afterwards removed to a larger house, opposite the Bank on College-Green and on the 6th January 1818, the new Post Office in Sackville Street was opened. Coaches left the General Post-office every evening at eight o'clock precisely.

The English mail was despatched every morning at seven o'clock, in a mail cart, to Howth-Harbour, whence it was conveyed by government steam-packets to Holyhead. All letters for Scotland and the north of England were sent by way of Donaghadee and Port Patrick, and to the South, by way of Waterford and Milford Haven.

The Penny-Post-office was opened in 1770, and was conducted in an expeditious manner, there being four collections and four deliveries of letters through the city every day, Sunday excepted; in the neighbourhood of Dublin there were two collections and deliveries daily; but for all letters delivered beyond the circular road, there was a charge of two pence postage.

Before the introduction of the uniform Penny Post in 1840 it was very expensive to send letters. However, Members of Parliament and certain State Officials enjoyed a very special privilege by order of the Monarch. They were allowed to send letters free of charge, provided that they signed the front of the letter on the lower left-hand corner. These letters then received a special free hand-stamp.

Under this new arrangement an Irish Secretary was appointed to supervise Ireland's Postal Service and reported directly to the Postmaster General in London until 1831. In 1840 Rowland Hill reformed the postal service by introducing postage stamps so that the sender paid for the postage. He understood that if people could be encouraged to exchange letters, postal charges could be greatly reduced.

After the War of Independence, the post office in Ireland came under Irish administration on April 1st, 1922, post boxes and mail cars were repainted, and the first Irish definitive stamp was issued in December, 1922.

1930

Back Row J. Finn, E. Cotter, T. McInerney, J. Ryan, M. McCarthy, E. O'Brien, E. Lee, T. McMahon, J. Tuhill.
Middle Row E. Mulhall, C. Grimes, C. Bartlett, M. Keane, T. Hughes, T. Heher, C. McCarthy, J. Barry, J. O'Connell, M. Pearse, J. Jackman.
Front Row J. Leddin, J. Power, N. Lynch, M. O'Brien, J. Nash, J. Griffin, B. Hourigan, J. McNamara.

Irish Republican Army, July 1922

1d Brown   2d Green   6d Blue

"An Post Poblacht na h-Éireann" ("Post of the Republic of Ireland"),

Date of Issue: July 1922.

Numbers Issued: The number of sheets originally printed is not known. Most, in any case, were destroyed when the Republicans burned their Cork headquarters prior to withdrawing from that city during the Civil War (August 1922). Most sources estimate that 250 copies of the 1d and 2d values, and 1000 copies of the 6d value, survived the fire.

The Irish Republican Army, which at the time controlled much of southern and western Ireland, and was headquartered in Cork, decided to issue a series of postage stamps. The Republican stamps of 1922 are perhaps the most philatelically legitimate of all the Irish forerunners, in that they were clearly prepared to serve a postal function, and were issued by a competent regional authority. But due to the destruction of most of the printed sheets, only a very few covers bearing these Republican stamps are known of.

1916 Erie Puist Labels

James Connelly

Design: Portrait of James Connelly, framed by shamrock. Inscriptions "ERIE PUIST" (top-bottom), "I. R." (left-right). This is one of eight designs making up the full set. 35 x 44 mm.

Printing: The full set of eight different designs or vignettes was printed se-tenant in sheets 4 x 2; thus, each sheet includes one example of every design. The Connolly label is located third from left in the top row of the sheet. Many commentators have speculated that the labels were printed in America, but there is no documentation to support this.

One of the important socialist thinkers in Edwardian Ireland and a key trade union organiser was James Connolly (1868-1916)

Some commentators have interpreted the misspelling of the Irish Gaelic Éire ("Éire Puist" is "Ireland Post") as an indication that the labels were printed in America, by Republican sympathizers. Dublin also argues for an American origin, but suggests that "ERIE" may not be a misspelling but rather a reference to Fort Erie, captured by the Irish-American Fenians fifty years before in their attempted invasion of Canada. The initials "I. R." presumably stand for "Irish Republic." There is no evidence that they were ever sold.

Dr. Charles Wolf
University of Notre Dame

The First Definitive Series of the Irish Free State 1922

With the creation of the Irish Free State imminent on 6th December 1922, a competition was held to design the first distinctive stamps of the new country. Unfortunately, only the basic 2d rate stamp was ready for issue on the day itself, the other low-value stamps being issued throughout 1923 were as follows:

$^1/_2$d: 20th April 1923 1d:23rd February 1923 1 $^1/_2$d:2nd February 1923

2d: 6th December 1922

2 $^1/_2$d: 7th September 1923 3d:16th March 1923   4d:28th September 1923

5d: 11th May 1923   6d:21st December 1923 9d:26th October 1923

10d: 11th May 1923   1/-:15th June 1923

These designs were extremely successful and formed the basis of the Irish definitive series, virtually unchanged until 1968. The principal variation which occurred over the years was in the watermark: originally the watermark consisted of a script letter "e" with a small "s" contained within the "e", representing "Saorstát Éireann" (Irish Free State), but following the introduction of the new Constitution in December 1937, when the official name of the country became "Éire" (Ireland), the watermark was changed from 1940 onwards to be simply a script letter "e". The $^1/_2$d and 1/- stamps of the definitive series were replaced from 1944 onwards by two stamps initially intended to be commemorating the tercentenary of the death of Bro. Michael O'Cleary and the "Annals of the Four Masters", so the original $^1/_2$d and 1/- stamps with the "e" watermark are quite valuable in unused condition.

Arwel Parry, 1997.

Georges Street, Limerick.

The Crescent - Postman Johnny Griffin with Customer, on left hand side.

UNIFORM PENNY POSTAGE

A PUBLIC MEETING

Of the Bankers, Merchants, and Traders, of the City of London,

Will be held at the

EGYPTIAN HALL OF THE MANSION HOUSE,

ON

Friday, May 31,

AT TWO O'CLOCK PRECISELY,

TO PETITION PARLIAMENT FOR THE ADOPTION OF MR. ROWLAND HILL'S PLAN OF A UNIFORM PENNY POSTAGE,

As recommended by the Select

Committee of the House of Commons.

THE RT. HON. THE LORD MAYOR

WILL TAKE THE CHAIR.

The Metropolitan Members are expected to attend.

PRINTED BY T. BRETTELL, RUPERT STREET, HAYMARKET.

NOTICE.

REPRESENTATIONS having been made to the Postmaster General, that some of the Letter Receivers have refused to Sell *One* Postage Stamp only, when required to do so, and having found from the enquiries I have instituted, such to be the case, I think it right to take this means of informing the Letter Receivers, that they are expected by the Postmaster General to Sell *only One* Postage Stamp (if such is required) as well as in larger quantities.

It has also come to my knowledge that some of the Letter Receivers have affixed Postage Stamps upon Letters that have been *pre-paid*; I think it right to ˙   ate, that *such a practice must not continue*, for as long as it remains optional for the Public to send their Letters under a Postage Stamp, or to pre-pay them, they must be allowed to do so.

When a Letter Receiver may require a fresh supply of Postage Stamps he must make application for them to me, *in writing*, at least Two Days before his Stock on hand is likely to be exhausted; and in every case he must pay up his instalments due for Stamps which have already been supplied to him, before a fresh supply can be sent.

R. SMITH,
Superintending President.

TWO-PENNY POST-OFFICE,
25th August, 1840.

The Penny Black

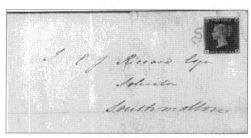

The introduction of the Penny Black stamp played an important role in the reform of the British Postal System during the 1830's. Before this time, postage fees were based on weight and on distance involved. Postage had to be calculated for each letter, and was typically paid by the addressee. The introduction of the Penny Black shifted the cost of postage to the sender and eliminated the complexity of postage computation by requiring a uniform, low rate.

The Penny Red

The Penny Red, issued in 1841, succeeded the Penny Black and continued as the main type of postage stamp in the United Kingdom until 1879, with only minor changes to the design during that time. The colour was changed from black to red because of difficulty in seeing a cancellation mark on the Penny Black; a black cancel was readily visible on a Penny Red.

The Two-penny Blue

One day after the introduction of the 1d black, its sister, the 2d blue was put on sale. 2d blue stamps, both imperforate and perforate, were printed through to 1876 and a similar (but smaller) variety of printings, containing watermarks and perforations can be found on this denomination.

GPO Cecil Street. Circa. 1950

GPO Henry St 1975

GPO Cecil Street. 2005

GPO Cecil Street. 2007

Entrance to Enquirey Office GPO Henry St

Symbol over Door ER Edward VII

Extension to Sorting Office GPO 1980

Sorting Office GPO 2004

Sorting Office GPO 2005

Spiral Stairs GPO Henry St 2004

LETTER BOXES

With the rapid growth of correspondence, following the introduction of uniform penny postage in 1840, a demand for more posting facilities arose and the public began pressing the Post Office to provide roadside posting boxes, similar to those which had been introduced in France sometime previously.

In 1851, Anthony Trollope, the Surveyor, suggested, in a proposal to improve postal services in Jersey (Channel Islands), that the scheme operating in France be tried in St. Helier, Jersey. The proposal was accepted and on 23rd. November, 1852 four boxes were erected. The scheme was a success and in 1855 six boxes were erected in London. Various changes in the design were made in the following years and the first boxes were introduced to Dublin in 1857. In a report to Parliament in 1861, the Postmaster General said that there had been a prejudice in Ireland against roadside boxes. This was "owing apparently to a fear of insecurity but the surveyor now reports that the public protect these boxes and that the prejudice is fast disappearing".

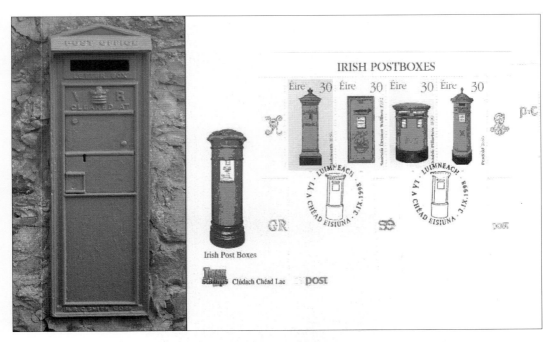

Oldest wallbox in Ireland Parteen, Co. Clare.	*Designer: Creative Inputs, drawings by Michael Craig*	*First Day Cover Envelop Courtesy of Dermot O'Brien*

A Penfold box, hexagonal box, called after the designer J.W. Penfold. They were manufactured by Messer's. Cochrane & Co. of Dudley. There are only Five of this type in the country. These are in Bray, Galway (1866), Kilmacanogue (Wicklow), New Ross and Skibbereen. Complaints about letters being caught up and delayed by faults in the construction of these hexagonal boxes, resulted in a reversion to cylindrical boxes. Some of these new boxes were made 1879 and 1883 and had their aperture very close to the roof, which caused large letters and newspapers to become lodged in the top of the box. The design was therefore amended, in those made between 1884 and 1887 by lowering the aperture a few inches. They were made by Messer's. Handyside and Co. of Derby. Surprisingly it was not until eight years after they were first made, that it was realised that the new cylindrical boxes did not bear the Royal Cypher, or any indication that they were Post Office property. By the end of 1887, a new design with the Royal Cypher VR on the door and the words Post Office on the collar below the rim of the roof had been approved.

Tricycle 1934.

EXTRACT FROM "IRIS AN PHUIST"

TO THE STAFFS

In taking over, on behalf of the Irish people the control of the Irish Post Office, I desire to say that the aim of the new administration is to make the Staff the most contented of staffs, and to make the Service as a whole the most efficient service in Europe. In its dealing with the Staff the administration will be guided solely by the interest of the service, and the extraneous considerations, which have in the past been allowed to influence service decisions will no longer operate.

For the first time, the Irish Staffs are working for an Irish Government; for the first time they are responsible for the providing of an efficient Service, to an Irish Government alone—to the Irish People alone. And, in the providing and maintaining of an efficient service, I feel confident that I can rely upon the whole-hearted co-operation of men and women of all grades.

SEAMUS BREATHNACH

Dated 15th March, 1922

Paddy Mitchel , 1940's.

CHARLES BIANCONI

Carlo Bianconi was born in the village of Tregolo, in the Lombard Highlands, near Lake Como in Italy on September 24th 1786. As he showed no talent at school, his father apprenticed him to Andrea Faroni, an art dealer. In 1801, Faroni, with Bianconi and two other apprentice boys set out on foot over the Alps and across France for Ireland. They arrived in Dublin in the autumn of 1802, where Faroni opened a little shop near Essex Street Bridge.

Soon after having learned a little English, Bianconi was sent down the country. Every Monday morning, with a supply of pictures in his pack and a few pence in his pocket and strict instructions to be back in Dublin the following Saturday night, he set off on foot through Leinster and Munster selling his wares. On one occasion he was arrested in Passage East, Co. Waterford, for selling pictures of Napoleon Bonaparte. He was released the following day. In 1804, his term of apprenticeship to Faroni having expired, Bianconi decided to set up his own print business. He travelled south, towards Thurles and followed the Suir Valley to Carrick where he opened a shop in 1806. The following year he transferred his business to Waterford and in 1809 he moved again, this time to Clonmel where he set up as "carver and gilder of the first class" at No 1 Gladstone Street.

Bianconi had long dwelt on the poor transport facilities in Ireland. Roads were almost non-existent, travel on the waterways was slow, and those who could not afford the stage coach fare simply had to walk. Bianconi decided to set himself to the problem of cheap public transport. The time was favorable; Napoleon's defeat at Waterloo enabled him to purchase horses bred for the army, at the price of from £10 to £20, while hay and oats were correspondingly cheap.

On July 6th 1815 the first Bianconi car ran from Clonmel to Cahir and back - a total of 22 miles. Traveling at 7 Miles per hour, it carried six passengers who were charged one penny farthing a mile. This service was so popular that soon Bianconi decided that his cars should run as far as Tipperary and Limerick. Before long, there were Bianconi cars or "Bians", as they were called, running to Wexford, Waterford, Cork and Kilkenny. Other places wanted Bianconi cars too.

THE ROUTES ESTABLISHED

Clonmel/Limerick 1815
Waterford (10a.m) 1816
Thurles 1815
Ross 1818
Waterford (regulator) 1820
Waterford (telegraph) 1821
Cork 1821
Kilkenny 1821
Tipperary (3oclock) 1828
Tipperary (nightmail) 1828
Dungarvan 1831
Roscrea 1842
Gould's cross 1849

Within the next thirty to forty years a network of communication, of which Clonmel was the centre, was spread over the whole of Ireland. Towns and villages which had never known public transport of any nature, were now linked together. Bianconi's workforce also grew rapidly. He was now hiring drivers, guards, agents and stable-hands besides entering into contracts with suppliers of oats and hay. Bianconi had his own factory where all his coaches were built. At first the coaches were two-wheelers but from 1833 onwards he built mainly "long cars". These had four wheels and some of them could carry up to sixteen to twenty passengers. Coach building and harness making became major industries in Clonmel

Bianconi was not interested in hotels or inns of his own but at Clonmel, Kilkenny, Waterford and other centers, he rented large premises, reserving to himself the outer yards, stables and corn sheds. He sublet the main buildings which he converted into hotels and "eating houses" for his agents. The Clonmel premises consisted of two or three private houses thrown into one, Bianconi's agent in

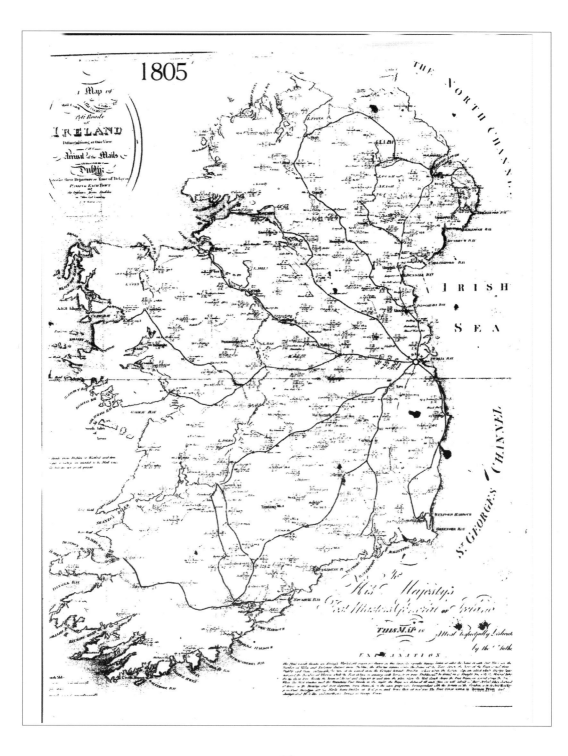

Clonmel was Dan Hearn. By 1845 Bianconi had cars running to all the principal towns in the West of Ireland.

In 1827 Charles Bianconi had married Eliza Hayes, daughter of a wealthy Dublin stockbroker. They had three children, a son Charles who died in 1864 at the age of thirty-one and two daughters, one of whom, Kate, died in 1854. The second, Mary Anne, married Morgan John O'Connell, nephew of Daniel O'Connell.

In 1832, Bianconi secured the lucrative mail carrying contract for the British and Irish post offices. In 1833 he bought a house called "Silver Spring", about a mile from Clonmel on the road to Waterford and Kilkenny. In 1834, the first railway line was opened between Dublin and Dun Laoghaire. Bianconi saw its advent as the beginning of the end of the coaching business. He bought shares in the different lines as they were built and he became a director of the new National Bank, founded by Daniel O'Connell.

1950s
Back Row: P. Patterson, B. Cleary.
F. McNamara, S. Hinchey, T. Byrnes, P. Kiely, J. Power,
Sam Malone

Travelling on Mail Cars

Travelling in those days was an affair very different from what it now is. The journey from Limerick to Dublin, a distance of 120 miles, was a serious undertaking. If you wanted a seat inside the coach, you had to secure it three or four days beforehand; if outside, a day or two before the day on which you meant to travel. The day coach, which carried 17 passengers, four inside and 13 out, nominally performed the journey in 14 hours, but practically took two hours more. The night mail, which was very punctual, did it in 12 hours; it carried only eight passengers, four outside and four in. Of the outside travellers, one sat on the box beside the coachman, and three on the seat behind him. The back of the coach was occupied by the mail-bags and the guard, or guards (there were sometimes

two), who were armed with brass-barrelled blunderbusses and pistols to guard the mails, as the mail-coaches were occasionally attacked and robbed. The coach was comparatively small, and, with people of any size, it was a tight fit to squeeze four into it. As soon as the four unhappy passengers were seated, and had put on their night-caps, the first thing was to arrange their legs so as to incommode each other as little as possible; the next was to settle which of the windows was to be open, and how much of it. This was seldom settled without a good deal of bickering and dispute. The box-seat which was the favourite in the day coach, was least sought for in the mail; can and rightly so, for it was hard to keep awake all night. If you fell asleep, you couldn't lean back - there was nothing to lean on; the box-seat had no back. If you leant to the right, you fell against the coachman, who awoke you with a shove, and requested you would not do that again; if you did it again, he gave you a harder shove, and used some strong language. If you leant to your left, you did it at your peril; the low rail at the side of the seat could not prevent your falling off; it was only about four inches high. How often have I wakened with a start, when I was all but over, resolved to sleep no more? Vain resolution! In 10 minutes I was fast asleep again, again to be awakened with another frightful start; and so on for the greater part of the night. A few years later, when I had constantly to travel by night, I adopted the device of strapping myself to the seat with a strong leather strap.

Seventy years of Irish Life.
By W. R. Le Fanu

THE CUSTOM HOUSE

The Custom House, of which we have given an elegant representation, was begun on the 9th of June, 1765, from a design drawn by Mr. Davis Dukart, engineer. It was completely finished in the year 1769 and cost the Commissioners of his Majesty's revenue near eight thousand pounds In order to prevent the smuggling of goods at the Pool, they also built a Surveyor's house on the North Strand, with four houses for boatmen.

The introduction of a new postal system in the 1840s whereby post was prepaid using stamps, meant that an office was needed in Limerick. Therefore, the Controller was encouraged to move his residence and a Penny Post Office was opened in the Custom House with its entrance onto Rutland Street. Between then and 1870 the balcony and steps were built to grant easy access. In subsequent years the Customs Officers have had to share their space with many Government Departments as well as with a dispensary.

The Custom House which was of the late 1860s was the Limerick GPO before it was moved to Cecil Street. When the change was mooted, the old Deanery in O'Connell Street was selected as the new G.PO. but the price was considered too high. The Deanery was bought by the Munster Bank, and later acquired by the Munster and Lenster Bank.

Photograph Courtesy of Tom Keogh
Coat of Arms from the Post Office in the Custom House

Post Office Rutland Street. 1846

Postmaster. Patrick MacNamara.

The mail from Dublin arrives every morning at thirty-three minutes past eight, bringing the English and Foreign letters, and is dispatched every afternoon at four, taking letters for the following places, viz.-Castleconnell, Newport, Killaloe, Nenagh, Moneygall, Roscrea, Borris-in-Ossory, Montrath, Maryborough, Kildare, Newbridge, Naas and Rathcoole.

The Cork Mail arrives every afternoon at half-past three, and is dispatched every morning at nine, taking letters also for Bruff, Kilmallock, Charleville, Buttevant and Mallow. The Waterford Mail arrives every morning at half-past five, and is dispatched every night at eight, taking letters also for Tipperary, Caher, Cork, Clonmel, Carrick-on- Suir and Pilltown.

The Galway Mail arrives every afternoon at half-past three, and is dispatched every morning at twelve minutes before nine, taking also letters for Bunratty, Sixmilebridge, Newmarket, Ennis, Gort, Ardrahan and Oranmore. The Mail from Clonmel arrives every afternoon at ten minutes before three, and is dispatched every morning at ten, taking also letters for Caherconlish, Pallas, Tipperary and Caher.

The Tralee Mail arrives every afternoon at twenty-five minutes past three, and is dispatched every morning at ten minutes past nine, taking also letters for Patrick's Well, Croom, Ballingarry, Adare, Rathkeale and Newcastle. The Listowel Mail arrives every afternoon at ten minutes past three, and is dispatched every morning at ten minutes past nine, taking letters for Clarina, Pallaskenry, Askeaton, Foynes, Shanagolden, Loughill and Tarbert. The Tulla Mail arrives every afternoon at half-past three, and is dispatched every morning at ten minutes past nine, taking letters also for Broadford. *The Office is open from half-past five in the morning till eight in the evening.*

Slater's Directory 1846

Mr William Roche of 96 George's Street Limerick.

Roches Hanging Gardens.

William Roche MP was a member of the Limerick banking family who established Roche's LIMERICK BANK in 1801 at Charlotte Quay which moved to 96 George's Street in 1804.

William Roche MP, a Catholic, represented Limerick at three Parliaments until his retirement from politics in July 1841. He was the first Roman Catholic to be appointed to the commission of the peace in Ireland. At a public meeting in Limerick, Daniel O'Connell said that "William Roche was the only man in Ireland from whom he would not demand a pledge." William Roche was a Life Commissioner of St. Michael's Parish Commissioners and an active member of the Limerick Literary Institution. He died, unmarried, in April 1850. His brother, Tom Roche and his nephew William Roche later became founder members of the Limerick Athenaeum.

"Though Limerick possesses so few places of public resort, yet it contains a curiosity, we believe, unique in the British empire, the offspring of the refined taste and singular ingenuity of a wealthy and respected private gentleman. In 1808, William Roche, Esq. being much occupied by the care of an extensive banking concern, devised a plan for his personal recreation, to obviate the necessity of occasional absence from his residence. He accordingly took some ground at the rear of his house in George's Street, and having raised a number of arches, converted the interior of them into stores for holding wine, spirits and other goods. The height of the arches is varied; the top of the two side ones being nearly forty foot from the street, and that of the middle arches twenty-five. On these he formed elevated terraces, the highest of which is ornamented with forcing or hothouses, heated by glass and flues. These hot houses produce grapes, pine-apples, peaches, others are orangeries and conservatories, and the hot houses are united in the angles by globular greenhouses. The middle terrace is devoted to vegetables and hardy fruit trees; the lower to flowers of every form, scent, and hue. A vacant space in the garden, also raised on arches is appropriated to forcing melons, cucumbers, etc. Flights of steps lead from one elevation to another, and the whole occupies more than an English acre of ground: the side terraces are one hundred and fifty feet long by thirty wide; the central terrace one hundred and eighty feet long by forty wide; and the lower two hundred feet long by one hundred feet wide. The façade of the building extends opposite the houses of the earl of Limerick and the Bishop, for about two hundred feet. The top of the highest terrace walls is seventy feet above the subjacent street, and commands a most extensive prospect of the city, and the windings of the Shannon, with the gentleman's villas on either shore spreading for a considerable distance. Several of our Irish Viceroys and other illustrious strangers have visited this singularly interesting curiosity existing in the centre of a large commercial city, and all have departed impressed with admiration of the taste and ingenuity of the worthy and intelligent contriver. Mr. Rollins description of the celebrated Hanging Gardens of Babylon exhibits a striking similarity to those (though on a larger scale) which we have attempted to delineate ...."

Rev. P. Fitzgerald and J.J. McGregor, the History, Topography and Antiquities of the Country and City of Limerick with a preliminary view of the History and Antiquities of Ireland, 1827, Vol 2, pages 614-617.

Post Office. Henry St. / Cecil St.

Wall on Henry Street: Originally part of Roche's Hanging Gardens. Existing walls of brick and rough stone formed part of the vaulting in which Roche stored mercantile produce, and supported the rows of terraces forming the gardens above.

Victorian: Red brick block on corner of Henry Street and Cecil Street. Cecil street façade contains a dramatic first floor Oriel window. Entrance (used by St Michael's Temperance Society) retains tile flooring and half-turn stair with landing. Some exterior brickwork patterns.

Edwardian: Red brick symmetrical block built in 1903 in a Neo-Baroque style including a pair of Diocletian windows in the gable ends and rusticated pilasters and curved pediment above the central entrance.

Branch building: Mid twentieth century Modernist structure. Ground floor street façade clad in black faience tiles topped with large canopy and large plate glass windows above lighting 'Banking Hall' behind.

Archway: Consisting of a brick arch inset into a classical stone pediment. Similar materials to and possibly contemporary with Wall on Henry Street, mentioned above.

Extant parts of **Roche's Hanging Gardens,** and a good example of Neo-Baroque mercantile architecture in the Georgian Newtown Pery. Branch building is a good example of early Modernist architecture, which succeeded in both its form and function.

Hanging Gardens in existence c. 1808, and acquired and re-developed by Post Office in 1885.

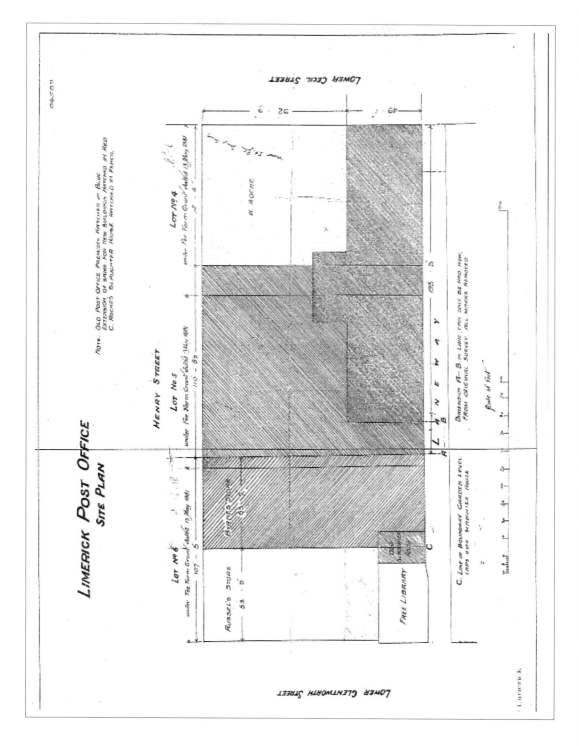

POSTMASTERS IN LIMERICK SINCE 1659

Name	Date of Present Appointment
Butterton R	1659
Wilkins R	1677 and 1682
Vincent E.	1769 to 1786 Nicholas St.
Bernard E.	1824
MacNamara P.	1838 to 1840 Ellen St.
MacNamara P.	1846 to 1856 Rutland St.
McNamara J.T.	1867
McNamara J.	1870 Rutland St.
McNamara J.	1875 Cecil St.
Conway M.J.	1877
Conway M.E.	1879/80
Hurley M.	1880
Conway M.J.	1884
Conway M.E.	1886
Downey T	17 May 1892 to 1902
Spraggon TH	9 December 1902 to 1907
Wright R W	17 September 1907 to 1911
Guerin M	9 May 1911 to 1920
Cleggett P	28 July 1920 to 1923
Twoomey J	1924 - 1925
Daly. T. A.	25 March 1936 to 16 October 1945
Timoney. P.J.	1 January 1946 to 1 January 1952
O'Neill E. J.	20 February 1952 to 8 April 1954
Lynch. P.	12 May 1954 to 17 January 1962
Naughton. P.	21 March 1962 to 1 January 1964
Haughey. T.	1 January 1964 to 15August 1976
O'Neill. D.	1977 to 31 March 1980
Lavelle. S.	1981 to 28 January 1984

Marnane. W. F.	1984 to 1986
Mularkey. S.	1986to 1989
Real. J.	1989 to 1992
Hourigan. F.	1992 to 1996
Carroll. P. (Acted Head Postmaster)	1996 to 30 November 2000

Exham, Vincent. Postmaster

Common Council burgess from 1757

Mon 14/08/1786: Died last Monday at Castletown Roche in the county of Cork, Greatly regretted by her friends and acquaintance, Mrs Vincent, wife of Exham Vincent late of Parteen in the county of Clare.

Subscriber to Ferrars History

Walsh, Philip BSNS Distributor of Stamps

Post Office, Nicholas St, 1788.

27/01/1785: Mayor acknowledges receipt of 41fines levied on printers for printing two unstamped papers 13/07/1786: Mr Hill acknowledges the receipt of two pounds sterling from Mr Philip Walsh, stamp officer, for the use of the House of Industry, being part of two fines he received for unstamped newspapers.

28/09/1786: Stamp Office, Limerick 25th September 1786. The Public are requested to take notice that in pursuance of the orders received from the commissioners for managing his majesty's stamp duties, I am determined to put the law in force against every person "Who shall buy or sell, or have or keep in his, her or their possession, any unstamped news papers," and also against every printer who shall print or publish the same. Philip Walsh, distributor of stamps. NB The penalty for buying or keeping in possession any unstamped news papers is five pounds.

Alms Houses, Corporation Widows Corporation Almshouse Nicholas St,

1838; 1870; 1906

Erected soon after siege of Limerick on ground where St Nicholas Church formerly stood, in Old Post Office Lane. Twenty widows have apartments in this house, with the use of a garden and 40s, a year.

Limerick Museum

A Postmaster's Lament

Now the junior staff had mentioned and at times I thought it too,
When you occupy the PM's chair you have little then to do.
But I've altered my opinion and completely changed my mind—
Since I've hit the masters' cushion now this is what I find...

You need a lot of patience and you need a little grit—
You need a lot of tolerance and a little bit of wit;
You need some perseverance and quite a bit of skill—
Whilst accuracy's important, and a "must" a sturdy will.

You need some understanding and be merciful as well,
But at times you must use power and be as strict as hell.
A memory like an elephant and a hide as tough as teak
And nerves as calm as millponds and a head that's just as weak.

At times as hard as tungsten and sometimes soft as down—
Though still maintain composure and smile when you could frown.
Suppress impending trouble, handle problems by the score
And then come up still smiling and look around for more.

You need a lot of wisdom and at times be very kind
Yet both real finely balanced or often you will find—
This is seen as signs of weakness and forces start to roll
To undermine authority and weaken your control.

You'll need to work for peanuts and p'raps a ten hour day
Eighty minutes to the hour with no increase in pay;
Persevere with staff not trying, handle those not worth a feed
And compliment the good ones—they're a most uncommon breed.

You'll need to be efficient and cover plenty ground,
And your framework strong and healthy and your constitution sound.
At times you'll feel like quitting for something not so rough,
But the challenge keeps you going then you're glad it's been so tough.

You'll need a sense of humour though at times could almost cry
And wonder if you'll make it, but you seem to just get by.
You'll need to know your workmates and just what makes them tick,
And if they're feeling happy or if they're feeling sick.

You'll need some dedication, love your job if people ask;
Love your office and it's duties, love your very complex task.
You must be diplomatic, conscientious, loyal and true—
If you don't possess these qualities—no PM's job for you.

R. L. GROS, Wollongong East.
Courtesy Australian Postmasters' Association.
The Postal Worker February 1974

Yard at GPO Henry St 2004

William Monsell, Postmaster General. 1871-1873

William Monsell - of Irish Protestant stock, Unionist by conviction, English by education (Winchester and Oxford) - sat as M.P. for Co. Limerick from 1847 to 1874; he held high office in the Liberal government (Paymaster General), and retired as Baron Emly of Tervoe. Under the influence of Cardinal John Henry Newman, he became a Catholic in 1850.

Born 21st Sept., 1812; died at Tervoe, Co. Limerick, Ireland, 20th April, 1894. His father was William Monsell of Tervoe; his mother, Olivia, daughter of Sir John Walsh of Ballykilcavan County Laois, and grandson of William Thomas (1754—1836). He was educated at Winchester (1826-1830) and Oriel College, Oxford, but he left the university without proceeding to a degree. As his father had died in 1822 he succeeded to the family estates on coming of age and was a popular landlord, the more so as he was resident. In 1836 he married Anna Maria Quin, daughter of the second Earl of Dunraven, but there was no issue of the marriage. After her death in 1855 he married Bertha, youngest daughter the Comte de Martigny (1857), by whom he had one son and one daughter. In 1847 he was returned to Parliament as a member for the County of Limerick in the Liberal interest and represented the constituency till 1874. In 1850 he became a Catholic and thereafter took a prominent part in Catholic affairs, especially in Parliament. As a friend of Archbishop Nicholas Wiseman, John Henry Newman, Comte de Montalambert, W.G. Ward, Bishop Felix Antoine Philibert Dupanloup and other eminent Catholics, he was intimately acquainted with the various interests of the Church, and his parliamentary advocacy was often of great advantage to the hierarchy. In the House itself he was successful and filled many offices. He was clerk of the ordnance from 1852 to 1857; was appointed privy councillor in 1855; was vice-president of the board of trade in 1866; under-secretary for the colonies, 1868-1870; postmaster-general, Jan., 1871, to Nov., 1873. Finally he was raised to the peerage as Baron Emly on 12th Jan., 1874. He lost much of his popularity in Ireland during his later years, owing to his opposition to the land league and to the Home Rule movement. His work being chiefly parliamentary, he wrote little, but published some articles in the "Home and Foreign Review" and a "Lecture on the Roman Question" (1860).

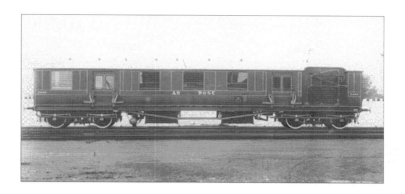

TRAVELLING POST OFFICES (TPO)

From 1855 to 1994, mail was transported by rail on special mail carriages, where postal staff sorted the mail as the train travelled through the night, stopping at stations across the country. In a major modernisation project in 1994, Letter Post shifted to the more flexible road transport and also opened a state of the art automated sorting facility, the Dublin Mails Centre.

Travelling Post Offices (T.P.O.s) were first introduced in 1838 on the London Birmingham line. A carriage on the train was specially fitted where letters were sorted for the various towns en route. The first T.P.O. to run in Ireland was on January 1st. 1855 on the Dublin Cork route. These T.P.O.s provided much needed relief to the Dublin Sorting Office and accelerated the mails. The earlier carriages had apparatus attached, which enabled it to despatch and pick up mail bags from special standards at railway stations, while the train was running at full speed. In 1909, this apparatus was in use at Clonsilla, Leixlip, Maynooth,

Kilcock, Enfield, Moyvalley, Hill of Down, Killucan, Castletown Geoghegan, Moate and Oranmore. A Postman at Oranmore was paid an allowance of ls.6d. a week to operate it and 15s.0d. a year to have it cleaned. By 1928 apparatus working had ceased.

Staffing was generally provided from Dublin. Additional allowances of 3s.0d. 3s.6d. and 4s.0d. were paid for trips of 9 hours, 10 hours and 12 hours duration respectively. It operated on the Down Night, Up Night, Down Day and Up Day trains. Since January 4th. 1943 the Down Day mail is walk sorted into the various delivery routes when it arrives in Limerick.

During the 1939-1945 Emergency, the trains were suspended for periods, which in turn affected the carriage of mails. The Up day mail was ceased from July to October 1941. The night mail was suspended from October 1941 and the day mail from April 1944. The day mail resumed on July 1945 and the night mail on November 4th. 1946. The day mail was again suspended on January 20th. 1947 and restored on May 31st.1948. The night mail from Dublin ran to Athlone only from January 20th 1947 and was not extended to until May 1948, C.I.E. provided a special lorry service during these periods to convey mails.

NIGHT MAIL

By W.H.Auden.

This is the Night Mail crossing the border,
Bringing the cheque and the postal order.
Letters for the rich, letters for the poor,
The shop at the corner, the girl next door.
Pulling up Beattock, a steady climb,
The gradient against her but she's on time
Past cotton grass and moorland border,
Shovelling white steam over her shoulder.
Snorting noisily, she passes
Silent miles of windswept grasses.
Birds turn their heads as she approaches,
Stare from bushes at her blank—faced coaches
Sheep—dogs cannot turn her course;
They slumber on with paws across.
In the farm she passes no one wakes,
But a jug in a bedroom gently shakes.

2

Dawn freshens. Her climb is done.
Down towards Glasgow she descends,
Towards the steam tugs yelping down a glade of cranes,
Towards the fields of apparatus, the furnaces,
Set on the dark plain like gigantic chessmen.
All Scotland waits for her:
In dark glens, beside pale green lochs,
Men long for news.

3

Letters of thanks, letters from banks,

Letters of joy from girl and boy,

Receipted bills and invitations,

To inspect new stock or to visit relations,

And applications for situations,

And timid lovers declarations,

And gossip, gossip from all the nations,

News circumstantial, news financial,

Letters with holiday snaps to enlarge in,

Letters with faces scrawled on the margin,

Letters from uncles, cousins and aunts,

Letters to Scotland from the South of France,

Letters of condolence to Highlands and Lowlands,

Written on paper of every hue,

The pink, the violet, the white and the blue,

The chatty, the catty, the boring, the adoring,

The cold and official and the hearts outpouring,

Clever, stupid, short and long,

The typed and the printed and the spelt all wrong.

4

Thousands are still asleep,

Dreaming of terrifying monsters,

Or a friendly tea beside the band in Cranston's or Crawford's:

Asleep in working Glasgow, asleep in well set Edinburgh

Asleep in Granite Aberdeen,

They continue their dreams,

But shall wake soon and hope for letters,

And none will hear the postman's knock.

Night Mail Trains

Prior to 22nd April 1918 Sorting Carriages were attached to the Night Mail trains between Limerick and Limerick Junction and between Waterford and Limerick Junction. In addition to the Indoor Staff a Postman travelled in each Carriage and the transfer of the mails at Limerick Junction between the main line trains and the branch trains was carried out by these officers.

As from the 22nd April 1918, in connection with alterations in Railway services, the TPO service ceased and it became necessary for a postman from Limerick and one from Tipperary to travel by the Night Mail trains to Limerick Junction to perform the transfer work. The man returned to their Headquarters by the Inward Night Mail trains but the train for Waterford was made a "goods" as from the date mentioned and, there being no other suitable means of locomotion available, the Tipperary Postman had to make the return journey on that train.

The Great Southern & Western Railway Company applied to the Department (on the 19th April 1918, file III) for an Indemnity in respect of the Postman's journey by "goods" train, and the matter was referred to the Secretary, London (12th June 1918) who agreed that an Indemnity should be given somewhat on the lines of one included in the contract with the Great Western Railway. The Great Southern & Western Railway Company would not, however, accept an Indemnity in the form proposed by the Department and a prolonged correspondence ensued. In a letter dated 5th November 1918 the Company definitely repudiated liability in respect of the Postman, while still allowing him to travel and the Secretary, London, agreed (9 July 1919) that matters might be left as they were, the alternative being to give an unqualified Indemnity.

The services of the Postman from Limerick were discontinued in August 1920 but, except for interruption due to the suspension of the Night Mail trains, the arrangement whereby a Postman from Tipperary travels to Limerick Junction for transfer purposes and return to his Headquarters by Mail Goods has continued up to the present and until the 3rd October last there was no further reference by the Railway Company to the question of an Indemnity.

Following the restoration of the Night Mails Trains (as from 28/8/1923) the Company was asked (8/9/1923) to attach to the Up Night Mails Train from Waterford a Sorting Carriage formerly employed on that train for the more conveyance of the Mails – in view of the heavy transfer at Limerick Junction – and it was in reply to this request that the fresh demand for an Indemnity was put forward. The Company intimated, on the 6th November, that the Carriage was ready for use but it has not yet been put on the provision of the carriage would facilitate the transfer work but it is not essential.

The question of providing for the transfer of the Mails at Limerick Junction by a Postman from that Office was considered in 1918 and 1919 (file III) and found impracticable. The Postmaster, Tipperary, was recently asked to reconsider this aspect of the case and he reported strongly (2nd and 12th November) against such a proposal, the chief objections being:-

(1) It would be necessary to convert an Auxiliary post at Limerick Junction into an established situation and the Postman who would become redundant at Tipperary could not be economically provided for at that Office, and he does not desire a transfer.

(2) The proposal would involve an awkward Night attendance for inward Night Mails Station Service at Tipperary (train time 1:15am). It would not be desirable, at present, to arrange for the retention of the Mails at the Railway Station at 1:15am. The retention of the Mails at the Station would also involve awkward indoor attendances and it would retard the commencement of the Town and Rural deliveries.

(3) While the existing arrangements are regarded as more satisfactory, the alternative under consideration, if practicable, would not involve any reduction in expenditure.

Post Office Memo

7th January 1924.

Daniel Kelly

Date of Birth

24-2-1880

Leaner unpaid 11-11-97 to7-12-97

Acting Leaner Paid 8-12-97 to 18-4-99

Sorting Clerk & Telegraphist 19-4-99

Resigned for purpose of joining the Royal Engineers

under conditions laid down in PO Circular

Returned on 10-6-1909

He also served in 1914/1918 War

Died in PO Service in 1937 aged 57

Limerick Post Office Annual Reunion Cruises Hotel 1941

Paddy Carroll

Telegram boy / Head Postmaster.

I attended school at C. B. S. Sexton St. where I shared classes with Paddy O'Brien. He told me about the exams for telegram boy in the P.O. and with his encouragement I did the exam in May 1956. We were both successful and we started in August, 1956.

It was a dream job for a sixteen and a half year old who was already interested in cycling and I enjoyed the job and the company for nearly three years. For the last year 1958/59 I was upgraded to postman to fill a vacancy and I found the job demanding and more physical than the telegram delivery duties. I spent one Christmas as a postman and it was a gruelling slog up at 4 am and not getting back to bed until twelve midnight. This operated up to Christmas Eve by which time I was only fit to sleep during the Christmas.

In 1959 the same Paddy O'Brien brought the upcoming clerks exam to my attention. We studied in Paddy's house in Chapel Street for about one hour per night and then we went chasing for two hours.

Thanks to Paddy's lessons we were both successful. We were sent to Kilkenny for training, we learned Morse for a while but then it was discontinued and then we started to learn the Teleprinter. We also were given practice at the counter where we were trained by Miss Frizzel. *"Don't smile at the customers and don't get into conversation, just keep the lines moving quickly"*. Customer care was not encouraged in those days.

I spent a month in Drogheda and then I was transferred to Portlaoise and about six months later I was moved to Thurles. While I was there I became engaged to

Rose with whom I had kept in touch and we were married in 1961. I was transferred back to Limerick in July 1962 and never left again.

In the following years I was appointed overseer in 1980, four years later I was appointed superintendent II. In 1992 I was appointed superintendent 1. Fred Hourigan became head postmaster in 1992 and retired in 1996 when I took over from him.

These times were times of great change and it was a very interesting time to manage the office. I was very fortunate to have been able to learn from Fred and before him Jim Rael, Bill Marnane, and of course Bernie Flannery. The staff in the head office and indeed the 93 sub offices were almost to a man diligent and pleasant to work with and I can safely say, that apart from delivering telegrams as a teenager it was a most satisfying time, as also was my time as superintendent and head postmaster.

The very same fair minded union representatives, with whom I dealt G. Leddin, J. Lyons, D. O'Brien, and G. Nolan, in particular also contributed hugely to a period of about seven years during which no section of staff lost wages through any dispute. I take great satisfaction from this. During this time my friend Paddy O'Brien became a surveyor in Dublin and then manager of counters.

I retired on the 30th of November 2000. As the Head Postmaster grade was abolished on the 21st of October 2000, I claim to be the last man to perform the role of Head Postmaster in Limerick.

Paddy Carroll HPM.

Liam Hanley

I joined the Dept of Posts and Telegraphs as a Post Office Clerk in 1964 having competed for the position through the open Civil Service Examinations.

After training in Cavan I spent short spells in Listowel and Kilmallock before arriving on appointment to Limerick in 1966— and there I have remained to this day having progressed through promotions from POCB to POCA to Overseer, Superintendent 11, Superintendent 1 and Delivery Services Manager for Limerick City in 2000.

Indeed I can claim to be the first Delivery Services Manager for Limerick City & Environs, as the old positions of Headpostmasters and their related districts were abolished some time earlier to allow for the introduction of three separately run business units operating within the Company, An Post, under the Area Office system.

That indeed was but one of the many changes I have seen and taken part in during my almost now 43 years with the Company.

In 1964 Telex and Teleprinter (the new inventions of the late 40's and 50's) and Telephones had taken over from Morse code and were the ultra modern communication systems used by the Post Office for transmitting Intemational and national telegrams. Telegrams! Do you remember Telegrams! Phonograms! Of course the use of those systems began to wane from the 1980's onward with the rapid development of new technologies such as computers, PC'S (The Internet and e-mail) and mobile phones etc. Amazingly all these are with us now —just as if they had always been there.

In 1984 the Dept of Posts and Telegraphs was taken from under the Government's wing and split into two Semi-state bodies — An Post and Telecom Éireann. Telecom Éireann was formerly known as the Engineering Branch of the Dept of P & T. This separation heralded huge changes, as both sections had to set up their own separate Companies under Chief Executives and Boards etc.

Our own Company, embarked on big change in the 1990s and with the arrival of Counter Automation, our Post Office counter services were revolutionised — for the customers and ourselves. Gone were the days of the long hours balancing, the long tots and manual calculations etc.

Likewise the computerization of the wages/payroll system made life so much easier for all of us from an accounting point of view.

On the mail's side the Company went from Rail to Road in 1993 and the famous 2 Deliveries ceased. Prior to this, the bulk of internal mail vouching was carried on through the Rail networks. People will remember the TPOs — Travelling Post (sorting) Offices. Mails were sorted on the trains and despatches were made to many offices throughout the country from that source. Needless to say, that system is now defunct and the most recent changes are even more staggering than people would have imagined in those times — 4 main Automated Sorting Hubs in Dublin, Portlaoise, Cork and Athlone, with a capacity to sort the major portion of all mails produced in this country plus incoming International mails as well - are now in full operation. Naturally this has had, and will have, massive implications for staff, staffing and the related old Despatching, Collecting and Delivering systems, right into the future.

As I write, further changes are imminent. From enjoying the once proud position of being the major processor and Deliverer of mails in the Mid West, Limerick (and Galway and Waterford in their respective areas) will become just another Delivery Office — albeit one of the biggest such offices in the country. It is sad to see, but that's progress.

Currently governed by a Regulator who decides the price of our stamps, we face into full open competition very shortly. Regulator or no regulator, and even in the teeth of open competition, I would be hopeful that a newer, stronger and more vibrant Post Office — as everyone still calls it — will emerge for the future, continuing it's proud tradition of dedicated (possibly unequalled in it's own right) public service to all the people of Ireland.

Liam Hanley

Jack Hourigan Limerick man
who had served in the First World War.

My father was in South Africa during the Boer War. He was a colour-sergeant in the Munster Fusiliers. He spent 22yrs in the army and retired with a pension.

Jack as a Postman, had spent most of his working life at the GPO Limerick.

This is his story.

I went down to the Strand Barracks ,towards the end of 1917, to enlist in the horse drawn field artillery. They told me that it was more or less obsolete, but they were recruiting for the heavy artillery , although there were some heavy guns 4.7s still pulled by horses They (the British army) had nothing (artillery)when it started only the 18 pounder field guns which fired a small shell they were being beaten in that war until the Yanks (the American army) came with tanks. Only for the Yank' they would have lost the war. They were good soldiers. I was stationed in northern France near Lille, at a place called Tourcoin. I was also in Roubaix and Montecat.

When you fired a 6 inch or 9 inch , or an 18 inch Howitzer it would recoil and I would have to set it again. After a while you got to know every twist of those guns. There were ten or twelve men on a gun, in what was known as a gun –bay. Each man had a different job, the shells were heavy and had to be carted over on a tray and put into the gun. An officer took the readings and called them out to another man who had a clinometer (for measuring height). Another set the readings. You waited for the instructions to fire. The guns were camouflaged but you had to watch out for German planes. If we saw a plane passing over we would all go under cover or else they would signal back to their own artillery to shell such and such a place.

The soldiers at the front, in the trenches, the Munster's and all those other regiments, had it tough. I saw the trenches. They were horrible. I don t know how men survived them. In the winter they were water-logged. We were safe enough in the rear as we were never water logged. The guns had to be on solid ground. You couldn't have them in swampy places. I was home from France and I remember meeting a Dublin Fusilier, who was muddy from the trench - he had just come off of the boat. He said he was going on holidays. He wasn't showing off or anything with all that mud on him. Before coming home we had to be fumigated and our clothes cleaned.

Other memories that I have are that we had tons of jam-it was a waste. At Tourcoin we saw the kids going to school in the morning. There was one young lad whom I saw there and I used give him bread and jam from our rations from the cook house. In 1920 that little boy wrote a letter to thank me-I still have it. Another time I had to bring 10 or 12 German pensioners of war back behind the lines. I didn't know where we were going but one of the Germans spoke French and he enquired as we went along.

I remember one day we weren't firing and we didn't know what was going on but we suspected something was happening. Then a Frenchman came along and was shouting at the top of his voice "La guerre finie - La guerre finie" (the war is over). That was the first we heard of it, and that was on the 11th of November 1918. When I came home I had a lot of keepsakes and souvenirs. I have only a few of them now.

Des Ryan, Historian.

World War I - Button from Postman's uniform, 1914.

Limerick Post Offices

Irish Name 1	Irish Name 2	Post town	Open Date	Close Date	Specialities
Mainistir na Féile		Abbeyfeale	1784		Newcastle
Áth Dare		Adare	1811		also: Adair
Gleann na gCreabhar		Anglesborough, Kilmallock	1873 – 1874		From Mallow to Kilmallock 1966
Ardach	Ardachadh	Ardagh, Limerick	1851		
Ard Pádraig		Ardpatrick, Kilmallock	1881 – 1882	2003	
		Ashford, Charleville	1859	1895	
Eas Géitine	Eas Géiphtine	Askeaton	1814		also: Askeyton
Áth an tSéibhe	Baile Átha an tSléibhe	Athea, Limerick	1853		
An tÁth Leacach	Áth Leacach	Athlacca, Kilmallock	1857 – 1859		
Sráid Átha an Longphuirt		Athlunkard Street, (Limerick)	1896 – 1899	1945	
An Bealach	Bealach	Ballagh, Limerick	by 1895		Charleville in COR
Baile na Corra		Ballinacurra, (Limerick)	1937 - 1950	22.09.1962	(resignation of postmaster), see New Street
Baile an Gharraí	Baile an Gharrdha	Ballingarry, Rathkeale	1815		
Balie an Gharráin	Baile an Ghráin	Ballingrane, Askeaton	1870 - 1871	10.02.1990	
Stáisiún Baile an Gháin		Ballingrane Station, (Ballingrane)	1905 - 1914	by 1959	
		Ballinleeny, Kilmallock	1857 - 1859	1909 -1914	
Béal Átha Grean		Ballyagran, Kilmallock	1875 - 1877		
		Ballybrood, Pallasgreen	1857 - 1859	1861 -1863	
Baile Dhá Thuile	Déal Átha Dhá Thuille	Ballyhahill, Loughill	1877 - 1879		Limerick
Baile hAodha		Ballyhigh, Charleville	by 1895	1915 -1918	PT in Cork
Baile an Londraigh		Ballylanders, Kilmallock	1856		
Baile Uí Neachtain Beag		Ballynantybeg, (Limerick)	01.06.1957		
Baile an Fhaoitigh		Ballyneety, Limerick	1852 - 1857		01.07.1863/01.01.1864 - 1881/82
Baile Uí Argáin	Balie Argáin	Ballorgan, Kilmallock	1885 - 1887	17.06.1989	
Béal Átha Síomoinn		Ballysimon (Limerick)	1873 - 1874	17.02.1964	(resignation of postmaster)

Irish Name 1	Irish Name 2	Post town	Open Date	Close Date	Specialities
Baile Stiabhna		Ballysteen, Askeaton	1885 - 1887		
Bánóg		Banogue, Kilmallock		1879 -1880	15.07.1967
Bearna		Barna, Pallasgreen	1852 - 1857	1901 -1905	
Barr i gCuan		Barrigone, Askeaton	1859 - 1860	31.07.1965	(resignation of postmaster)
Droichead Barrington		Barrington's Bridge, Lisnagry	06.11.1833	1925	Limerick
Sráid an Droichid		Bridge Street, (Limerick)	08.05.1943		Limerick
An Briotás		Brittas, Pallasgreen	17.12.1887		
Béal an Átha	Baile an Átha	Broadford, Ráth Luirc	1870 - 1871		PT in COR
Sráid Leathan		Broad Street, (Limerick)	08.12.1930	10.05.1970	replaced by Garryowen
An Brú	Brugh na nDéise	Bruff, Kilmallock	1800		
Brú Rí	Brugh Ríogh	Bruree, Kilmallock	1848		also: Buree
Buílgidín	Béalgadán	Bulgaden, Kilmallock	1883 - 1885		
Cathair Chinn Lis		Caherconlish, Pallasgreen	1822		Limerick, also: Cahirconlish
Cathair Dháibhín	Cathair Daibhin	Caherdavin, (Limerick)	01.04.1933		also: Cahirdavin
Cathair Aili	Cathair Ailigh	Caherelly, Kilmallock	1885 - 1887	2003	
An Cheapach Mhór	Ceapach Mhór	Cappamore, Limerick	1849		Limerick
Carraig Chiarraí	Carraig Chiarraighe	Carrigkerry, Ardagh	1909 - 1914		
Caisleán Uí Chonaill	Caisleán O gConaing	Castleconnell, Limerick	1805		Limerick
Caisleán Mai Tamhnach		Caisleán Mathghamhna		Castlemahon, Limerick	
Baile an Chaisleáin, Charleville, alsoCastleconyers	Baile Chaisleáin Mhic Innéirghe			Castletown Conyers, Kilmallock	1896 - 1899 5-7-2002 1849 - 1852 2003
Caladh an Treoigh	Calathna Uí Threo	Castletroy, Limerick	1905 - 1909		
Sráid Chliara, Uachtarach		Clare Street, Upper, (Limerick)	1892 - 1896	09.01.1965	(resignation of postmaster)
Clár Aidhne	Clár Einigh	Clarina, Limerick	1844	12.2001	
Cluain Cath	Cluain Catha	Cloncagh, Rathkeale	1909 - 1914	14.07.1986	
Plás Cluain Tarbh		Clontarf Place, (Limerick	06.11.1974		see The Crescent
Craobh Chomhartha	Craobh Chumhra	Crecora, Patrickswell	1892 - 1894		Limerick

Limerick Post Offices

Irish Name 1	Irish Name 2	Post town	Open Date	Close Date	Specialities
Cróch	Cruach	Croagh, Rathkeale	1852 - 1857		
Cromadh		Croom, Kilmallock	1796		also: Croome
An Dairtheach		Darragh, Kilmallock	1857 - 1859	28.12.1925	
Dún	Dún Bleisce	Doon, Limerick	1854		
Tuar an Daill		Dooradoyle, (Limerick)	05.07.1971		
Drom an Chomair		Dromacomer, Kilmallock	1885 - 1887	1998?	
Drom Caoin	Druim Caoin	Dromkeen, Pallasgreen	1880 - 1881		Limerick
Drom Collachair	Druim Chollchoille	Drumcollogher, Ráth Luirc	06.10.1833		also: Dromcolliher
Sráid Eadbháird		Edward Street, (Limerick)	1885 - 1887		
Eifinn	Eimhin	Effin, Kilmallock	22.08.1928		
Eiltiún	Cluain Eiltin	Elton, Kilmallock	1873 - 1873	2000?	
Bóthar na hInse		Ennis Road, (Limerick)	19.09.1939		
Feadamair	Fiadh Damair	Fedamore, Kilmallock	1872 - 1873		
Fíonach	Fiodhnach	Fennagh, Kilmallock	1852 - 1857		
An Fheothanach	Feóchanach	Feohanagh, Limerick	1877 - 1879		
Faing		Foynes, Limerick	1837		
An Gallbhaile	Gallbhaile	Galbally, Tipperary	1845 - 1849		PT in Tipp
An Galbhóin	An Ghall Mhóin	Galvone, (Limerick)	21.02.1972		
Garraí Dúlas	Garrdha Dubhlais	Garrydollis, Pallasgreen	1896		Limerick
Garraí Phaghain	Garrdha Fionn	Garryfine, Kilmallock	1871 - 1872	29.07.1988	
Garraí Eóin	Garadh Eoin	Garryowen, (Limerick)	25.01.1971	closed	
Garraí Uí Spealáin 01.06.1939	Garrdha Uí Spoláin	Garryspillane, Kilmallock	1885 - 1887		also: Garryspellane, 1922/25 -
		George's Street, (Limerick)	1849 - 1852	1852 -1857	also O'Connell St.
Gleann Bruacháin		Glenbrohane, Knocklong	1883	07.01.1924	
An Gleann Rua	Gleann Ruadh	Glenroe, Kilmallock	01.03.1938	closed	
An Gleann	Gleann Chorbraighe	Glin, Limerick	1828		

Irish Name 1	Irish Name 2	Post town	Open Date	Close Date	Specialities
Greanach		Granagh, Kilmallock	1909 - 1914	30.07.1988	
An Ghráinsigh	Gráinseach	Grange, Kilmallock	1849 - 1852	1988	
Gráinseach		Grange, Pallasgreen	1931 - 1937	1959 -1964	
Baile Hiobaird	Cathair Fuiseóg	Herbertstown, Kilmallock	1849 - 1852		Knocklong
Baile na gCailleach		Holycross, Kilmallock	01-04-1864		
An tOspidéal	Ospidéal Ghleann Áine	Hospital, Kilmallock	1837		Knocklong
Baile Shinéad		Janesboro, (Limerick)	13-03-1970	26-2-2002	
Sráid Eóin		John Street, (Limerick)	1905 - 1914	07.12.1930	
Coill Bheithne		Kilbeheny, Mitchelstown	1855		Pt in Cork, also: Kilbeheny
Cill Chormáin		Kilcolman, Ardagh	1877 - 1879		Limerick
Cill Chormáin		Kilcornan, Limerick	1872 - 1873	31.10.1963	(resignation of postmaster)
Cill Díoma		Kildimo, Limerick	1857		also: Kildemo
Cill Fhionáin		Kilfinane, Kilmallock	13-05-1832		also: Kilfinan, Kilfinnane
Cill Fhingín		Kilfinny, Limerick	1881 - 1882	07.11.1964	(death of postmaster)
Cill Mocheallóg		Kilmallock	1803		HO
Stáisiún Cill Mocheallóg 1959		Kilmallock Station, (Kilmallock)	1905 - 1914		1955 -
Cill Mide		Kilmeedy, Limerick	1857 - 1859		Ballingarry, also: Kilmeady
		Kilpeacon, Limerick	1857 - 1860	1892 -1894	
Cill Tíle	Cill tSíle	Kilteely, Limerick	1852 - 1857		
Cnoc an Doire		Knockaderry, Newcastle West	1861 - 1863		
Cnoc Áine		Knockainy, Kilmallock	1883 - 1885	closed	
Cnoc Loinge	Cnoc Luinge	Knocklong, Kilmallock	1849 - 1852		
Stáisiún Chonc Luinge 1959		Knocklong Station, (Knocklong)	1905 - 1914		1955 -
Luimneach		Limerick	1653		HO
Stáisiún Luimnigh		Limerick Station, (Limerick)	1922 - 1925	1955 -1959	Telephone exchange also operated

Limerick Post Offices

Irish Name 1	Irish Name 2	Post town	Open Date	Close Date	Specialities
Lios na Graí	Lios na Groighe	Lisnagry, Castleconnell	1845		Limerick
Leamhchoill		Loughill, Limerick	1941	31-5-2005	
Castlemahon		Mahonagh, Newcastle West	1883 - 1885	1896 - 1899	also: Mahoonagh, replaced by
An Mhainistir		Manister, Kilmallock	1895 - 1896		also: Monaster
Baile Mháirtín	Bhaile Mártin	Martinstown, Kilmallock	1877 - 1879		also: Baile Mhic Máirtin
Méanus	Mianghus	Meanus, Kilmallock	1885 - 1887	23-4-2002	
Cnoc Uí Choileáin		Mountcollins, Abbeyfeale	1881 - 1882	1-6-2002	also: Mount Collins
		Moyne, Clarina	1845	?	existence doubted
Mungairit		Mungret, Limerick	1883 - 1885		
Maigh Rua	Murbhach	Murroe, Limerick	1849 - 1852		Newport in TIP, also: Moroe,
Morroe (until 1906)					
An Caisleán Nua	Caisleán Nua	Newcastle West	1805		also: Newcastle
Corach Fhraoich		New Street, (Limerick)	1892 - 1896		merged in Ballinacurra
An tSeanphailis	Sean-Phailis	Old Pallas, Pallasgreen	1849 - 1852	30.11.1944	Limerick, 1852/57 - 1885/87
Ulla	Na h-Ulla	Oola, Tipperary	1849 - 1852		Pt in TIP, also: Na h-Ubhla
Pailis Ghréine	Pailis Gréine	Pallasgreen, Limerick	1811		
Pailis Chaonraí	Pailis Caonraighe	Pallaskenry, Limerick	1811		
Irish Name 1	Irish Name 2	Post town	Open Date	Close Date	Specialities
Sráid Phádraig		Patrick Street, (Limerick)	24-01-1964		replaced Ruthland Street
Tobar Phádraig		Patrickswell, Limerick	22-12-1832		also: Patrick's Well
Ráth Caola		Rathkeale	1726 - 1729		
Roighne	Ríghne	Reens, Ardagh	1865 - 1867	13-7-2004	Limerick
Sráid Réaltan		Rutland Street, (Limerick	1873 - 1874		Replaced by Patrick Street
Seanhualainn	Seana-Ghualainn	Shanagolden, Limerick	1805	10.11.1963	

Irish Name 1	Irish Name 2	Post town	Open Date	Close Date	Specialities
Baile an Fháinne		Sherin's Cross, Kilmallock	1881 -1882	12.11.1966	
An Trá	Traigh	Strand, Ballagh	1896 - 1899		Limerick, also: Traigh Caisleán Atha
Teampall an Gleanntán	Tempall Gleanntán	Templeglantine, Limerick	1877 - 1879		
An Corrán		The Crescent, (Limerick)	1896 - 1899	06.11.1973	replaced by Clontarf Place
Na Dogaí		The Docks, (Limerick)	1892 - 1896	21.12.1972	(death of postmaster)
		The Markets, (Limerick)	1875 - 1877	1905 -1914	
Sparr Thuamhan	GeataThuathmhumhan	Thomondgate, (Limerick)	1889 - 1892		
Tuar na Fola		Tournafulla, Ballagh	1871 - 1872		Limerick
Sráid Uilliam		William Street, (Limerick)	1892 - 1896	1905 -1914	changed to Upper William Street
Sráid Uilliam, Uachtarach		William Street Upper, (Limerick)	1905 - 1914		

Harold Frank and Klaus Stange, updated by Frank O'Connor.

Post Offices in Limerick

(1) Limerick GPO / HPO

1824		Located Lower Cecil Street
1832	Vol 2 / 46	Limerick P O Cholera raging at.
1843	Vol 14 / p247 / No357	Reference removal of the Post Office to the Custom House. May be carried out without delay 17 March 1843

But was it in fact moved – see separate entry (1A) for Custom House

1844 onwards		
1846		Located Russell Street / Maybe Mallow Street
1856	Vol 43 / 49	Pillar letter boxes. 5 Erected (in Limerick)
1858	Vol 46 / 156	Pillar letter box. Additional one erected.
1859	Vol 46 / 325	(early 1859) Central Railway Station. Wall box erected.
1859	Vol 48 / 318	Further wall box erected at Quay,
1870		Located Russell Street / Maybe Mallow Street
1874	Vol 24 / 757	MO & SB Business to close at 4pm on Saturdays instead of 6pm
1875		Located Cecil Street
1880		Located Lower Cecil Street
1884	Vol 42 / 2275	Establishment. List of officers, dates of appointment.
1886		GPO Located 5 Cecil Street
1897		Postmaster T. Dowey.
1901	Vol 91 / 428	Postmaster T. Dowey. Sick leave. Three months.
1906	Vol 103 /12	Post Office enlargement. Byrnes store taken by Dept. Further rent
1907	Vol 108 / England 12455	Mr T.H. Spraggon, Postmaster, was appointed Postmaster Sunderland
1907	Vol 110 / 1985	Mr R.W. Wright appointed Postmaster
1911	Vol 1911/ England 3428	Mr R.W. Wright, Postmaster, was appointed Postmaster Middlesborough

1911	Mr M. Guerin appointed Postmaster
1912	GPO Located 5 Cecil Street Lower
1920	Mr P. Cleggett (ex Londonderry) appointed Postmaster
1931	GPO Located Lower Cecil Street
1969	Located Lower Cecil Street
1977	Located Lower Cecil Street

(1A) *Custom House Receiving Office*

1844	Vol 15 / 142+339+365	Objections on the part of Customs collector to transfer.
1844	Vol 15 / 428 + 440	Arrangements for removal of the PO to the Custom House
1844	Vol 15 / 479	Respecting alteration of Custom House for purposes of the PO
1844	Vol 16 / 437	Occupation of the Custom House for PO purposes
1844	Vol 16 / 27 + 71	Alteration of Custom House for PO purposes
1844	Vol 16 / 310	Proposed transfer of PO to Custom House.
1844	Vol 16 / 530	Application for establishment of a Receiving Office
1844	Vol 16 / 534	Application for its being in a more central position than Hartstongue St. (Was this Custom House or Glentworth St ?)

(2) *The Crescent*

1898	Vol 82 / 2690	The Crescent M O TSO established
1899	Vol /England 299	The Crescent TSO Miss Mary A Hannan (now Mrs M A Dilworth) appointed Sub Postmistress
1901	Vol /England 18846	The Crescent TSO Mrs C O'Connor appointed Sub Postmistress
1905	Vol 1905 / 440	The Crescent TSO Paid P O £5.12.1 destroyed by fire.

(3) Northumberland Buildings

1871	Vol 16 / 488		The Deanary. As to the sale of and concentration at Branch Office. *I assume that this is referring to acquisition of land for new (Head) Post Office*
1871	Vol 19 / 51		New P O Proposed acquisition of the Deanary
1871	Vol 19 / 127		New P O Proposed acquisition of the Deanary
1871	Vol 20 / 575	)	
1871	Vol 20 / 586	)	New P O Proposed acquisition of the Deanary
1871	Vol 20 / 628	)	
1872	Vol 20 / 893		Northumberland Buildings, George Street. Purchase of by Dept for Post Office
1872	Vol 20 / 963		New Post Office. Proposed purchase of part of Northumberland Buildings (Cecil Street) for.
1872	Vol 20 / 1064		New P.O. Acceptance of Mr Roche's offer of Northumberland Building.

Presumably Northumberland Buildings (or part thereof) was sold by a Mr Roche

1873	Vol 21 / 11	Northumberland Buildings. Completion of purchase.
1873	Vol 21 / 88	New P O Northumberland Buildings. Purchase of remainder not proceeded with.
1873	Vol 21 / 214	New Post Office. Draft to Treasury.
1873	Vol 22 / 723	New P O As to progress of

(4) Edward Street

1885	Vol 44 / 1014	Edward Street Receiving Office established Allowance for collections from
1900	Vol 86 / 901	Edward St TSO Marriage of Sub Postmistress to SC & Telst. Office declared vacant.
1900	Vol 86 / 1197	P McGrath Temporary Postman, Irregularity in signing papers in name & on behalf of his sister Sub Postmistress Edward St TSO

1900	Vol England 15637	Edward St TSO. Elizabeth Carroll appointed Sub Postmistress
1907	Vol 110 / 2113	Edward St Telephone extension
1919	Vol 1919 / 315	Edward St TSO. G.B. Bruce, appointed Sub Postmaster

(5) *The Markets*

1875	Vol 25 / 699	The Markets. Proposed B O in.
1876	Vol 26 / 465	The Markets. Allowance for collections.
1876	Vol 27 / 749	The Markets B O. Risk allowance
1876	Vol 27 / 897	Rutland St BO closed & RO (Receiving Office) substituted Market St (= The Markets?) RO hours altered
1877	Vol 27 / 372	The Markets office. Transfer of bond of Clerk in Charge (Mrs O'Hanlon) to her husband and Mr O'Hanlon to be Clerk in Charge (Tels) [Mr J. L. O'Hanlon]

Was The Markets office only a Telegraph Office for the despatch (and receipt) of telegraphs relating to prices obtained, at this point in time ? With Clerk in Charge

1881	Vol 34 / 1492	Markets B O. Supervision of accounts
1883	Vol 38 / 1521(or 1571?)	Markets B O. Transferred from Mr to Mrs O'Hanlon
1885	Vol 43 / 326	Market St B O. Insanitary conditions
1887	Vol 49 / 1739	O'Hanlon Mrs S Clk + Telst Withdrawn from (being in) charge of Markets B O through drink.
1887	Vol 49 / 1739	O'Hanlon Mrs S Clk + Telst Appeal for compassionate allowance through the death of her husband who contracted Phthisis from a brother clerk.
1888	Vol 51 / 1154	The Markets B O. 1st Class male telegraphist to be placed in charge in lieu of female. Telegraphist 1st Class Additional authorised.

1888	Vol 51 / 1154	The Markets B O. Postal and Supervising allowances to cease. Does this minute confirm that The Markets B O was not conducting any postal business – just telegraphic business?
1897	Vol 76 / 520	Markets B O. Sanitary accommodation. Proposed increase of rent.
1901	Vol 91 / 363	The Markets B O. Extension of tenancy
1906	Vol 1906 / 1171	Markets B O and William St TSO abolished. Upper William St TSO established.

(6) Athlunkard Street

1895	Vol 71 / 1343	Athlunkard St M O TSO Established
1896	Vol Engd 1473	Athlunkard St TSO Mrs C Quinlan appointed Sub Postmistress
1896	Vol Engd 10133	Athlunkard St TSO D Quinlan apptd Sub Pmr
1901	Vol 89 /1391	Athlunkard St TSO Sub Pmr allowed to retain position as Sanitary Officer for Corporation
1913	Vol 1913 / 1343	Athlunkard St (Application) for Tel Office at

(7) Mulgrave Street

1875	Vol 25 / 699	Mulgrave Street. Proposed B O in
1875	Vol 25 / 963	Mulgrave Street. Proposed B O. Counterpart of lease
1876	Vol 26 / 202	Mail Contractor. Increased allowance for collecting from Mulgrave S B O

(8) Hartstongue Street (note spelling)

1844	Vol 16 / 530	Application for establishment of a Receiving Office was this Hartstongue Street ?
1844	Vol 16 / 534	Application for its being in a more central position than Hartstongue Street [Refers to Custom House]
1845	Vol 17 / 132	Mrs Braxton declining situation of Receiver in Hartstongue Street.

(9) *Hart Street*

| 1845 | Vol 17 / 437 | Proposed Receiving Office in Hart Street Did Hart Street open? |

(10) **The Docks**

1892	Vol 61 / 1067	The Docks M O TSO Established
1892	Vol 61 / 1778	The Docks TSO Tel extension
1893	Vol 62 / 270	The Docks TSO (Mr) Hall apptd Sub Postmaster
1893	Vol 63 / 835	The Docks TSO Mrs M.C. O'Brien nominated as Sub Postmaster
1894	Vol 68 / 1266	The Docks TSO Mrs O'Brien Sub Pmss resigns
1894	Vol 68 / 1470	The Docks TSO Salary reduced.
1894	Vol 68 / 1540	The Docks TSO Miss Waters appt as Sub Postmistriss
1895	Vol 69 / xx34	The Docks TSO Miss Waters as to appoint as Sub Postmistriss
1898	Vol 81 / 1908	Limerick Docks TSO Allowance for indoor tel work
1900	Vol England 12879	The Docks TSO Elizabeth Flynn appointed Sub Postmistress

(11) *Thormondgate*

1888   Notifications of Office   Thormondgate A new office, under Limerick, in County Clare Vacancies. It appears that the office did not open in 1888, but it is interesting that it was shown as "in County Clare"

1891	Vol 57 / 602	Thormondgate New M O Receiving Office estabilished
1891	Vol 58 / 1209	Thormondgate RO Robert Moorhead appointed Receiver
1894	Vol 68 / 1455	Thormondgate TSO Salary
1912	Vol 1912 / 1082	Thormondgate Miss E.Cashin appointed Sub Postmistriss
1913	Vol 1913 / 1343	Thormondgate (Application) for Tel Office at

(12) Glentworth Street

| 1849 | Vol 28 / 144 | Glentworth Street. Receiving Office established |
| 1872 | Vol 19 / 367 | Glentworth Street. Offer of premises for P O |

(13) Butter Market

1872	Vol 21 / 1498	Butter Market Proposed temporary Tel Office
1873	Vol 21 / 431	Butter Market Tel Office opened
1875	Vol 25 / 28	Head Office and Butter Market Office. Allowance for office expenses

(14) John Street

| 1914 | Vol 1914 / 584 | John St TSO   Call office opened |

(15) Irishtown

| 1913 | Vol 1913 / 1246 | Irishtown   (Application) for TSO |

(16) Clare Street

| 1871 | Vol 16 / 320 | Clare St office closed and business removed to telegraph offices in George Street. |
| 1893 | Vol 64 / 1180 | Clare St M O TSO estabd. Became Upper Clare Street almost immediately ? |

(17) Upper Clare Street

1893	Vol 65 / 1883	Upper Clare St TSO Nomination as Sub Postmistriss of Miss M. Geary
1905	Vol England 9451	Upper Clare St TSO Mrs M. A. McCartie apptd Sub Postmistriss
1905	Vol England 12613	Upper Clare St TSO Miss S. A. Kavanagh apptd Sub Postmistriss
1913	Vol 1913 / 1343	Upper Clare St (Application) for Tel Office at

(18) George Street

| 1844 | Vol 15 / 452 | George Street. A Receiving office established at Mr Goggins' house |
| 1849 | Vol 28 / 409 | George Street |

		Receiver – Mr Transdell refuses appointment
1849	Vol 29 / 17	George Street Vacancy for a Receiver
1849	Vol 30 / (481?)	Salary of George St Receiver fixed at £5.12 a year
1863	Vol 7 / 348	George St Large Pillar box substituted for .... (smaller) ....
1870	Vol 16 / 995	Tels - George St B O Allowance for cleaning
1870	Vol 16 / 908	George St B O Tel Office opened
1871	Vol 16 / 194	Tels - George St B O Extension of lease of premises
1871	Vol 16 / 320 (330?)	Clare St office closed and business removed to telegraph offices in George Street
1872	Vol 20 / 433	George St Additional allowance for cleaning office
1872	Vol 20 / 801	Further expenditure on premises in
1873	Vol 21 / 231	George St Allowance for opening and closing shutters (tel)
1874	Vol 24 / 610	George St premises. Question of cancelling lease
1875	Vol 25 / 265	Old Tel Office 44 George Street. Subletting Mr Quinlan & Mrs Von Esbeck
1875	Vol 25 / 38	George St (44) Proposed surrender of old telegraph office lease

(19) New Street

| 1893 | Vol 62 / 459 | New St M O TSO Established |
| 1913 | Vol 1913 / 1343 | New St   (Application) for Tel Office at |

(20) William Street

1892	Vol 61 / 1463	William St M O TSO Established
1894	Vol 66 / 560	William St (Memorial) for Tel Office
1896	Vol Engd 4369	William St TSO Miss G Hurley appointed Sub Postmistriss
1904	Vol 99 / 1805	William St TSO Sub Postmistress carelessness. Revision of salary. Warned, etc.

| 1905 | Vol 1905 / 412 | William St TSO   Tel extension refused |
| 1906 | Vol 1906 / 1171 | Markets BO + William St TSO abolished. Upper William St TSO established |

(21) Upper William Street

1906	Vol 1906 / 1171	Markets BO + William St TSO abolished Upper William St TSO established
1906	Vol 1906 / 1873	Upper William St TSO Miss E Humphries appointed sub postmistress
1907	Vol 1907 / 2918	Upper William St TSO Tel Office established
1911	Vol 1911 / 69	Upper William St TSO Marriage of Sub Postmistress (Mrs Roche)
1920	Vol 1920 / 499	Upper William St TSO Attempted robbery. E. Roche Sub Postmistress commended and rewarded

(22) Rutland Street

1875	Vol 25 / 585	Rutland St Mr Kehoe removed from. Misconduct.
1875	Vol 25 / 838	Rutland St BO Receivership conferred on Mr J. Harrington, Tel Clerk
1876	Vol 27 / 897	Rutland St BO closed & RO (Receiving Office) substitutedMarket St RO Hours altered
1877	Vol 27 / 266	Rutland St New RO not to be a Tel office
1894	Vol 68 / 1724	Rutland St TSO Tel Office refused
1899	Vol 83 / 788	Rutland St PO Fraudulent savings bank transaction for Patk McCarthy depositor
1901	Vol 91 / 507	Rutland St TSO (Application) for Tel Office at (Mr Joyce MP)
1902	Vol England 10474	Rutland St TSO Miss Sarah O'Dell appointed Sub Postmistress
1905	Vol England 4234	Rutland St TSO P Webster appointed Sub Postmaster

1909	Vol England 16150	Rutland St TSO S B (Savings Bank) irregularity. Sub Postmaster cautioned
1911	Vol Engd 5711	Rutland St TSO Saving Bank fraud. Sub Postmaster fined & warned
1920	Vol 1920 / 498	Rutland St TSO Attempted robbery. P. Webster Sub Postmaster commended & rewarded

(23) Limerick railway Station

1858	Vol 47 / 325	Central Railway Station. Wall box.
1872	Vol 20 / 731	Railway Station. Opening for tells.
1905	Vol 1905 / 1020	Limerick Station G W & S Railway (sic - should read G S & W Railway). P Box at station not accessible to other than passengers for late posting. P Box at Booking Office to be cleared before departure of mail trains.
1909	Vol 1909 /926	Railway Station Tel Office improved ventilation, lighting & w.c. accommodation.
1909	Vol 1909 / 1103	Station Tel Office – alleged inadequacy of office. Memorial from staff.

Extracts From Limerick Leader and Limerick Chronicle.

THE POSTAL TELEGRAPH FIFE AND DRUM BAND

Limerick (says the Weekly Independent) enjoys the privilege of being the only city in Ireland in which there is a band connected with a post office. The Limerick Postal Telegraph Fife and Drum Band, as it has been named, is the latest addition to our local bands. It was started in 1896 under the patronage of the present courteous and popular postmaster, Mr. T. Downey and Mr. D. O'Keeffe, the efficient and genial telegraph superintendent. The instruments were the gift of the citizens. The members are enthusiastic musicians. The practices are well attended, and though it was all up-hill work from the start, the band now enjoys a high reputation for excellence. Politics of course, are rigidly excluded, and the band has never taken part in any public demonstrations. In other ways however, it compensates for the deficiency by giving evening performances during the summer at Lansdowne Pier. Really enjoyable music, under the circumstance, is provided for the citizens now and again.

When the English members of Parliament visited Limerick at the commencement of the tourist development movement, the Post Office Band was the first to bid them a Ceád Míle Fáilte. The visitors were very agreeably surprised when at dinner in Cruise's Hotel the band serenaded them for over half hour. Before giving the names of the band members, it might be well to mention that the origination of a band was not the first indication given by our local postal and telegraphic employees of a love for music. Many years before a splendid string band was established by them. Its members attained a high degree of efficiency – the band was warmly welcomed by the citizens on the few occasions it appeared in public. Why it was allowed to slowly die away is a matter that I could never understand. We have many capable amateurs in Limerick who are occasionally brought together to form a scratch string band at amateur theatricals and concerts, but we have no permanent society which would help to keep them together for even a winter session. Appended is the list of the members of the present fife and drum band:

Flutes, B Flat – T. Donnelly, W. Donnelly, P. Lynch, P. Salmon, M. O'Dwyer, J. Toomey.

2nd B Flat – B. Guilfoyle, B. Waters.

3rd B Flat – J. Fennan, P. Flynn, S. Lynch.

F Flutes – P. Guerin, T. Garvey, F. Lynch.

Piccolo – M. Egan, M. O'Callaghan.

Bass Drum – J. Lahiff.

Side Drum – W. Egan, M. O'Connor, M. O'Brien, W. Reynolds, J. Guinane, J. Cherry, M. Hogan.

Tenor Drum – P. Cronin.

Drum Major – M. Clifford.

Triangle – M. O'Donnell.

Cymbals – P. McMahon.

Limerick Leader 22 December 1899

POST OFFICE BAND

Victoria arrived in Dublin on Wednesday, 4 April. In Limerick, the only visible sign of the Queen's imminent arrival was the Union Jack, which flew over the prison and some other government buildings. Later that evening, the Post Office Band came out on parade and played in front of the police barracks on William Street. When they struck up God Save the Queen it was met by hisses from the indignant spectators, while a few loyalists among the crowd gave a cheer. The band then proceeded into the police station.'

Limerick Leader 4-4-1900

POST OFFICE WISDOM

The Postmaster General, replying to a memorial from the Association of Chamber of Commerce asking that all printed matter open to inspection might be carried for a halfpenny, says that the financial effect of such a concession would be serious, and that he is unable to recommend His Majesty's Government to adopt it. This is another of those things which the great department does badly, The Post Office will carry an illustrated magazine all printed matter 3 or 4lbs in weight for halfpenny but a commercial circular is quite another matter. It is really difficult to see why.

Limerick Chronicle 19 June 1902

THE G.P.O. & G.S.W.R.

Under the present arrangement of conveying the mails westward from Limerick by mail car, passengers travelling from the city on any morning by train but particularly on Sunday morning at 8:45am and intending to reach Ballingarry by mail car from Rathkeale (as was the convenient custom before the introduction of the new system on the first instance) are hindered from doing so, owing to the fact that the Ballingarry mail car has arrived at its destination, some three hours before the train has touched on Rathkeale. If the Postal authorities and the Great Southern and Western Railway Company would agree, pending the expected removal of other grievances to have the mails conveyed by train, at least on Sunday mornings from Limerick, it would necessitate the junction once more of the mail car at Rathkeale station and serve the popular double purpose of again conveying both passengers and mails to Ballingarry.

The following letter has been received from Mr. R, G. Colhoun on the matter: ---
Dear Sir, ---- In regard to the train service on the North Kerry section of the Company's line you have doubtless seen by this time the intimation in the local Pressto the effect that on and from the 1st proximo the Company will run a train from Limerick to Newcastlewest at 10.15am, returning from the latter station at 4.30pm. The Sunday service on the section of the line mentioned remains practically the same as heretofore but of course the option of using this service for the conveyance of the mails lies with the Post Office authorities.

Limerick Chronicle 19 June 1902

POSTAL INQUIRY

The Rutland Street Office

In the House Of Commons, Mr. Joyce asked the Secretary to the Treasury as representing the Postmaster General, if he can say when the result of the inquiry, now been held at Limerick Post Office, will be made known and whether the Postmaster at Rutland Street branch office, Limerick, has yet got a residence in the locality.

Mr. Austin Chamberlain, The Postmaster General, expects to receive the report in the course of a few days. The sub Postmaster of the Rutland Street Office, Limerick has secured suitable premises and will probably be installed to-day.

Limerick Leader. 2 July 1902

WORK OF THE POST OFFICE

The Annual Return

The forty-eighth annual report of the Postmaster General issued on Saturday shows the total number of postal packets delivered in the United Kingdom during the last year was 3,919,000, an increase of 5.2 per cent and the average number to each person of 94.2. These included 2,451,500.000 letters an average of 58.9 per person and 445,000,000 postcards an average of 10.7. Out of 10,000,000 undelivered, nearly 9,000,000 were re-issued or returned. Property found in undelivered letters included £18,231 in cash and bank notes, and £651,000 in paper money. Letters without address and containing property, numbered 3,800 the contents including £179 in cash and bank notes and £3,500 in cheques. Articles found loose in the post included coins to the amount of £1,000 and cheques to the value of more then £6,000.

Telegrams totalled 90,432,041 an increase of 8555,000, the receipts being £2,821,866, an increase of £55,000. Ordinary inland telegrams numbered nearly 75,000,000, an increase of 1,500,000 and £64,000 in receipts. Inland Press telegrams numbered nearly 6,250,000, a decrease in number and £4,800 in receipts. On the night of the announcement of the price terms the Department dealt with 740,000 words as press telegrams. The total number of employed in the Post Office is 179,202. The weight of correspondence carried by the various Public Offices in Ireland was as follows: - Agriculture and Technical Instruction Board 757,763 ozs; Chief Secretary, Dublin Castle 547,119 ozs; Constabulary 385,059 ozs; Inspector of Fisheries 114,424 ozs; Inland Revenue3, 765,886 ozs; Irish Land Commission 638,809 ozs; Local Government Board 1,156,974 ozs; Public Education 1,000.664 ozs; Registrar General 1,000.061 ozs; Commissioners of Works and Buildings 768,058ozs.

Limerick Leader 18 August 1902

LOCAL MAIL SERVICE

An almost complete dislocation of the mail service between Limerick and the West has arisen owing, I'm informed, to the unpunctuality of the Dublin to Limerick mail train. The partial interruption of traffic has occasioned great Inconvenience to business people. ----Cor.

Limerick Leader 10 September 1902

GPO LINESMAN FOR THE WAR

Complimentary Presentation.

A number of the employees of the Engineering branch G.P.O. met at the Telephone Exchange, Cecil Street (Mr E. O'Callaghan in the chair), on Sunday to present a Congratulatory address, silver cigarette case etc. to Mr. B. Benn linesman, on his departure to join the Royal Engineers (Signal Section). He volunteered in the early stages of the war but was not released from duty until the present. He carries the hearty wishes of the staff with him for a safe and speedy return.

Mr. W. Ford, who acted as Hon. Secretary, read the address which stated "We the undersigned take this opportunity of congratulating you on your patriotic action in joining the Royal Engineers (Signal Section), and beg to present you with a small presentation as a token of our esteem and regard. Knowing you as we do so well we have no hesitation in predicting for you a brilliant career in the regiment you have chosen, and we are sure you will bring further credit on the service to which you so creditably belong."

Mr. Benn thanked the members for their kindness and said he did not expect any such mark of recognition for what he had done. He thought it his duty to do his bit for the war, and he hoped he would always find such good comrades as he had in Limerick.

The meeting concluded with the singing of "For he's a jolly fellow."

Limerick Chronicle February 1st 1916.

REVISION OF POSTAL SERVICES

Revision of public postal service is now in progress, and in a short time there will probably be few localities where the war will not impose some curtailment. The movement has been dictated by shortage of labour and the need for economy. The new restrictions roughly consist (except in the case of larger towns) in the cutting down of mail deliveries to two per day, and the shortening of the hours during which post offices are open to the public.

Limerick Chronicle February 8th 1916.

LIMERICK POSTAL RESTRICTIONS

The Post Office authorities propose announcing further curtailments of the hours for closing. Recently the hours were changed from 10pm to 8pm, and now it is proposed to change from 8pm to 7pm. At the meeting of the Corporation last night, the Mayor in the chair, the following resolution with regard to the seven o'clock closing hour was proposed by Alderman McNeice and unanimously adopted – Resolution: That we, the members of the Limerick Corporation, in meeting assembled, hereby enter a strong protest against the present and prospective curtailments of postal and telegraph facilities in Limerick, as we believe there is no urgent necessity for it, and as such retrenchment is likely to operate adversely against the trade of the city. We therefore call on the Postmaster General to restore the former local service forthwith and to point out that if he wants to effect a saving in the expenditures of the Irish Postal Service he ought to consider the abolition of the surveyors department in Dublin as suggested by the Association of Irish Post Office Clerks at their Conference a few weeks ago, and we invite the co-operation of the Chamber of Commerce, the board of Guardians and other public bodies in securing the full restoration of public rights which are necessary for the welfare of our native city. That copies of this resolution be forwarded to Mr. John E. Redmond. M.P. Alderman Joyce, M.P. and Postmaster General.

At the annual meeting of the Mechanics Institute Delegate Board held yesterday, the following resolution was adopted, "That we view with alarm the proposed changes that are about to be made by the Postal authorities in the postal service in Limerick, and we strongly protest against such changes, as it would mean the lowering of the city to the status of a village and interfere greatly with the commercial and other interest of the city; also it would deprive some of the employees of their livelihood, thereby adding more of our people to the ranks of the unemployed. And we call on the Parliamentary representatives in city and county to appose these changes by every means at their disposal. Copies of the above to be forwarded to Messrs Joyce London, and O'Shaughnessy. M.P's."

Limerick Chronicle. February 24th 1916.

GENERAL POST OFFICE LIMERICK

Sweeping Changes in Public Arrangements.

We have received the following official announcement;

Restrictions of hours of attendance for public business at Provincial Post Offices, owing to the war. The scheme referred to above will be applied to the Limerick Post Office and the town sub offices as from the 12th prox, from which date the hours of attendance will be;

HEAD OFFICE.

Sundays-8:30am to 10:00am.
Week Days- 9:00am to 12:30pm
2:30pm to   7:00pm
TOWN SUB – OFFICES.
Sundays – No – attendance.
Week Days – 9:00am to 7:00pm

There will be no suspension of telegraph work at the Head Office between the hours of 12:30pm and 2:30pm telegrams should be handed in at the Enquiry Office, Henry Street between these hours.

Limerick Chronicle February 26th 1916

LETTER FROM THE POSTMASTER GENERAL

The following is a copy of a letter received by Alderman Joyce, M.P. from the Postmaster General, and transmitted by the Alderman to the Town Clerk;

"His Majesty's Post Master General" 1st March 1916.

Dear Mr. Joyce,

This is to acknowledge your letter of yesterday enclosing a resolution of the County Borough Council of Limerick with regard to proposed changes in the postal service. Also resolutions of other bodies.

I shall be glad to give the matter my personal consideration, but I am afraid I should do wrong if I held out any great hopes of being able to accede to the Council's wishes, in view of the serious difficulty which is been experienced in maintaining the postal service during the present emergency, and of the urgent need for economy.

Yours very truly,

Joseph A. Pease.

M. Joyce, Esq. M.P,

Alderman Joyce states he will also have a personal interview with the Postmaster General on the subject.

Limerick Chronicle March 4th 1916

POSTAL SERVANTS

The Postmaster General has informed an Irish member at all post offices that servants are under a general liability to serve in any office in the United Kingdom where the Postmaster General may think proper to employ them, but he has no intention at present of transferring officers from Ireland to Great Britain to take the place of officers who have gone on military service. The question whether, if officers were so transferred they would become liable to military service under the Military Service Act did not, therefore arise.

Limerick Chronicle March 11 1916

P.O. BUDGET

The war has taken £3,320,000 off the Post Office profits, and though the changes and increases in charges recently brought into effect naturally swelled the receipts in a substantial manner, the effect in one department at least, viz, 'the telephone. phone, was decrease in revenue

These, and many other interesting details, were disclosed by Mr. J. A. Pease, Postmaster-General, on the vote in Parliament yesterday of £14,937,149 for Post Office salaries and expenses.

THE IRISH REBELLION

Eulogising the word of the women who went on with the work while Zeppelins were dropping bombs, he said that in Dublin, especially during the rebellion, they stayed at their work while bullets were flying and fires were raging. It was really through telephonic communication that the authorities were able so speedily to secure the assistance of the military. It had been suggested that there were a large number of Sinn Féiners or sympathisers with the movement in the Irish postal service. Generally speaking that charge was wholly unjustified. After careful investigation, he had thought it necessary to discharge two or three of the staff. Men who had been arrested had been cleared and were now being reinstated. There were 40 postal servants under suspicion, and he was, referring their cases for inquiry. Among a staff of 17,000 there must be a few black sheep, but the number was so small that he thought the house would agree there was no justification for a general charge of sedition. He was not prepared to say what the cost would be of the alterations consequent upon the damage to the Dublin G.P.O.

Limerick Chronicle 4 July 1916

West Clare Postal Service

Further Restriction Threatened

At the adjourned meeting of the Kilrush Urban Council, Mr. M. O'Shea presiding, the town clerk read letters from Colonel A. Lynch M. P. and Mr. J. A. Pease P. M. G. on the postal service for West Clare. In his letter, Mr. Pease having outlined the circumstance which rendered the present alteration necessary, continued "I am afraid it is not improbable that the week day service may have to be altered when the contract expires next February, as it would be difficult to justify additional expenditure to maintain the existing service" Colonel Lynch. M.P. stated he would do all in his power to co-operate in the matter with the Urban Council and all other public bodies interested. After a discussion, in the course of which much dissatisfaction was expressed by the members present, the Chairman said the question of the mails would stand over for the consideration of a large meeting, and probably they would call a meeting of the representatives of the other public bodies of West Clare to protest against the threatened drastic action of the Postal authorities.

Limerick Leader 8 December 1916

Superintendent

Richard George Hetherington joined the post office at the Kilmallock in 1883. From there he went to Knocklong, Clonmel, Limerick junction, and Mallow. He came to Limerick in 1901 as assistant superintendent. He was promoted to superintendent II in 1908 and became superintendent I in 1911.

His son Private Arthur Hetherington, 1st Grenadier Guards died as a result of wounds received in action in France in 1915.

He was carrying a wounded comrade from the firing line when he was shot in the neck. He had been in the trenches since February 1915.

Death notice appered in the Limerick Leader 4-10-1916

Enlistment of Civil Servants in the Volunteer Reserve.

The question of the facilities to be afforded to Civil Servants in connection with enlistment in the Volunteer Reserve (as distinct from the Army Reserve, an announcement respecting which appeared in Iris an Phuist of the 7th August, 1929) has been under consideration, and it is desired that Civil Servants who wish to join the Volunteer Reserve should be facilitated as far as possible, consistent with the uninterrupted maintenance of the Public Service. Further, every effort must be made to avoid expense on the substitution of released officials, though it is realised that in certain cases such expense may be unavoidable. In this connection it should be made known to members of the staff who are not in the Reserve that the grant of ordinary leave to them, in the month in which the training of Reservists takes place, must be curtailed in so far as this may be necessary to facilitate releases without involving expense.

So far as Post Office employees are concerned, written permission to enlist must be obtained from the Secretary, who will determine to what extent the Post Office Staff may be permitted to join. Applications in the matter should, of course, be forwarded through the usual official channels. Any officer who may have already joined the Volunteer Reserve should now report the fact.

Officers who are members of the Volunteer Reserve, and who attend for the full period of annual training in camp, may be granted leave of absence as follows :—

(a) Officers entitled to twelve days annual leave or less to be allowed six days special leave without pay;

(b) Officers entitled to more than twelve and less than eighteen days to be allowed, in addition, six days special leave without pay, subject to a total leave of twenty-one days;

(e) Persons not ordinarily entitled to annual leave to be allowed twelve days special leave without pay

(d) Officers entitled to annual leave allowances of eighteen days or more to be allowed no special leave.

The special leave without pay will reckon for increment of salary, and Civil Servants who enlist will be allowed the appropriate bounty payable to members of the Volunteer Reserve.

Iris an Phuist 4th December 1929

Thomas Downey

Thomas Downey was born in 1891 in what is now the Holy Ground public-house in Church Street, off John Street, in the Irishtown, Limerick.

His parents, Thomas and Mary, had two other children, Michael and Mary Bridget and the family lived over the pub.

When Thomas was about eight years old, his father sold the pub in Church Street and moved to a larger premises at 47 Parnell Street (now Dempsey's Chemists), at the entrance to Hunt's Lane. Although this street had been renamed in 1890, the old name of Nelson Street was still being used when the Downey's moved in.

Young Thomas attended the Christian Brothers' School in Sexton Street, and showed particular aptitude for English and Geography. Outside of school hours, he spent much of his time in Singland and Garryowen with his cousins, the Murphys and the Cunneens. It was here that he developed a strong interest in rugby football.

During their long summer holidays Thomas and his brother Michael would set off for the 'Table Rock' in the Shannon Fields or to the Railway Bridge (the 'Metal Bridge'), near the Salmon Weir Bank in Corbally, for a swim. Before the motor car came into general use, a trip to the seaside was a rare luxury for most people: consequently, local swimming places on the Shannon and Abbey rivers were popular spots, particularly with working class children, well into this century.

In 1906, when Thomas Downey was fifteen years old, the Limerick City Football Club (also known as 'Young Garryowen' and later to be nicknamed 'The Gaubies') was formed. The team's members came from the Pike, Garryowen and Mulgrave Street and were mostly C.B.S. past-pupils. Young Downey's love of the game, his frequent visits to Singland and Garryowen, and his social status as a C.B.S. past-pupil ensured for him a place on the team. In the 1911/12 season the club won the Munster Junior Cup — no mean achievement at anytime—and Thomas Downey filled a place on the winning side.

Limerick City Football Club (The Gaubies) winners of the Munster Junior Cup 1911-12
Thomas Downey is third from the left in the back row.

When he finished school at the age of fourteen he went to work as a boy labourer at Spaight & Sons Ltd., on the Dock Road, Limerick. His brother Michael had secured employment as a post office clerk in the Midlands, but on one of his visits to his family in Limerick, tragedy struck. In the summer of 1911, while swimming at his boyhood haunt at the 'Metal Bridge', he drowned. His early death not only robbed the Downey parents of their eldest son, but the loss was to continue to haunt them to the end of their lives. Thomas's sister, Mary Bridget (usually called Mary B.), helped their father to run the public-house, but Thomas had other plans. Life behind a bar- counter, surrounded by the teeming, poverty-stricken lanes off Parnell Street, held little attraction for him; he had set his sights on a much larger, faraway and unknown world.

In November, 1913, at the age of twenty-two, he left home. The Limerick railway station, his first point of departure, was little more than a hundred yards away. Some weeks later, at Christmas time, he arrived at the house of his uncle, William Downey, at 61 Fig Street, Pyrmont, Sydney, New South Wales. Following the example of his dead brother, Thomas became a post office clerk and started work in Sydney.

But his spirit of adventure and wanderlust was not satisfied with this secure and pensionable position, and he soon headed into the outback to work on a sheep farm. By this time, however, Europe had been plunged into the First World War, and, somewhat like Ireland, Australia found itself sucked inexorably into the conflict.

Like many of his fellow Limerick men 13,000 miles away in Ireland, Thomas Downey heard, and — despite the strong anti-conscription campaign in both countries — heeded the call. When the war was in its sixth month the 17th Battalion was raised and embodied as a unit of the Australian Imperial Force. On 13th December, 1915, just two years after his arrival in Sydney, Thomas Downey joined this battalion. In his search for adventure in far-flung Australia he could hardly have envisaged the circumstances of his return to Europe, but he was destined to spend nearly three years in the 'futile hell' of that war-torn territory.

The Australians were to make a major contribution to the British imperial war effort of 1914-18: its army maintained five infantry divisions on the crucial Western Front; its soldiers won high praise as fighters, especially during the closing period of the war. The total number of Australians killed in the conflict has been estimated at just under 60,000.

Each of the five Australian divisions deployed on the Western Front comprised three brigades, each made up of four battalions. The 17th Battalion, along with the 18th, 19th and 20th, was attached to the 5th Infantry Brigade, which, in turn, was embodied in the 2nd Division. After an initial training period under Chief Instructor Lieutenant G. Costello, the Battalion marched to its own band through Sydney. Under its new commanding officer, Lieutenant H.A. Goddard, the 17th set off for Europe on Monday, 17th March, 1916, the Battalion embarked on the 5.5. Arcadian for Marseilles — though it is unlikely that Thomas Downey and the other Irishmen on board had much opportunity to celebrate St. Patrick's Day. The men of the 17th all came from the New South Wales area. It was the strict policy of the Australian Army to keep men from the same region in the same battalion: for instance, New South Wales men and Queenslanders were never brought together in the same battalion. This policy gave the Australians a unique cohesiveness and a definite advantage in morale.

Wounded and sick soldiers were sent to their own depots and then brought back to their former units. By contrast, the staff at the British depots did not take the trouble to sort convalescent reinforcements, and, not understanding a soldier's love of his unit as his war home, despatched him to the first unit which required its ranks refilled, The Australians, therefore, were kept together as a corps; as a result of this policy, they had a team-spirit which Highlanders thrust into county battalions, or Londoners drafted into Welsh battalions, could not be expected to acquire—it was a true esprit de corps.

Another unique feature of the Australian Army was that it did not impose the death-penalty for desertion, although its rate of desertion and absence without-leave was high. Douglas Haig, the British Commander- in-Chief, considered the Australians a danger to the discipline of the allied forces. Even in the last months of 1918, when the Australians were fiercely demonstrating their valor, Haigh was still pressing for the extension of the death-penalty to their ranks for cases of desertion.

On 1st July the Battle of the Somme began, and throughout the rest of the war the 17th Battalion never moved far away from that fatal river, which became the borderline around which the decisive battles were fought between 1916 and '18.

Private Downey found time to write regular letters and postcards to his home, but none have survived. He also managed a visit to Limerick during his leave and was seen parading around the city in the unusual uniform and hat of the Australian Army.

August 1918, was to prove the decisive turning-point of the war, and the 17th played a crucial role at this time. On 8th August, a major British attack destroyed 11 German divisions, captured 16,000 prisoners and thousands of guns, and made the enormous advance of six to seven miles along an eight mile front. This attack was sustained until the 21st, when a two- pronged but slower assault was made to the north and south, the Australians serving as the southern prong.

The Germans fell back to a line of defense which included Mount. St. Quentin, a hill on a bend of the Somme, above the approaches to the crossings of the river. The Australian General, Monash, decided to gamble on capturing the hill, and gave this dreaded task to the 5th Infantry Brigade, and specifically to the 17th and 20th battalions.

By this time the men of the 5th Brigade were badly fatigued, but had to continue the advance. During the night of 28th August they prepared to attack.

They advanced and fought throughout the next day and assembled for another attack that night. Despite their exhausted state, at dawn, on 30th August, they were marched back again to a spot near Frise, where they had expected to be able to take time out for a sleep, but, instead, after washing, shaving and breakfasting, were moved at 10:30p.m. along the Somme tow- paths and bridges to Clery.

On 31st August, as they were moving into position west of the hill (Mount St. Quentin), waiting for an attack, dawn broke. Each of the two battalions was divided into four companies, plus the H.Q. staff which was roughly company strength. At this stage the 17th had 18 officers and 357 men.

The task ahead was one of the most formidable ever faced by the Australian infantry. Mount St. Quentin was already a familiar sight, as it had faced the attacking battalions most of the day before, and, as they came over Clery Bridge, it commanded the centre of the landscape, which was completely bare except for the village trees, the trenches and bands of rusty wire. As 5p.m., the hour set for the barrage, drew near, few officers or men in the war-weary companies of the 20th (averaging only 60 rifles) and the 17th (70 rifles) believed they had any chance of success. The men had no hot meal that night, but the 18th Battalion brought up dry rations, and at 3a.m. an issue of rum arrived. On this occasion the old Australian Army practice of keeping the rum until after the action was broken as a concession to the weariness of the men.

German resistance proved less than had been expected and Mount St. Quentin was taken — but at a price. In the three-day period from August 31st to 2nd September the 17th had a casualty rate of about 45% —eight officers and 151 men of the other ranks. Trooper Downey was one of the lucky ones: he merely suffered a neck wound.

The capture of this stronghold turned the assault of the German forces to the Somme, and they then had to fall back on their final defensive system, the Hindenburg Line. A further attack at the end of September blew a hole in this line and Ludendorff, the German Commander-in-Chief, decided the position was hopeless: it was time to start seeking terms.

The Armistice followed on 11th November. The 17th Battalion spent Christmas, 1918, at Silenrieux, and, in January, 1919, moved on to Montignyle-Tilleul in preparation for their return to Australia. On 24th April the 17th left for England on the first part of the journey home.

Trooper Downey and his Battalion returned to Sydney. On 19th September, 1919, he was discharged and given his Martin Henry' suit. He had served the full term of enlistment of three years and 251 days, most of it in the front line of battle.

Limerick Railway Station at the turn of the Century

In the early 1920s Thomas Downey returned to Parnell Street, Limerick. The street had seen little change since his departure, almost ten years before. While the streetscape had not altered, the attitudes of many of those who had remained there during the previous decade had — almost beyond recognition. He had come back to a 'new' Ireland where Sinn Féin thinking was predominant, and where there was anything but a feeling of pride towards those who had fought in the British imperial war effort. This attitude created an uneasy atmosphere for exsoldiers, perhaps even to the point where they were made to feel little better than traitors to Ireland's 'cause' — that flexible, catch-all term, so successfully exploited by the contending political forces of the day.

Work was scarce and money even more so in the Limerick of the 1920s. Although he did not find the work of a publican conducive to his free spirit, Thomas Downey was glad to avail of whatever was on offer.

The six feet tall, slow-walking Downey was a talkative man, especially when the subject of rugby came around — and sport has often proved to be a useful way of breaking down barriers in Limerick. However, he said little about the horrors of the Somme, or his part in 'the defense of small nations. During the next few years he helped in the family's pub, but took time out to stroll up the road to Wolfe Tone Street to whisper some tender words to Mary Agnes O'Halloran, who worked in Goodwin's shop in William Street. In 1926 the couple married at St. Joseph's Church, Quinlan Street, Limerick. Soon after they emigrated to New York and made their home on West 92nd Street, Manhattan, where their sons, Michael and Robert, and daughter Mary, (who died in infancy) were born. In New York Thomas Downey secured employment at various types of office work, and his income was supplemented by his wife Mary, who worked at Woolworth's Department Store.

In late 1931 his father died in Limerick. Thomas and his family returned to Parnell Street to run the pub, with the help of his sister. Mary B. had not married, and continued her job in Toppin's Shannon Laundry in Parnell Street, serving in the pub on a part- time basis.

During this period the street was a hive of diverse activities. There was a number of other licensed premises there, including Thady Coffey's, Lynch's, ('Cheap John's'), St. George's, Frawley's, Winter's, the Railway Bar, McDonnell's, Costelloe's, Tracey's and Walsh's, which doubled as a chemist of sorts, and went by the name of the 'World's Wonder'. The customers of these premises were mainly workers from the flour mills, the docks, McMahon's timber yards, the bacon factories and the railway, most of whom lived in the small two-storey houses in the narrow laneways (Lady's, Hunt's, Dixon's, Robertson's and Gorman's) running off Parnell Street and Carey's Road.

In the tiny backyards of many of these houses were kept small numbers of pigs, which were sold to the local bacon factories. The nearby Matterson's bacon factory (now demolished) is still remembered for the pungent smell which permanently emanated from it and which permeated the surrounding streets and laneways. Occasionally lice-filled mattresses were to be found mouldering in these lanes, with no trace of their former owners. On religious occasions during the year little altars, decorated with flowers and lighted candles, were set up at the bottom of each lane.

Among the other business premises on the street were the offal shops of 'Nonie' Maher, Carey's, Culhane's and Mullane's, which was situated next door to Downey's at number 48. There was also a variety of other shops:

Culhane's and McCormack's, drapery shops; Reidy's animal feed; Naughton's and Marcello's, fish and chip shops; Carey's jewellers; Hackett's and O'Mara, barbers, and Parker's pawnshop.

The railway station was a bustling centre of activity, with up to thirty trains coming and going from Limerick daily. Imports of coal and other commodities to the docks were hauled by horse-and-cart to the station by the Cusacks, Shannys,

Quilligans, McNamara's and many more carters, including the legendary 'Doggy' Cross.

Like all other pubs in Limerick at the time, Downey's was a 'man's' pub, but occasionally a few brave, blackshawled women ventured sheepishly over the threshold, across the saw dust covered floor and into the 'snug'. Thomas Downey served up the porter at 8d and (later) 9d a pint; twenty cigarettes — Gold Flake, Woodbine, Golden Spangle and Primrose — were sold at 11_d. One of the perennial topics of conversation, of course, was Young Garryowen, and he had some lively discussions with members of the 1928 Young Munster Bateman Cup-winning team, such as Charlie St. George, Henry Raleigh, Frank Garvey and Michael 'Cock' O'Flaherty.

All day on the street outside a passing parade of horse-drawn carts, cyclists and pedestrians moved up and down, and the Corporation's dung-car also did its daily round. Bare-footed children played 'Dobbie-off' (marbles), 'Cat' (a similar game to cricket), 'Hoop' (with tyreless bicycle wheels), and also sent spinning-tops dancing across the roadway.

At night large numbers of men would leave the congested lanes to assemble on the street and amuse themselves by singing to the accompaniment of 'bones' and jew's harps, These sessions were occasionally interrupted by outbreaks of fighting, which usually ended as quickly as they had begun.

Thomas Downey took his son Michael swimming to the Table Rock during the summer months. On Sunday afternoons they would wait near the railway station for the Boherbuoy Band, made up of their neighbors, such as the Bensons, Murphy's, Glynns, Connors, Dillon's and Fitzpatrick's, to make its appearance en route to the bandstand in the nearby People's Park.

By the mid-1930s Thomas Downey's health was beginning to fail. He lived to see the clearance of the laneways and the departure of many of his friends and neighbors; most were re-housed in the newly-built estate at St. Mary's Park. Towards the end of his life he often saw some of these 'displaced persons' strolling up and down the street, like returned 'immigrants', looking forlornly at what had been left of their old homes and at the labyrinth of hide-and-seek lanes.

In June, 1937, Thomas Downey fought his last battle, his early death being brought on by a severe chest ailment, caused by the hardship and suffering he had endured in the war. He was aged forty-six years. His burial at Mount St. Laurence's cemetery in an unmarked grave was a simple ceremony, attended by his family, friends, neighbors and Young Garryowen comrades.

His end, like his life in Limerick, was quiet and undramatic, and there was no band on hand to play 'Waltzing Matilda', or even a trumpeter to sound the 'Last Post'. Trooper Thomas Downey, 17th Battalion, had made his final journey. All he left behind from his days in Sydney and the Somme was his faded certificate of discharge (No. 5341) from the Australian Imperial Expeditionary Force.

Sources.

Michael Downey, Island Road, Limerick.

Kevin Hannan, Pennywell, Limerick

Ned Kirwan, Corbally, Limerick

Ned Delaney, Sexton Street, Limerick

Charlie St George, Corbally, Limerick

John Minahane, Waterloo Road, Dublin

Frank Kearney, West Melbourne, Australia

Cartha Maloney, Bentleigh, Australia

The Story of the 17th Battalion A.I.F. in the Great War 1914-18, by Lt. Cal. K.W. MacKenzie MC.

British Official History of the War 1918, Vol. V by Brig-General Edmonds. p-p. 178-179

Australian Official History of the War, Vol. VI by OW. Bean, pp. 806 end 809-810

The Old Limerick Journal

Bobby Downey, Thomas Downey's son.

No. 5.

SURCHARGES.

INTRODUCTION OF "POSTAGE DUE" LABELS.

On and after the 20th of April all surcharges on letters, parcels and other postal packets, posted unpaid or underpaid, will be denoted by means of "Postage Due" Labels to be affixed to the covers and date-stamped before delivery.

On and after that date no surcharge should be paid on delivery of any letter, parcel, or other postal packet, unless it bears a "Postage Due" label or labels of the face value of the amount demanded.

The new system does not apply to Customs Duty on parcels, to Trade Charges on Cash on Delivery packets, or to Express Fees.

"Postage Due" Labels are of the following denominations and colours:—

½d.—green.	2d.—agate.
1d.—red.	5d.—brown.

Each label bears at the top the words "Postage Due," in the middle its face value in figures, and at the bottom its face value in words.

By Command of the Postmaster General.

GENERAL POST OFFICE,
14th April, 1914.

[10840] 26500   Printed for His Majesty's Stationery Office by W. P. Griffith & Sons Limited, Prujean Square, Old Bailey, E.C.   4/14 S

Billy Whyte Having Lunch at Carmorry Quary

Put and Take

On the afternoon of Monday 25th January 1922, the staffs in the sorting office of the GPO in Henry Street were awaiting the arrival of mail from the railway station. Some of them were passing the time away by playing Put and Take. In this game, a small six sided top is spun and, falling over, shows on its upper side a brief order, which may be 'Put one or Take two,' or the face may show all Put or Take all. A series of spins had resulted in 'Put all' turning up for six consecutive spins. As the six players were playing for pennies, the large sum of three shillings was in the kitty. It was at this point in the game when the excitement was high that three Ford cars filled with armed men halted outside the gate on Henry Street. The men entered the sorting office with revolvers at the ready and ordered the staff to put their hands in the air. They then ordered the postmaster to open the safe.

The postmaster, suspecting their intentions, pointed out to them that any interference with her Majesty's mails carried a possible life sentence in prison, and as they were young men, surely they did not want to spend the rest of their lives in jail. He further pointed out that their intended action was a breach of Post Office Regulations, an extract from which clearly states - not more than one pound may be withdrawn from the Post Office without giving a weeks notice in writing. He suggested that they follow the regulations by filling in an application in duplicate and return in a week's time, as he had no intention of endangering his position or pension by negligence in the performance of his duties. The pressure of a gun on his ribs suggested that his position and his life were in greater danger than by non-compliance with a lawful order issued on behalf of the Irish Republic.

He then opened the safe, which contained almost two thousand pounds in notes of small denomination. The raiders extracted the contents, taking all. They also removed some sacks of mail destined for the British Military and sped away in their Ford cars.

The six players were about to resume their game of Put and Take, when the supervisor coming on the scene confiscated the kitty, taking all. While these events were taking place, the attention of the British military and the citizens was concentrated on the Theatre Royal, a hundred yards away. (Smyth's Toys now occupies this site) It had taken fire and the flames were being put out by the fire brigade and military. This was the day of Put and Take.

Old Limerick Journal Winter 2003

Mr. James Francis Burrowes.

Sorting Clerk and Telegraphist.

Date of Birth: 24-12-1867.

Date of employment 23-1-1885 to 12-4-1886 6/- shillings.

13-4-1886 to 26-6-1888 12/- shillings

Civil Service Cert. 27-6-1888

Dismissed, on 13-12-1905, He is strictly forbidden, on pain of dismissal, to become security for any fellow officer. Rule 135 of the Post Office.

Reinstated on 8-1-1906

Absence to be regarded as suspension.

Wages 50/- shillings.

May 1927.

Limerick (Indoor).

IN MEMORIAM.

It is with feeling of deepest regret that we have to announce the death of one of our oldest and most highly esteemed colleagues Mr. J. F. Burrowes, which took place on 30th March, at, his residence, St. John's Avenue, Limerick. He had been ill for some months and although we were aware of the grievous nature of his ailment we were reluctant up to the last to admit even to ourselves that he would not fight his way back to us again. The news of his death cast a gloom over the whole office and his large circle of friends.

Jim was a fine type of Irish manhood and was well known in athletic circles, particularly distinguishing himself in the Rugby field. He played his part as a dashing forward in the renowned Garryowen team, sharing in many of their earlier triumphs.

The Funeral was most representative and was attended by all available members of the staff It was "in every sense of the word" a remarkable tribute to the esteem in which our lamented colleague was held. Wreaths were sent on behalf of the Postmaster, Supervising Officers and Indoor Staff, the Ladies of the Telegraph and Telephone Department and the Outdoor Force.

Mr. Burrowes was a life long member of our Union contributing to our every appeal in a generous and whole-hearted manner. Of an unassuming and kindly disposition, he preferred to abstain from any executive office in our Branch or Union but nevertheless, he was one of our most reliable bulwarks when occasion demanded it. In all his actions he lived up to his old motto — to always remember a good turn and appreciate it, and to forget those in the other category.

"An Díon"

LIMERICK'S MEMORABLE STRIKE
Trades Council Defies Alien Military Might
POST OFFICE CLERK'S HEROIC PART

On Whit Sunday, 1915, the Volunteers, led by Patrick Pearse, marched through the streets of Limerick. In the district known as the Irishtown, the crowds, who watched from the footpaths, indulged in screams of abuse, cries of derision, jeers, sneers and missile throwing. This took place only a couple of hundred yards from where Limerick men and women defended the city twice in the seventeenth century. Pearse could not be blamed for thinking that patriotism was at a very low ebb in that once proud city. Was it possible that Limerick could ever redeem itself from the shameful exhibition of its citizens on that Pentecost Sunday?

James Connolly, wounded in the Easter Week 1916 Rising and about to face a firing squad, spoke four prophetic words. "We shall rise again," he said. Those words were to give hope and inspiration to a nation after the noble, the gallant and the heroic Connolly demonstrated that courage is much more the prerogative of those who face rifles than of those behind them.

Before the lordly Shannon could smoothen many, if any, of the edges of the Rocks of Curraghgour, the workers of Limerick, under the leadership of their Trades and Labour Council, were to atone for Whit Sunday, 1915. They were to make posthumous amends to Pearse and show the world that Connolly did not die in vain.

It is interesting for us, as a Post Office clerk figures so prominently in the story, that one is safe in saying that he was indirectly responsible for a stand against tyrannical oppression that has no precedent.

BOBBY BYRNES

Robert J. (Bobby) Byrnes, Post Office clerk, was in Limerick Prison in 1919 serving a sentence of twelve months' imprisonment for possession of firearms.

Others, whose avowed intention was to get what Connolly died for,—an Irish Republic— were also serving terms of imprisonment in Limerick Prison. The prison authorities regarded them as prisoners of the worst criminal type and treated them as such. Byrnes and his comrades, on the other hand, considered they were entitled to treatment as political prisoners. Byrnes led in resisting the ill treatment and in January, 1919, the resistance was so strong that the prison staff had to be augmented considerably. Then followed ill-treatment so typical of the barbarity which England either reserved for or perfected in this country. Prisoners were strapped in their cells, deprived of clothing, handcuffed night and day, placed on bread and water diet on flimsy excuses, etc. Jim Casey, an ex-Mayor of Limerick, in a splendid article, draws a comparison between the treatment afforded to Byrnes and his comrades and that afforded to a prisoner who was serving twelve months for the manslaughter of a girl "in circumstances of revolting brutality." Every comfort was afforded the latter by the authorities because, as Casey very aptly put it, "he was one of their Iike."

The Late James Casey, former Major of Limerick, whose signature appears on the Limerick Currency Notes.

The Irish political prisoners went on hunger strike and on March 15th, 1919, Bobby Byrnes was removed to the Limerick Workhouse Hospital in a very weak condition. He was then 28 years of age. Although the authorities made no secret of his condition, they maintained a guard of five constables and a prison warden while he was in what was described as "protective custody."

I will be forgiven for a digression here. Five days after Byrnes was removed to the Workhouse Hospital, a meeting of Post Office workers was held at the Town Hall. The Limerick Chronicle, which devoted almost two thousand words to a report of the meeting, tells us that it was held under the auspices of the A.I.P.O.C. and that it was arranged by a joint committee of the A.I.P.O.C., the Postmen's Federation, and the Engineering and Stores Association. Byrnes, who prior to his imprisonment was very prominent in Trades Union affairs, would surely have been pleased that at that meeting what he wanted and what he preached was done, A committee comprised of all grades present was set up because, the report tells us, that the speakers stressed the necessity "for a united front against a common employer." The A.I.P.O.C., we are also told, decided to put apathy aside. It was from meetings such as this that the Post Office Workers' Union was formed, but, as Connolly did not live to see freedom for all, but his beloved North-East, neither did Byrnes live to see the birth of the P.O.W.U., which he with others shared in conceiving.

BYRNES' RESCUE

While Byrnes was lying ill in the Workhouse which, incidentally, is now known as the Limerick City Home and Hospital, friends were making plans to rescue him. On Sunday, 5th of April, the sensational rescue was effected. Constable O'Brien, one of the guards over Byrnes, was fatally' wounded. Byrnes received a bullet wound which was to prove fatal some hours later He died at Ballycannon, a few miles from Limerick, to where he was taken from British custody.

Extraordinary measures were taken by the authorities on the day of the funeral. Armoured cars, which had been rushed to the city, were placed at selected sites. Extra police and military were drafted into the city and aeroplanes flew over the funeral procession. It had been thought that an impressive display of military strength would overawe the citizens but the opposite was the case. St. John's Cathedral was crowded for the Requiem Mass and many thousands, unable to gain admission, filled the square in front of the Cathedral. Twenty-five priests preceded the coffin as it was carried to the hearse. The Mayor, with mace- bearers and the members of the Corporation followed. The funeral cortege wound itself through the Irishtown and the many thousands who lined the footpaths raised their hats in respectful tribute. Men and women made the Sign of the Cross and uttered prayers for the gentle and noble soul of Bobby Byrnes. So it was in every street through which the funeral passed. Even newspapers with an anti-national bias recorded that the crowds were "immense."

THE STRIKE

As a result of the sensational rescue of Byrnes the British military authorities in this country acted swiftly. On April 9th, Limerick City was proclaimed a special military area. Strong forces of military and police were placed at all points leading to the city. Workers were ordered to obtain permits to enable them to proceed to their places of employment. The police and military adopted a most provocative attitude. They made one grave strategic blunder, however. The operation was apparently planned without reckoning on a body which, on February 1st, 1919, had not been silent on the question of the ill-treatment of political prisoners. The Limerick United Trades and Labour Council was a vigilant body which jealously safeguarded the interests of the workers. It did not matter whether the workers were attacked by employers or military authorities, the Council could always be relied upon to repel it. It is not surprising, then, that in spite of tanks, armoured cars, large forces of military and police, the representatives of 35 trades unions met on April 13th to consider the position. After two long sessions it was decided that there would be a general strike as from the following morning. The citizens were informed of the decision by the following notice which, like magic, made its appearance in every part of the city.

Limerick United Trades and Labour Council.

PROCLAMATION

The Workers of Limerick, assembled in

Council, hereby DECLARE CESSATION OF

ALL WORK from five am. On MONDAY,

FOURTEENTH OF APRIL, 1919, as a Protest

against the DECISION OF THE BRITISH

GOVERNMENT IN COMPELLING THEM

TO PROCURE PERMITS TO EARN THEM

DAILY BREAD.

By Order of the Strike Committee, Mechanics' Institute.

A note at the bottom stated: "Any information with reference to the above can be had from the Strike Committee."

The following Manifesto was issued by the Bishop and Clergy: —

(1) That we consider the Proclamation of the City of Limerick in existing circumstances to be quite unwarrantable without investigation of any kind. The citizens of Limerick are being penalized for lamentable incidents in the Limerick Workhouse.

(2) That the military arrangements at the funeral of the late Mr. Robert Byrnes were unnecessarily aggressive and provocative. The presence of armoured cars on the route and the hovering of aeroplanes over the city during the funeral procession were quite an uncalled for display, in the circumstances, of military power and calculated to fill every right-minded person with feelings of disgust and abhorrence.

(3) That in fixing the boundaries of the military area the responsible authorities have shown a lamentable want of consideration for the convenience of the citizens at large and especially for the working classes.

The manifesto was signed by the Bishop (Most Rev. Dr. Hallinan) and ten priests representing the parishes of St. Munchin's, St. Patrick, St. Mary's and St. John, and the following Orders: —The Franciscans, Augustinians, Dominicans, Jesuits, and Redemptorists Canon Keane of the Diocesan Seminary, and who was to succeed Most Rev. Dr. Hallinan as Bishop, was also a signatory.

TRADES COUNCIL CURRENCY

One would imagine from reading the Proclamation and the Manifesto that the Clergy and the Trades Council were working hand-in-hand. In actual fact the decision to stage a general strike was not communicated to the Bishop before that action was taken. There was no time for discussion as the decision to strike at 5 a.m. on the 14th of April was only arrived at on the 13th of April after 11 p.m. Sub-committees were immediately set up to deal with every aspect of life as we live it. Very naturally there was a Finance Committee but in this case it was a Finance Committee that was different. The Finance Committee issued its own, currency. The Propaganda Committee had taken over a printing works, the proprietors of which were in full sympathy with the objects of the strike. Notes for 1/-, 5/-, and 10/- were printed. They indicated that "The Workers of Limerick promise to pay the bearer, for the Limerick Trades and Labour Council" the sums for which the notes were issued. The notes indicated also that the workers were honoring the notes "Against British Militarism." One experienced no difficulty in purchasing one's requirements with the now famous Strike Currency. Here was more than a challenge to armed tyranny. The bastion of sterling, the Bank of England, was being attacked. These notes were printed in Limerick and issued under the supervision of the Accountants employed by the biggest firm in Limerick and the bearer was guaranteed that the notes would be redeemed in Limerick by the workers of Limerick. (As I write, a £1 note of the Central Bank of Ireland lies on my table. It tells me that "One Pound Sterling" is "payable to Bearer on Demand in London.")

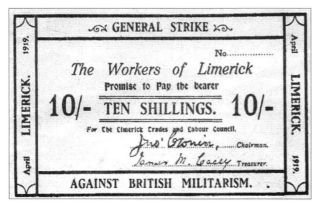

The Ten Shilling Note Issued by the Limerick Trades Council

The Propaganda Sub-committee availed of a golden opportunity to make known the true position of the strikers to the world. Many foreign newspaper correspondents were in Limerick at the time. The principal news agencies of the world also had representatives there in connection with a proposed transatlantic flight.

The Commercial and Western Union Cables were fully availed of, and when word reached foreign countries there were many messages of encouragement and offers of financial aid.

The Strike Committee published a daily paper and kept the citizens fully aware of the true position. Space does not permit a full account of the activities of the Committee and the various Subcommittees which assisted. The following will indicate the thoroughness of the arrangements. A Permit Committee was established and the only permits valid were those which it issued. These were for handling perishable goods, the transport of coal, butter and flour from the railway. The Strike Committee assigned the necessary staff to maintain gas and electricity plants. Major Woods, who was to make the transatlantic flight, was given a permit for the removal of petrol. It was impressed upon the Major that his flight would only take place by permission of the Strike Committee. Doctors and journalists were also given permits, as were the owners of the vehicles. Any vehicle which appeared on the streets had to display a notice that it was "working under the authority of the Strike Committee."

All public houses were closed for the period of the strike. The Committee replenished traders' stocks of food at agreed prices .and supervised the sales to the public. The citizens responded to instructions in a magnificent manner and it is to Limerick's credit that during the period a spiv, a blackmarketeer, a scab, or a looter was unknown.

UNITED AND UNCONQUERABLE

The Irish have always been a generous race and so during those critical times the farmers of the adjoining counties of Clare, Tipperary and Kerry joined their Co. Limerick brethren in sending food to the city, The military authorities, seeing the people so well disciplined, tried the old dodge of divide and conquer; and so it was that they posted up notices regretting the serious inconvenience caused to the citizens and assuring them that His Majesty's forces in Ireland were in no way responsible. Quickly the Strike Committee replied:

"Fellow Citizens,—As it has come to our notice that the military authorities are endeavouring to spread the falsehood that it is we, rather than they who are trying to starve you, we hereby disclaim any such intentions, as we have already made every arrangement whereby foodstuffs will be distributed to our fellow-citizens. Our fight is not against our own people but against the inhuman and tyrannical imposition of martial law by the British Government which is solely responsible. As peaceful workers we only desire that we be left alone to exercise the right of free men in our own country." The manifesto continued by exhorting the people to stand firm and bear any suffering that would be necessary so that the proud traditions of Limerick's men and women of earlier years would be maintained.

Brigadier General Griffin, Commandant, Limerick Military Area, then empowered the employers of labour through the Chamber of Commerce to issue permits to employees rather than through the permit office. The Chamber of Commerce passed an emphatic resolution demanding the removal of martial law, which was forwarded to Bonar Law.

THE WORKERS WIN

The workers were victorious, as they always will be, if they stand united. Martial law was removed and the Strike Committee called on the strikers to resume work on the 28th of April. The final proclamation states, inter alia, "that during the past fortnight the workers of Limerick have entered an emphatic and dignified protest against military tyranny and have loyally obeyed the orders of the Strike Committee."

MEMORIES

Sometimes a young Clerk or a Learner asks what is the use of being affiliated to the Limerick Trades and Labour Council as the Limerick Indoor Branch of the P.O.W.U. is perhaps this article may help to supply the answer. It is our duty and it is an honor to be affiliated to the body responsible for staging the most spectacular strike in the history of trades unionism It is no mean boast that the Limerick Trades and Labour Council by its action not only restored the good name which Limerick lost on the Whit Sunday preceding the Rising of 1916. It gave that hope, courage and inspiration to the people of Ireland which was to be sorely needed in Ireland's next two years of suffering.

I am indebted to the late James Casey for placing much data at my disposal to enable me write this article. The article was indeed written before he died and he looked forward to seeing it in THE POSTAL WORKER. God ordained otherwise and Jim, as he was affectionately known, was called by Him to his eternal reward. James Casey, a stalwart of the Strike and the man who was called upon to wear the mayoral chain after George Clancy was brutally murdered by the British, gave me a helping hand as he gave to all who sought it, and to his memory I humbly dedicate this article.

The Editor of the Limerick Chronicle placed the files of his newspaper at my disposal. In a leading article, after work was resumed, the Limerick Chronicle referred to the strike as an afait accompli. One issue covered so many dates that comment is not necessary. The Editor of 1919 is not the same person as my courteous friend.

I am also grateful to Mick Hartney, Limerick Leader. Mick marched with Pearse on Whit Sunday, 1915, and so was amongst those who were given the "charity of its silence" in the issue of the following day's Leader.

To the Editor, who has promised to illustrate the article by a picture of one of the Strike Currency Notes which he holds, I say thanks, and he can rest assured that any Limerick worker will be proud to redeem the notes if given half an opportunity.

By R. A. GLOSTER.
The Postal Worker November 1954

Post Office duties in Limerick in the 1940s

There were 33 duties. Despatches at 8am and 4.45pm.
14 Town, 8 Rural, 5 Drivers, 4 Postmen night duty, 1 Customs, 1 Cleaner.

TOWN DELIVERIES

No.1 Duty

O'Connell St. 64-74 Upper Mallow St., Upper Hartstonge St., Catherine Place, Barrington St., Pery Sq Joseph St., Bowman St Barrack Hill, Roden St Wolftone St., Edward St., Boherbuoy.   Town sorting for 2nd Delivery.

No.2 Duty.

Quinlan St, O'Connell Ave, Mount Vincent Cottages, Ryan's Cottages, Clonard Tce, Fitzgerald Cottages, Quins Cottages, Donnellans Buildings, Halls Range. Town Sorting for 2nd Delivery.

No.3 Duty.

O'Connell St 34-42 - 106-112, Roche's St, Catherine St Lower, Thomas St, Wickham St, Upper Geraldgriffin St, Sexton St, Roxboro Rd C.B.S. to Loco, Careys Rd, Dickons Place. Open Parcel Mail off day mail.

No. 4 Duty.

O'Callahans Strand All North Circular Rd.

No.5 Duty.

William St, Upper William St, Mulgrave St to Boru House, Markets Field Tce, Geraldine Tce, Gratten villas Garryowen, Ryan's Farm to St. Johns Cathedral. Rossa Ave + Rossa Villas, Pike on 2nd Delivery.

No.6 Duty.

Corbally, Island Road, Island Field, + Indoor 6:30pm to 8:30pm.

No.7 Duty.

O'Connell St 54-63, Glentworth St, Upper Catherine St, Cecil St, Dominic St, Pery St, Reeves Path, Davis St, Parnell St, Indoor Hang and label bags for day mail and night mail.

No.8 Duty.

Shannon St, Bedford Row, Lower Henry St, O'Connell 113-133 + 12-33, Ennis Rd to Union X, Shelbourne Rd on Left, Clanmorris Ave.

No.9 Duty.

O'Connell St 75-93, Lower Glentworth St, Henry St GPO to Gerard St, Lower Mallow St, Lower Hartstonge St, Mount Kenneth, Newenham St, Windmill St, O'Curry St, Clontarf Place, Gerard St, Quin St, South Circular Road, from Gerard St to Mc Grath's Shop, Laurel Hill Ave, Crescent 1-20,

Up Town Restricted after 1st Delivery.

No.10 Duty.

Lower Cecil St, Clancy's Strand, Thomondgate, Farranshone, + Shelbourne Rd and Ave on 2nd Delivery.

No.11 Duty.

Docks, Alphonsus St, South Circular Road Training Collage to Ballinacurra House, New St, Ballinacurra.

No.12 Duty.

Honans Quay, Francis St, Arthur's Quay, Rutland St, St. Mary's Parish. Parcel Delivery on Tricycle; Mallow St, Barrington St, Hartstonge St, Davis St, Glentworth St, Upper O'Connell St,

No.13 Duty.

O'Connell St 1-11, 134-140,Patrick St, Ellen St, Punches Row, Watergate, Broad St, Back Clare St, Clare St, Lower Lelia St, Pennywell, Killalee, Sarsfield Ave, Newcastle View Terrace.

No.14 Duty.

O'Connell St 43-52 / 96-105, Denmark St, Robert St, Carr St, Cornmarket Row, High St, Little and Lower Gerald Griffin St, James St, Barrack St, Summer St, Brennans Row, Smyth's Row, Cathedral Place, Canters Row, St. John's Square, Church St, John's Tce, Lelia St Upper, Roxtown Tce, John's St, Doyle's Cottages Davitt St, Mitchell St, Gratten St, Mungret St, Restricted Down Town.

RURAL DELIVERIES

Parteen

Shelbourne Rd and ave, Union X to Hassets X, Castlepark, Quinpool, Parteen, Munroe Valley, Blackwater, Indoor 2pm to 4:30pm.

Gortcarraun

Ennis Rd – Union X to Clondrinagh. (Including) Elm Park, Lansdowne Park, Caherdavin, Coonagh, Redgate, Pass, Meelick, Brennans X, Knockalisheen. Indoor 7pm to 9:30pm.

Castletroy

Dublin Rd Corner Pennywell to Ballyclough cold stores, (including) Plassy, Castletroy, Golf Links Rd, Monaleen Rd, Kilmurry, Rivers, Shanbally, Lower Park. 2nd Delivery, Ashbourne Ave, Cement Factory, Mungret College, and Father Punch's.

Ballysimon

Ballysimon Rd Munster Fair Tavern to Killonan X, (Including Fairgreen, St. Patrick's Rd) Commons, Toureen, Morrison's to Major O'Dwyer's, Monaleen to O'Shea's Pub

Back Rd Singland. Indoor 2pm to 4:30pm.

Cahernorry

Blackbuoy Pike, Wallace's Range, Bengal Tce, Cork Rd to Red Bridge, Back Rd Clonlong, Donoughmore. Donoughmore X to Coolreigh House, Cahernorry Quarry via Knockea House, Drombanna to Ratuard Castle. 2nd Delivery Wallers Well, Glenmore Ave, Janesboro, Rathbane Tce.

Ballysheedy

Wallerswell, Glenmore Ave, Janesboro, Rathuard, Ballysheedy, Spellacy's Pub to Knockea Church, via Oatfield and Raheen, Bushy Island. Indoor 7pm to 9:30pm.

Sheehan's X

Cork Rd from red Bridge to Greenbarry's House Including Power, Knockea, Ballyneety Village, Boher Load, Carrigmartin, Ballinagarde, Stone Park, R'town, Off Duty in Ballyneety 12 noon 1:15pm, Indoor Parcel Office 8pm to 9:30pm.

Lisnalta

Ashbourne Ave, Rosbrien Rd to Kilpeacon Rectory via Ex solders Houses, Mill Rd, Spellacy's Pub via Furnell Ballyclough to Friarstown to Lisnalta Creamery, Return via Dooradoyle. 2 Delivery Union X to Coolraine Tce Including Elm Park, Lansdowne Park.

Postman Drivers

1 Whitegate 6:30am to 7:30pm and 1 Shannon, New Market on Fergus, Quin, Cratloe, Sixmilebridge. 6:30am to 1:30pm.on Alternate Days.

2 Station Service Evenings.

1 Night Duty.

Nights.

1 Town Letters and Date Stamps.

1 Town and Sub Parcels + Furnace.

1 Help Driver on Station and sort Sub and Town News with him.

Parcel Delivers

Tricycle Centre of Town, Lower O'Connell St, Bedford Row, Shannon St, Roche's St, Thomas St, Patrick St, Rutland St, William St, + letter Delivery Morning to Customs House, Employment Exchange and Tax Office.

Parcel Delivery to Rest of Town in Horse and Cart with Driver, Except Cycle Delivers No.4, No.6, No.11

Customs

Postman, 9am to 5:30pm.

By Paddy Hayes. Postal Sorter. (Retired)

Total number of staff in Limerick Head Office in 1987 was 190 consisting of: 100 Postmen, 47 Clerks, 16 Postal Sorters, 12 Overseers, 4 Superintendent II, 3 Inspector of Postmen Class II, 1 Inspector of Postmen Class 1, 1Clerk Typist, 4 Cleaners.

Postal Strike Committee 1922 Names that are known at the back left Denis Looney, in the middle Daniel Kelly holding his son Sean Kelly

IRISH POSTAL UNION
FIRST ANNUAL CONFERENCE
REPRESENTATIVE GATHERING
STRIKE AGREED TO IN EVENT OF WAGE CUT

The first Annual Conference of the members of the Irish Postal Union was held on February 21st and 22nd1922, at the Oak Room of the Mansion House, Dublin.

Mr. John Normoyle, Chairman, presided, and in opening the proceedings said the Lord Mayor was to have performed the ceremony, but, unfortunately, he was ill, and would be unable to be present. Mr. Cleary, Hon. General Secretary, was also confined to bed, and his duties at the Conference would be undertaken by Mr. D. R. Hogan, Asst. Hon. Secretary.

The following Branches were represented as indicated: Executive—Messrs. J. Normoyle (Chairman), -D. R. Hogan (Acting Hon. Gen. Secretary), P. J. McPhillips (Hon. Gen. Treas.), J. C. McCloskey (Hon. Organising Secretary), J.J. Roche (Guardian Manager), W. Norton (Dublin, D. Dempsey (Belfast), F. Cussen (Cork), M. McGrath (Limerick), T. Johnson (Ballymote), P. O'Kane (Carlow), F. Hughes (Armagh).

DUBLIN:—Postal: E. W. Mahon, P. 3. Leonard, P. McLoughlin, C. R. Dixon, P. J. Grace, J. Connor; Telegraphs: Misses. McCleary and McCough, Messrs. Wisdom, Frewen, Brennan, O'Connor, Skelly, Larkin, Butler, and O'Hara; Telephones: Misses Egan, R. Murray and Louth; Boy Messengers: Messrs. Dargan and Clarke.

BELFAST:—Postal: Messrs. R. P. McGann and D. Dempsey; Telegraphs: Messrs. P. Trodden, P. L. Kelly, and J.J. O'Rourke; Telephones: Miss M.-Gunning, Mr. A. F. McGann.

CORK:—Postal: Messrs. 3. Kelleher and 1 W. Curtin; Telegraphs: F. Cussen and O'Driscoll. ATHLONE:—Mr. T. J. Malone. ARMAGH —Mr. F. Hughes.

BUNCLODY:—Mr. F. J. Wall. BALLINA:—Mr.: McGlade. BALLYMOTE:—Mr. T. Johnson. BALLYHAUNIS:—Mr. J Clune. BOYLE:—Mr. J.J. Callan.

CARRICK-ON-SHANNON:—Mr. J.J. Sheerin. CAVAN —J.J. Clarke. CARLOW — Cathal Mac Raghnaile, J. Carr. GOREY:—Mr. P. J. Brennan.

COBH:—Mr. M.G. Loane. CLONAKILTY —Miss N. Bruton. CLAREMORRIS — Mr. W. Ramsay. CLONMEL:—Mr. F. T. Scanlan.

DROGHEDA:—J. P. McGushin. DUNDALK:—Messrs. P. Daly and ENNIS:—Mr. T. F. Gill. FERMOY —Mr. M. J. Burke. FERNS:-—-Mr., M. J. O'Neill.

GALWAY:—Seaghan de Burca. KILKENNY:—Messrs. P. Haran and J. Read.

KILMALLOCK—Mr. Edmund Dinneen. LIMERICK:—Messrs J. White, D. Kelly, J. M. O'Sullivan.

LIMERICK JUNCTION:-—-M. O' Dochartaigh.

LONGFORD:—Mr. J. V. Kelly.

MALLOW:—Mr. G. F. Greene - and Mr. J Gardiner (Banteer).

MARYBORO:—Mr. J. Kearns. MULLINGAR—Mr. P. Kelleghan.

NAAS:—Mr. J. Hackett. PORTADOWN:—Mr. D. Cordon.

PORTARLINGTON:—Mr. J.J. Donoghue.

ROSCREA:—Mr. M. Delaney. SWINFORD —Mr. J. M. Kyle.

THURLES:—Messrs. J. J. Joyce and W; Clear.

TIPPERARY:—Messrs. P. J. Heffernan and D. O'Donnell.

TRALEE:—Mr. D. O'Connor. TULLAMORE:—Mr. F. Armstrong.

WATERFORD: ----Messrs, T. White and C. O'Sullivan and Miss Kenny

WESTPORT:—Mr. R.W. Joyce. WICKLOW:—Mr. P. Kehoe.

The Chairman proceeded to deliver his address as follows:-

The period covered was one of great difficulty, nevertheless a great deal of useful work had been done. A good many of the members were imprisoned and many dismissed from the service. Steps had been taken to get these men returned to their work, and he hoped that in a week or two they would be re-installed.

The speaker went on to say that with the General Secretary he had called -on the new Postmaster-General, and left with him a memorandum on the question of wages and bonuses in the Irish service. They urged that the bonus cut due on March 1st should not be carried into effect, as the cost of living had not fallen in

Ireland in the same proportion as in England, and moreover owing to the low basic wage any reduction could not be borne. They also pointed out that the Board of Trade figures were fallacious, even as regards England.

The President then pointed out that the average salaries of sorting clerks and Telegraphist ranged at the rate of 1rpm 37s. 6d. to 44s. 6d. this, of course, was without bonus. Mr. Normoyle then said, as regards the large number of resolutions on the agenda, he would not give any lead in order that the decisions reached by the Conference may reflect accurately the opinions of the membership in the country. Having briefly reviewed the Union's activities during the past year and suggested certain lines of policy for the future, he said if the Irish Free State was to be a Free State at all, it would have to be free as regards labour of all kinds

The several reports were, on the motion of the Chairman, seconded by Mr. Dempsey (Belfast) taken as read.

Mr. Frewen (Dublin.) called attention to the reply of the P.M.G. as to the wages question. It was important to know what - it really was, as the newspaper reports were vague and unsatisfactory?

Mr. D. R. Hogan replied the answer of the P.M.G. was that they had no financial control over the Post Office, and could do nothing.

The Hon. General Secretary's report was adopted unanimously.

The Chairman moved the adoption of the report of the Hon. Treasurer, and was seconded by Mr. J.J. O'Rourke (Belfast).

Mr. P. J. MacPhilips, Hon. General Treasurer, stated the current account had been reduced by £500, bringing the cash on deposit account to £3290. After some other explanations, Mr. MacPhilips said that their assets- amounted to £4,016, and that was the outstanding matter.

The report was carried unanimously.

The Chairman moved the adoption of the report of the Hon. Organising Secretary, the motion was seconded by Mr. Sheerin (Carrick-on-Shannon) and passed unanimously without discussion.

STRIKE RESOLUTION

Mr. MacPhilips moved the following resolution: — That this Conference declares that the wages of Irish Postal employees are totally inadequate.

That whereas the majority of the Irish Civil Service recently gained substantial additions for their permanent remuneration, the wages of the Post Office Staff are on practically the same level as those of thirty years ago.

That any further reduction will bring Post Office wages to starvation level. -

That this Conference demands that, pending an adequate increase in the permanent wages, no further reduction be made in the Bonus.

Resolved—That the Executive is hereby instructed to take the necessary steps for an immediate withdrawal of labour in the event of a: reduction being enforced.

In moving the motion, Mr. McPhillips said he had a very deep and full appreciation of what it entailed. The motion dealt with a very serious crisis in their fortunes as wage-earners, and also with a desperate remedy. He did not think the Conference needed any assurance that the Executive in deciding to table the resolution, had not acted hastily. The resolution was not decided upon hastily, but was the outcome of their profound conviction that to negotiate on the wage question, with any hope of success, they must send their negotiators armed (hear, hear). It was true they were already armed with Reason, Right and Justice, but it was their bitter- experience that these weapons -had brought them very little advance in the past. They had been forced now to the conclusion that - -to negotiate with a reasonable chance of success, and on level terms, they must take up the only weapon that had proved its efficiency -applause). - In short, they must approach the matter with the spirit, that if they were refused a living wage they would refuse to work -for less.

They knew they had reason and justice on their side, but it is well they should take care to state their case in public. They were prepared to prove the truth of the first declaration in the - resolution; for not only were their present day wages inadequate but that had been the case throughout the history of the service. During the twenty-one years of the existence of their Organisation it had been one ceaseless struggle for a living wage.

Let them make a comparison between their wages-history and that of other bodies of civil servants. Take three other civil service bodies which they claimed, were on about the same status as themselves; these bodies had their wages recently increased as follows: — Assistant Clerks—old minimum, £50, new-minimum, £80; old maximum, £200, new maximum, - £250. Second Division—old minimum, £70, new minimum, £100; old maximum, £300, new maximum, £400; Customs and Excise— old minimum, £80, new minimum, £100; old maximum, £350, new maximum, £420; National Teachers, Men— (Normal) old minimum, £78, new minimum, £170; old maximum, £102: new maximum, £370; Male National Teachers (Super-Normal)—old minimum, £110, new minimum, £79; old maximum, £134, new maximum, 415; Women Teachers (Normal—old minimum, £64, new minimum, £155; old maximum, £88, new maximum, £300; Women Teachers (Super-Normal)—-old minimum, £94: new minimum, £306; old maximum, £114, new maximum, £330. In the case of the Teachers the old minimum and maximum given were subject to war bonus, the new minimum and maximum were stabilized wages. The Irish Bank Clerks—and in passing he (the speaker) remarked that neither the Teacher or Bank Clerks could thank Right or Justice for what they have won; they won on the eve of a strike—the Bank Clerks instead of the old maximum of £150 now went to £4 free of Income Tax plus 20 per cent bonus. The Postal Workers wage history was very different. In 1891 the maximum wage earned by a Postal Clerk in Dublin was £2 16s. 0d; to-day it was £3 Is. 0d; so that the right and justice on their side had got them 5s. in 30 years.

The 3rd paragraph in- the resolution made a startling statement, but startling as it was, it was but too true; For the purpose of having documentary evidence of the truth of this, the Executive had compiled weekly domestic Budgets, by men of known reliability, at the maximum of their pay, and men with average responsibilities. There was nothing perfunctory or loose either in the task set these men. The compiler of each budget had to account for every pound of bread, every pint of milk, and every penny of his wages. If most of them were not in the same boat these human documents would -make appalling reading. In no case did the wage suffice for the bare necessities of life and even with the balance eeked' out by the-slavery of overtime the standard of living fell far short of what we are entitled to expect.

The crisis they were face to face with was desperate and that brought him (the speaker) to the last paragraph of the resolution—the desperate remedy. He had not the slightest doubts that that remedy would be judiciously used by those who had the handling of their affairs. Arbitration might be offered—and he had no doubt that when it was, it would be carefully considered—but, taking their stand on the admittedly insufficient wages, he thought it was not their business at this stage to seek arbitration. They should instead decide to give their negotiators a fair chance to argue the case on level terms with the other party to the dispute.

That was all he had to say, but before sitting down he wanted to tell those who might be going to vote against the motion to consider carefully what they were about. Every vote given against the motion was a vote for the handcuffing and disarming of those who had to fight their cause. If they turned down the motion they said to the other party to the dispute "Proceed, and if you refuse to pay us a living wage, we won't fight. Turn a deaf ear to reason and justice, we won't fight. Do your demand tha we won't fight—we'll starve instead (applause).

Mr. Cussen (Cork) seconded.

Mr. Norton (Executive, Dublin) said he feared that the course suggested in the resolution must be adopted if they were not to go back to conditions of slavery. Far better to fight and go down than to exist under such slavish conditions. If it was necessary to face the issue indicated in the resolution let them do so

The Conference proceeded to next business.

The following resolution was agreed to on the motion of Mr. White (Limerick) seconded (Athlone)

"That this Conference demands that the Executive ask for an immediate revision of subsistence allowances for Special Surveying and Relief duty consistent with the value of money and the cost of living."

Mr. B. McGann (Belfast) moved:—

'"That this Conference demands an: immediate settlement of wages on the terms ready communicated to the English P.M.G."

The weekly wage of both services, he contended, should be levelled up to the Union's claim

Miss McGoff (Dublin) seconded.

Mr. Conlon (Portadown) thought it was not a fair demand. He - agreed that the increments should be 10s. Per week and that the maximum should be reached after 10 years' service.

Mr. Gill (Ennis)—Are we to understand this scale of pay applies to postmen?

The Chairman—Oh, no.

Mr. McPhillips explained that when the resolution was put down first they were an Association of Post Office Clerks.

The Chairman said the question did not deal with post- men in any shape or form.

Mr. McPhillips asked people who were talking about exorbitant sums to leave that alone. They would get plenty of other people to point that out to them (hear, hear).

Mr. O'Donnell (Tipperary) said he would be in favor of the resolution being withdrawn as the outdoor staff were not included.

Mr. McPhillips said the bulk of the Irish postmen were not members of that Union, and until they were nothing could be done.

The: Chairman said it would be an extraordinary thing to formulate a claim for men who had other bodies speaking for them at present.

The mover decided to withdraw the resolution.

Mr. Sheerin (Carrick-on-Shannon) moved

"That non-members be excluded from all benefits and privileges enjoyed by members of the Irish Postal Union, and that the rule which prohibits members from associating with non-members be strictly carried out by all branches."

Mr. Joyce (Wexford) seconded. There were non-members in Wexford who, in vulgar parlance, had the leg of the surveyor. People who hung about the Union and would not join, but benefited, should be outside the pale.

After discussion the following was passed, on the motion of Mr. Hughes (Armagh) seconded by Mr. Mahon (Dublin)

"That this Conference demands that after the maximum of each class has been reached, an additional long service increment of 5s. weekly be granted at the end of every five years of approved service."

On the motion of Mr. Kelleher (Cork), seconded by Mr. Burke (Galway), it was resolved

"That all officers in the Post Office, 50 years and upwards, - be allowed to retire, if they so desired, on full pension under the new Government."

Extracts from *The Irish Postal and Telegraph Guardian March 1922*

Strike Suspended

IN our last number we had to announce that the issues were then knit for a struggle of a character hitherto unknown in the history of the Post Office. The men and women workers of the Irish Post Office, driven to desperation because of the proposed cut in their already absurdly inadequate remuneration, were about to withdraw their labour in order to assert their right to a living wage.

The situation has so far altered that for the moment a truce has been called. We have been offered and have accepted an Independent Commission of Inquiry into wages, etc., and the terms of reference to that Commission have been mutually agreed to, though after some difficulty, by the Department and ourselves. The Commissioner's report regarding the recent cut is due to be furnished before the 15th of May, and thereafter it will be the duty of the same body to inquire into the Wages and Salaries, Organisation of Work, and Conditions Generally in the Post Office, and to report what alterations, if any, are desirable.

For the moment their interest centers on the question of the March cut in bonus— on the question whether or not the cut could be borne by basic Post Office wages. It is urged by the Department that because the bonus system applies generally to the Civil Service, the Post Office employees must come under survey every six months as do other Civil Servants. This, we agree, would be but the mildest form, the very fundamental of logical reasoning, had the Post Office worker a basic wage on a level with that of the other grades of the Civil Service. He has no such scale and therefore we say his case is one for special treatment. For this reason our offer to the Government is: (I) Leave us free from cuts (the March one included) "pending an adequate increase in our permanent wage," or, (2) Place us on the same scale as other Civil Servants and apply the cuts as they become due. Surely this is a sane suggestion. Simplicity itself, Anybody mistaking this situation is therefore threading upon the proverbial thin ice.

The Post Office especially in Ireland is essentially a key industry in the class of Civil Service callings, and its employees should have first call on the Government's consideration when they claim not privileged treatment, but the right to live in modest comfort and citizen decency, It is true that this claim has repeatedly been turned down by the old control. It is by no means clear that the members of the Provisional Government are alive to the gravity and-the urgency of the Irish Post Office wage question. It is unfortunate, too, that in the earlier phases of the issue as between the Heads of the Department and ourselves unworthy motives on one side and the other were allowed or alleged to obtain. For our own part, our conscience is perfectly clear and we are disposed to accept the view that after a clash of. arms on both sides, the situation as regards the future may be all the better that that clash has taken place thus early. The Post Office worker is not a pampered Civil Servant. He is a labour man. He is a worker not only in the people's service as a servant, but also in the people's cause as a unit, and like all workers, a not inconsiderable unit in that ingredient that goes to make up what is called the National Entity. We refrain from recording our little deeds in the days just passed.

Let us see what the remuneration of the Post Office worker is at the moment. Since bonus has never, not even in the case of the poorest paid classes, exceeded the increase in cost of living, an examination of regular wages, affords "the acid test. '. In 90 per cent, of the offices a Sorting Clerk and Telegraphist has as average basic wage 37/6 a week, a Postman has 28/- a week and a Female S.C. & T. has about the same amount. The Telephonists and the other classes for which the Union speaks are on a lower level still.

An interesting, in fact a highly illustrative, example of the effect of recent bonus cuts is revealed by a comparison of the earnings of our members in August last and this month. Taking offices in the category of I, II, III, we find the following reductions in weekly wages of officers at their maximum:—

> Dublin. Cork. Galway.
>
> Male S.C & T £1:8:5 £1:7:4 £1:4:11
>
> Female S. C. & T....£1:2:5 £1:1:7 £1:0:5
>
> Postman.............£1:2:5 £1:1:7 £1:0:5

Scarcely less interesting is an examination of the average weekly wages (including bonus) in the Class Ill, offices (90 per cent, of all the offices in Ireland) consequent on the recent bonus cut. The figures are as follows :-

> Male Clerk......................... £3:15:5
>
> Female Clerk.......................£3:1:6
>
> Postman...........................£2:17:5

There is work before the Independent Commission. There may be work before our members: For the moment the duty of the latter is to keep their powder dry and their machinery intact.

AGREED TERMS OF REFERENCE.

The Terms of Reference as agreed to between the Postmaster General and the Union are as follows:—

COMMISSION OF ENQUIRY INTO WAGES AND SALARI ES.

ORGANISATION OF WORK AND CONDITIONS

GENERALLY IN THE POST OFFICE.

TERMS OF REFERENCE.

That an Independent Commission of five members be set up to enquire into the Wages and Salaries Organisation of Work and Conditions generally in the Post Office, and to report what alterations, if any, are desirable.

That in the cases of the principal classes of Post Office Servants, and of such of- the other classes as the Commission may think necessary, the first task of the Commission shall be to determine whether the present basic wage can bear the recent cut, this to be determined by the 15th May, 1922, and that the Commission shall be empowered to recommend in the case of Classes where the cut is regarded as not being justified, an increase of the basic wage as from the 1st March, without prejudice to the general findings.

That the Commission shall then consider the general question of Wages and Salaries, Organisation of Work, and Conditions generally. - -

That the Commission shall have the fight to determine what subjects may properly be regarded as coming under the terms of reference, and what evidence is admissible.

That three be the quorum, of which one must be a nominee of the Irish Labour party.

The Commissioners to be:

MR. J. G. D0UGLAS Chairman.

SIR T. ESMONDE,

MR. H. FRIEL,

Nominated by the Provisional Government.

MR. T. J. O'CONNELL (IRISH NATIONAL TEACHERS ORGANISATION)

MR. L. J. DUFFY (DISTRIBUTIVE WORKERS AND CLERKS UNION);

Nominated by the Irish Labour Party.

The Irish Postal and Telegraph Guardian April 1922

IRISH POSTAL STRIKE

Statement issued for the information of our Fellow-Citizens by the Joint Committee of the Limerick Post Office Staffs.

The strike of Irish Postal Officials is justified on the ground of a reasonable grievance which other means have failed to remove.

REASONS why we are compelled to strike :—As the result of our fight in last March we won from the Post Office Commission of Inquiry the "cut" then threatened, and the award of the Commission was to be retained until an Irish cost of living figure was **agreed upon** (vide par. 10 to Post Office Commission Interim Report). The Government cost of living figure is **not an agreed one**. It is the production of the Government, and it is nothing more than a perversion of economic facts.

In justification of its index cost of living figure the Government quotes prices of commodities that no Irish wage earner can obtain from shop-keepers. Here are a few quotations :—

FOOD.	Prices in June, 1922.	CLOTHING
	s d	£ s d
Beef, per lb — 1 1½		Women's Clothing 3 16 4
Mutton ,, — 1 3½		Men's Tailor-made
Bacon ,, — 1 7		Suits — 5 12 7
Milk (fresh, per quart) 4¾		Men's Boots — 1 2 9
Eggs (1st grade, per doz.)— 1 5³⁄₁₀		,, Shirts — 6 4

RENT, per week, 5s. 2d

Upon figures like these an index figure of 85.2 has been arrived at, and reductions varying from 10s. to 20s. have taken place.

[...] six minimums [...] the miserable cut into operation and consistent with [...] [...] drawn on the recommendations of the Postal Commission set up to deal with the case in view of a threatened strike at that time. Now the Government has in effect repudiated this Commission and enforced a cut in our wages which reduces the majority of our members below a bare subsistence level.

This is the THIRD wages cut since Sept., 1921.

The cost of living has not fallen to such an extent as to justify **any of the reductions.**

If this is not **labour sweating,** what is it? Is it the wage earner's share of Irish freedom? Is it an advance sample of a reactionary **capitalistic policy** to drive wages down to a bare subsistence level?

Issued by Publicity Dept.
Limerick Joint Postal Strike Committee.

Sept. 12th, 1922.

CHRISTMAS ARRANGEMENTS 1947

Extract from report of An Maistir Poist, Limerick, in papers R. 4630/42

The expeditious disposal of the unprecedented and abnormal volume of traffic at this office this Christmas was hampered, to some extent by lack of adequate accommodation in the existing building and for next Christmas season it is proposed if obtainable, to acquire suitable temporary premises outside for the period 14th to 24th December inclusive, in which all outward and inward Parcel traffic could be dealt with, the Sorting Office being used exclusively for letter traffic. The very appreciable increase in traffic this Christmas season over that of previous years, especially Air Mail traffic, reaches phenomenal proportions and needs a much extended special section to itself at Christmas, renders imperative the provision of the additional accommodation referred to and no doubt this matter will be extracted for separate consideration in say, September next, unless in the meantime, the structural alterations, envisage in other papers, are carried out.

———————

For the Building Section.
4th Marta 1948.

Maistir Poist
Limerick.

It may be accepted that structural alterations at Limerick P.O. are to commence this year and that the temporary accommodation you propose will be required next Christmas at all events.

An Runai,

Additional temporary accommodation for dealing with Christmas traffic can be obtained from the. Limerick P.Y.M.A., who are willing to let their Badminton hall for 14th to 24th Nollaig, inclusive, for a rent of £20, the Department to bear the cost of all light and heating in addition

The hall, which is 55' X 27' X 18' is situated' at the rear of this office and is admirably suited to the purpose for which it is required. It is well lighted and heated. Letting terms are considered reasonable. No other suitable accommodation is available in the city and it is recommended that the offer of the L.P.Y.M.A. be accepted

Maistir Poist
Limerick 15/10/1948.

Maistir Poist
Limerick.

Read.
Now the assumption that no better terms are negotiable, authority is given for hiring of the Limerick L.P.Y.M.A. Badminton Hall during the period 14th to 24th December next at a charge of £20, plus cost of light and heat, for handling Parcel mails.

Necessary arrangements for transfer of furniture fittings etc and renovations of temporary fittings may be made with the Boards District Architect.
How is it proposed to arrange the charges for light and heat? Will we have to pay the Furnace Attendant, please.

19-10-1948.

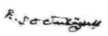

L.P.Y.M.A.
97 O'Connell St, Limerick.
28 Dec 1954.

Postmaster
GPO.
Limerick.

Sir,

As the cost of living has increased and you have recently increased the Post Office staffs salaries, perhaps you could see your way to give me an increase in my remuneration for extra work here during the Post Office period here. I have had later hours and extra cleaning as the public have had the right of way through the front entrance. I have had to give up some of my outdoor work to meet this.

Thanking You,
Yours Faithfully,

George Coslir

An Maistir Poist
Limerick.

Read.   In the circumstances, authority is given for the additional payment of 17/- to the caretaker.

Fraher
Brts.
2/2/55

An Runai,
B. and S. Section.

Read and noted. The additional payment has been made to the Caretaker and he is satisfied.

Maistir Poist, Limerick
4-2-1955

H. Simon

POWU Annual Conference Limerick 1950

Standing in the centre William Norton An Tánaiste, Minister for Social Welfare. Others that are known Autie Gloster, Ms. Terry Ryan, Maurice Fitzgerald,Mr. Terry Quinlan (Waterford), Gerard O'Shea, Jim Jackman, Eamon O'Brien, Mick Keyes, Tom Sullivan, Jimmy Curran, Brendan Brinn.

Twenty-Seventh Annual Conference

The Twenty-Seventh Annual Conference of the Union was held in Cruise's Hotel, Limerick, on June 14th, 15th and 16th, 1950. Miss M. J. McPartlin presided.

The attendance included Mr. Wm. Norton, An Tánaiste, Minister for Social Welfare; Mr. James Everett, Minister for Posts and Telegraphs, and Mr. G. A. Stevens, Fraternal Delegate from the Union of Post Office Workers of Great Britain. Members of the outgoing National Executive present were: Messrs. T. K. Igoe, Drogheda Outdoor; S. Wadding, Waterford Outdoor; M. G. Keyes, Limerick Indoor; H. Blackmore, Cork Clerks; E.. T. Devine, Cork Outdoor; D. Burke, Dublin Motor Drivers; S. Murray, Drogheda Indoor; L. Swift, Waterford Indoor; J. L. Lynch, Glenamaddy; J. Jackman, Limerick Outdoor; P. McCann, Dublin Motor Drivers; O'Callaghan, Ballina Outdoor, and D. O'Connor, Killarney.

At the outset, a civic reception was accorded the delegates by the Mayor, Councillor G.B. Dillon. Welcomes were also extended by Very Rev. Canon Maloney, P.P., St. Munchin's, on behalf, of his Lordship the Bishop, Most Rev. Dr. O'Neill, who was unable to attend; and by Mr. Synan O'Mahony, President, Limerick Trades and Labour Council.

The Mayor, in his address to the delegates, said that this was the second Postal. Congress to have been held in Limerick in 20 years, and, in the intervening years, the Post Office Workers' Union had grown to full maturity. Their return visit to the city was much appreciated by the citizens. The public, too, appreciated the very efficient and courteous manner in which Post Office workers discharged their multifarious duties under the most trying conditions and gave general satisfaction.

Referring to Limerick G.P.O., the Mayor said it was in urgent need of extensions and it was altogether too small for a growing city and for the substantial growth of the service. It' was about time the Department provided a public office to meet these requirements. He hoped there would be no undue delay in having the new telephone exchange installed. Their telephone staff deserved adequate treatment and consideration for they had to work under trying conditions; and how well they were doing their duties was ably demonstrated during the recent rail strike.

The Mayor concluded by saying that it was with pleasure he learned that the Government had decided to deal by arbitration with the Civil Service staffs, and he hoped their grievances would be dealt with promptly and satisfactorily through that machinery.

Very Rev. Canon Moloney apologized for the absence of the Bishop, who was attending the Liturgical Retreat. He joined with the Mayor in welcoming the splendid men and women of the Post Office Workers' Union, whose members, by their patience, courtesy and consideration commanded the respect and confidence of the whole Community.

"In fact," said the Canon, "the work and the services which you render to the public are so .thorough, so quiet and smooth and so reliable, that we may be tempted to take it for granted and-perhaps to overlook or forget it. I can assure you, as a man in the street, that, though we may be tempted to do so, we cannot forget that splendid, patient work of yours. You display a most gracious spirit in the discharge of your very onerous, exacting duties. The fact that you have such 'a fine and quiet sense of duty is the best guarantee that the public will eventually see that you will obtain your rights." -

Canon Moloney said he hoped the generous spirit they had displayed in the past would continue in the years ahead. He referred to the important position Limerick occupied as a strategic centre for trade and commerce and said he hoped it would get a place in the sun, worthy of its place and people.

"On behalf of the citizens," he said in conclusion, "and on behalf of the Bishop and my own behalf, we all hope and pray that the gracious spirit which has presided over all your deliberations for all these years may continue to animate you and your deliberations in the future."

Mr. Synan O'Mahony welcomed the delegates on behalf of the Limerick Trades and Labour Council. The members of the Union were, he said, an important body of civil servants and they commanded the high regard and esteem of their fellow workers in all branches of trade and industry. The silent, courteous workers in the Post Office were, in literal fact, civil servants for the operative word was "civil" (laughter). They were amongst the pillars of the State and in that position they deserved to be adequately requited for their signal services to that State and to the citizens. He wished the Conference every success and hoped their deliberations would be fruitful.

The Chairman, on behalf of the delegates, returned thanks to the Mayor, Canon Maloney and Mr. O'Mahony for their gracious words of welcome compliment and said that she had no doubt delegates would carry back with them pleasant recollections of their visit to Limerick.

Delegates Present from the Limerick Office were;

Robert Autie Gloster, Ger O'Shea, E. S. Fitzgerald, (Indoor) Jimmy C. Curran, Eamon C. O'Brien, John M. Ryan, (Outdoor)

Kilmallock (Outdoor) D. Cusack. Newcastle West M. J. Healy.

CHAIRMAN'S ADDRESS.

Miss M. J. McPartlin, in her address to Conference, said: —

COLLEAGUES,

In extending to you a céad mile fáilte to this the 7th Annual. Conference of the Union, may I express pleasure in being asked to preside at this meeting in Limerick, where we are again holding our Annual Conference after a lapse of nineteen years.

It is only right that I should refer to the loyalty which the members of the local Branches have given to the Union and of the support for Trade Unionism which has been a characteristic of the Post Office Staff in Limerick, and I feel I am ex pressing your sentiments when I say how glad we are, on this account, to revisit this old Irish City by the Shannon, for the purpose of taking stock of the work which has been carried out during the past year preparing the ground for the work of the coming year. There is, approximately, 75 per cent, more delegates assembled in this hall than the number who participated at Annual Conference in 1931. Throughout the intervening years we have built up the Union and increased our strength to such an extent that I believe we can claim, that by tenacity of purpose, the members with good leadership, have succeeded in having the Union established to-day as the most powerful organisation in the Civil Service and a Union whose opinion is highly respected in the Labour and Trade Union Movements.

May I add how pleased we are to have with us to-day, in his capacity as Minister for Social Welfare, our General Secretary, Mr. Wm. Norton To his able leadership we may attribute a great amount of the credit for the present status of the Union.

Speaking of the Labour and Trade Union. Movements, I have to say how encouraging it is to know that there is unification in the Labour Party, and that the Party is prepared to work with a political programme in accordance with Christian principles and national ideals. Workers will be heartened in the thought that, for the future, a united voice will look after their interests in the Legislature.

The acceptance of the principle of Irish- based and Irish-controlled Unions to cater for all Irish workers will commend itself to Trade Unionists in this country. We can only hope that when the members of the Party meet representatives of the two Congresses, a full measure of goodwill and friendship will abound on both sides and the opportunity taken to register agreement on the desired principles and reach complete solidarity in the Trade Union world.

Conference will have no hesitation in extending to the representatives conducting the negotiations, an earnest wish for the success of their meeting and a speedy termination to the good work.

COST OF LIVING

In this small Green Isle of ours, of which we are so justly proud, and where in this Atomic Age we take no part in the scramble for power with other nations, we should at least be able to undertake the task of adjusting our economic position— so as to give a headline to the world—in establishing a Social Order which will conform with the Christian way of life and cater for both the State and people. Unfortunately, we are not progressing as we should in this direction. In a Christian community such as ours, a more determined effort must be made to assist in developing family life. As the basic unit of the State, the family must be afforded every possible facility for full development. In this respect, the two problems demanding urgent attention and remedy are the high cost of living and the housing shortage. With regard to the former: the present official Cost of Living index issued under the direction of the Government can scarcely be regarded as a correct reflex of prices. The machinery for computing the figures will have to be overhauled if a true picture of the present position is to be given and the ordinary citizen to have confidence in the results obtained. With so many depending upon the production of a true figure in order to successfully prosecute demands for a just wage, the necessity for the compilation of a representative Cost of Living index is very apparent and one which the Government must tackle without delay. We know, for instance, the increase in the price of necessities such as food and clothing has been abnormal during the last ten years. It is true the workers have secured increases in wages but not in proportion to the increase in prices. There are many workers to-day whose standard of living is much below that which obtained for them in 1940, before the Wages Standstill Order was introduced, and yet to-day their output is not less than it was at that time. While there is abundant evidence of the need for increased wages, most thoughtful workers are of the opinion that further increases in wages are not the remedy if, as heretofore, the wages increase is used by employers as a pretext for raising prices. Prices of essential goods must be kept down and Trade Unions would be well advised to concentrate on securing effective control of prices as a preliminary measure towards raising the standard of living for all classes of workers. The housewife, who has the job of balancing the family budget, has no doubt that at present a reduction in the prices of food, clothing and rent would make her duties much easier than an increase in her husband's wages which helpings with it an increase in the price of essential goods.

ACCOMMODATION

While the Government must be congratulated on its efforts to solve the housing problem, it was very disquieting to learn in December last, that had not the

Government taken action, the housing programme in Dublin would have come to a standstill because of the refusal of the banks to lend the necessary money with which to carry on. In view of the fact that private builders of the luxury type of house appear to have no difficulty in getting money from the banks, the Government should assume the necessary powers with which to super- vise and control Banking policy, in order to ensure that the community's savings, as represented by bank deposits, shall be utilised for the financing of necessary State and Local Authorities' projects, before the granting of credit for luxury transactions would be considered. It is not unreasonable to suggest that the Government should see that houses are made available at a rent within the reach of the lower paid groups so that the average workingman may be provided with suitable accommodation for his family. There is no doubt - that if there were better housing conditions for the people in Ireland there would be less need for the erection of Sanatoria.

When speaking on the housing question, I would like to say a word on the very bad conditions under which Post Office staffs work, owing to the lack of suitable and adequate accommodation in Post Office buildings. The National Executive is aware, from the number of complaints reaching Union Headquarters, of the defective and unsuitable buildings being used for Post Office business and of the urgent need for more up-to-date premises, in order to provide for the services now administered by the Departments services which were not in operation when the majority of the present buildings, were erected. As a consequence of the large number of transactions required by present day traffic, there is overcrowding, not only so far as the staff are concerned, but also the public, for whom the facilities available are totally inadequate to conduct business which is very often of a private nature. We read a great deal about the progress being made in the development of the Telephone Service, but nothing to suggest the hardship which is being imposed on Telephone Operators, when an unlimited number of switchboards is hoisted into premises which are not sufficiently extensive to accommodate them. The overcrowding and lack of suitable accommodation for Post Office staffs throughout the country is a disgrace to any Administration and requires immediate remedying. It should be appreciated that working in ill-ventilated buildings does not lend itself to the efficient discharge of duties and can only be a constant source of danger to the health of the staff.

ARBITRATION

In the past year of the Union's achievements, I think the introduction of the Conciliation and Arbitration Scheme may be considered a success of major importance. The coming into operation of the scheme marks a new era in the method of representation open to the Union and will enable us to go forward and discuss claims with Departmental representatives in an endeavour to reach an amicable conclusion. If this is not possible, it will be open to the Union to seek the intervention of the Arbitration Board and obtain Independent judgment on the issue involved. The formal opening of the General Council on the 1st June marked the introduction of the trial year for the new machinery, and I am sure we all hope that at the end of twelve months, in the light of experience in working the scheme, we will be enabled to agree on the perpetuation of Conciliation and Arbitration machinery which will provide us with the long-awaited opportunity of an effective means of securing improved conditions for Civil Servants. We are hopeful that by conciliation and negotiation we will succeed in enlightening the official side on the merits of some of our long outstanding claims. The responsibility for the success or failure of the scheme rests equally with the Official Side and the Staff Side. There is no reason why a scheme for Conciliation and Arbitration should not prove a successful means of bringing about a better understanding and relationship between the State and its employees.

As decided by Annual Conference, the National Executive has given priority to the question of Steeper Increments and it has been the first claim to be put before the Departmental Council now functioning. The long and low incremental scales paid to Post Office workers have no parallel in the Civil Service and certainly are unknown in outside employment. It takes ordinary members of the staff from 11 to 22 years to reach the maximum rate of wages; we know from experience that these long incremental scales impose severe hardship on our members and are in need of early improvement. We recall that twelve months ago the Minister, replying to our claim for Steeper Increments, stated that the matter could not be considered in advance of the inception of Arbitration for the Civil Service. We hope the outcome of the claim, which we have submitted, will be satisfactory to all concerned and that, as a result, the financial position of members of the Union will be improved.

WAGES

Apart from any benefits which may result from the submission of our claim for increments, we have also to consider the general position of our wage standards. The wages paid to Post Office workers are meagre and the Union has at all times maintained that the staff are not sufficiently compensated for the important and responsible work undertaken by all sections of the Department in rendering service to the State. The work of endeavouring to rectify this position will be continued until a satisfactory conclusion is reached. Under the Wages Consolidation Agreement, 1948, wages of Civil Servants are due for review next November. While the agreement provides "that salary levels will be re-examined in the light of the then economic conditions, the Exchequer position and the trend of remuneration outside the Civil Service in so far as that trend is affected by the Cost of Living." When we consider that present wage, levels are only 72 per cent above pre-war levels and the increase since pre-war in living costs amounts to at least 84 per cent and that as a result of devaluation, further increases in prices are inevitable, the members may be confident the National Executive will give careful consideration to the question of submitting a claim for a further increase in wages at the earliest opportunity.

As you are aware, since the Emergency, we have had a great number of temporary staff employed. It cannot be stressed too often the enormity of the social evil which this type of employment presents. However, we are glad to see that some effort is being made by the Department to reduce the number of those employed in a temporary capacity, but we feel that a greater effort still could be made by promoting more frequent opportunities for establishment to temporary officers. Indeed it is imperative that, as an initial step towards the goal of equal pay for equal work, temporary service be abolished. As long as we have temporary officers performing the same work and the same hours of attendance at reduced rates of pay, I feel there is very little prospect of ever successfully grappling with that feature of equal pay, which is related to the discrepancy between the rates paid to men and' women. In fact, I should like to comment here on how disappointing it was to me to learn from the report which I read on "Women's Place, in the Postal, Telegraph and Tele. phone Administration,", which was submitted 'to the International Congress, 1949, the lower status of women in the Post Office Services in Ireland as compared with those of other countries who are also' members of the P.T.T.I. In Great Britain women in the Post Services are not limited to the extent that women are in Ireland, with regard to promotion outlets. The Union of Post Office Workers has by its policy of "A Fair Field and no Favor" secured equal opportunities for women as regards promotion: Since 1935 women in the Post Office Services in' Britain are eligible for benefit under the 1909 Superannuation Act. Let us hope it will not be long more before the provisions of this Act will be available to women here; it would improve our status to some extent and relieve us, a little, from the awful feel- tug of oppression from which we are at present suffering.

On the question of pensions, I speak of the keen disappointment felt at the recent decision conveyed to the Union regarding the provision of pensions for Auxiliary Postmen. Although the Social Security Scheme contains provision for people like Auxiliary Postmen who would otherwise be neglected, the Union view is that, irrespective of any such scheme coming into operation, our colleagues in this Class should have adequate reward for long service. They can be assured that the Union will continue its efforts to secure justice on this question.

OUTSTANDING ACHIEVEMENTS

The Secretary's Report reveals many outstanding achievements, most outstanding amongst them being the extension of the main meal relief to one hour, the privilege of taking two days' uncertified sick absence and the extension of the provision of Unestablished Appointments to long-service temporary officers in the Post Office Clerk and, Telephonist Grades. The Report is a tribute to Mr. W. Bell, Deputy General Secretary, who worked under a very great handicap throughout the year, and is a credit to his ability in serving the members. I think you will agree that the progress recorded in the Report leaves us confident of the Union's future.

The Organising and Financial Reports show that the membership continues to increase and that the Union is in a sound financial position. To Mr. Horan much credit is due for the efficient and 'competent manner in which he has presented these reports.

- To my colleagues on the National Executive, I should like to express my deep appreciation of the kindness and consideration shown to me at all times during my term of office and to say how impressed 1 was by the earnestness displayed by them in their endeavour to fulfil their obligations to the members.

To the staff at Union Headquarters, I should like to return my sincere thanks for the courteous service which I received from them during my term of office.

Bearing in mind the gigantic struggle which the Trade Union pioneers had in the early part of this century in establishing Trade Unions in Ireland I would, before concluding, exhort you to place great value on your Union: Never let it be said that Post Office workers were guilty of abusing the power of their organisation, but rather let it be said that we have worked together at all times to further the Christian ideal of Social Justice for all men.

Extract from the Postal Worker July-August 1950

Boy Messengers of the 50s N. Clancy, M. O'Dwyer, E. Nash, P. O'Brien.

Dermot N. O'Brien
Boy Messenger 1950-1954.
Postman 1954 to 1998

Along with twenty or so 14 to 16 year old boys, I sat the open competitive examinations for appointments to situations as boy messenger in the Department of Post and Telegraphs in late 1949. The examination was held in the L.P.Y.M.A hall 97 O'Connell Street, Limerick, under the supervision of Mr. Dennis Looney superintendent in the G.P.O.

Some extracts from the syllabus of the examination:

The standard of the examination papers in Irish. English, Arithmetic and Geography will be that of 6th class primary school.

Excess marks not exceeding 10 percent of the marks gained for geography and not exceeding 5 percent of the marks gained for arithmetic will be awarded to a candidate who answered the paper wholly in Irish.

Should the aggregate marks of two more candidates be equal, priority will be given to the candidate whose marks for Irish are the higher.

Some samples of the questions in the examination:

GAEILGE:

1. *Aiste (leathanach ar a laghad) a scríobh ar cheann amáin diobh so: -*

a) *An Lá is fearr a chaith me ar mo laethe saoire*

b) *A scéal féin á insint ag sean-scilling*

c) *Bhí cluiche peile ann idir buachailli do scoile-se agus buachailli scoile eile. Scríobh litir chuig cara leat ag cur sios ar an gcluiché.*

ENGLISH PAPER

Write a short essay (one page at least), on any of the following subjects:

a) *Describe a camping holiday you spent with some friends last summer.*

b) *The best movie you ever saw.*

c) *A day in the life of a schoolboy as told by himself*

d) *Give an account of a funny story you read or heard*

e) *A dialogue between an aeroplane and a motor-car*

You left a parcel on the bus. Write a short letter to the bus conductor, describing the parcel and asking him to recover it for you

ARITHMETIC PAPER:

Find the cost of repairing 19 miles, 6 furlongs and 25 perches of road at £6 19s. 6d. per mile. Answer to the nearest penny

If .25 of my money is £300 more than .125 of it, find .05 of my money.

How many years would it take £40 principal to amount to £80 at 5% simple interest?

A profit of 15% was made by selling a horse for £460. Find the selling price of the horse if 20% profit was made.

GEOGRAPHY PAPER:

On the accompanying map of Ireland show and name: -

a. *Ennis. Athenry. Arklow. Coleraine. Drogheda Clonmel.*

b. *The Sperrin Mountains the Mourne Mountains, the Comeragh Mountains, Slieve Bloom, the Ox Mountains, the Mountains of Connemara*

c. *Howth Head, Mizen Head, Malin Head, Carnsore Point, Achill Head, Hag's Head*

Select any five of the following towns and give (a) the name of the country in which it is situated and (b) any other information you have regarding it: - Barcelona, Milan, Cologne, Geneva, Marseilles, Oporto, Helsinki, Leningrad.

The examination would be very challenging to our present day second-level students.

After some weeks I was notified by the Civil Service Commissioners that I was successful in the examination. I was required to pass a medical exam and an oral

Irish test before I was appointed. The medical exam specified that a boy must be in height (without boots) not less than 4 feet 6 inches at 14 years of age, or not less than 4 feet 7 inched at 15 years of age or not less than 4 feet 8 inches at 16 years of age. Failure to pass the oral Irish test meant disqualification for appointment.

After satisfying the Civil Service Commissioners as to my height, health and "Cupla focal" I was appointed a boy messenger on the 15th January 1950 at the tender age of 15 years. Rate of pay 25s 8p per week.

Boy messengers were required to live with their parents and reside within 3 miles of the G.P.O. They were also compelled to attend night education classes in the schoolroom at the G.P.O. for a minimum of 4 hours a week for the first 2 years of service Failure to give regular and punctual attendance involved dismissal.

Messengers were employed on delivery of telegrams and express letters and on indoor duties in the telegraph office and in the telephone exchange. Boys over 16 years of age "acted up" as Postmen (P.O.) during the summer months as cover for Postmen on holidays. They also assisted Postmen as helpers during the Christmas rush. While "acting up" yielded extra money, you attended for duty at 6:30am in summer and 5am at Christmas. Under present day labour-legislation, boys of 16 years would not be allowed to work before 8am.

Delivering telegrams in the highways and byways and environs of Limerick City for 4 years (1950-1954) was an education, indeed an apprenticeship to what was to be for me a 44-year career as a Postman.

I was promoted and appointed a Postman on 31 January 1954 at 19 years of age to Limerick head office, It was a 6 day 48 hour week on a wage of £3.3.5 per week = €4.04 rising to £5.00.9 per week = €7.15 after a 9 year incremental scale.

 Being the "junior man" I spent the next number of years as a leave-substitute, which meant covering the range of postmen's duties, i.e. town and rural deliveries, indoor and night duties. Pleading, not knowing a delivery, was met with the curt response from the inspector of postmen "you will know it when you come back". A feature of the night parcel-duty was stoking the furnace during the winter months. Parcels in the city center were delivered by hand carts: these were large wicker baskets on similarly large wheels and were fitted with shafts. They were affectionately referred to as "Rickshaws". Fully loaded, they were a hazard, especially on frosty mornings.

Postmen's duties were allocated after an "auction" on a seniority basis. Failure to secure a duty after an auction meant going from "post to pillar until such time as a duty became vacant or until the next auction. I spent 5 years in that sort of limbo.

In 1956 I was selected for driver training and was sent to the Post office driving school at John's Road Dublin. After two weeks let loose on the streets of the capital city, I duly "passed out" and returned to Limerick a fully qualified driver. Nelson's Pillar survived for another 10 years.

In the early sixties I was assigned to a new driving duty to cater for expansion at Shannon airport. The mail order stores were flourishing, the Industrial estate was developing rapidly and a new town was being built on Drumgeely hill. I was the first delivery Postman in the new Town.

The mid-sixties saw the end of handcarts and tricycles and the beginning of motorization of rural posts in Limerick. Extra driving duties were created. I claimed one of the new driving duties, a split attendance 8:30am- 12:15pm town parcels, 4:15-7:00pm Pallasgreen sub office collections. Split attendances spread over 14 hours were a feature of Postmen's duties up until the mid-eighties.

In 1968 I found myself on the Ardnacrusha motorized rural delivery. The route was created by amalgamating Ardnacrusha and Kilmore auxiliary posts and adding on bits of Parteen, Meelick and Clonlara. Little did I think I was going to spend the next 30 years delivering letters in that beautiful corner of East Clare. I could write a book about it. "The life and times of a long-distance Postman."

By and large I enjoyed my work in the Post Office. I declined promotion several times preferring to be on the open road. There were great friendships made, you could always depend on a colleague for a "dig out." Characters were there in abundance (another book). I retired undefeated on 15th May 1998.

By Dermot O'Brien

By S. Spillane (Dasher)

White's Lane

There's been ructions all the night
Down White's Lane.
Have you ever heard the wild wives fight
Down Whites Lane.
All the gang, they are on a booze,
They are giving but some wild abuse.
There is skin and whiskers flying loose
Down White's Lane.

Chorus
Down White's Lane, if you don't believe me, Come and see
They will present you with a pair of black eyes free -
Ah 'Tis then you will shout for liberty
Down White's Lane.
Katie Elligott and Jack Tar they came
Down White's Lane,
Just to try their hand at the boxing game
Down White's Lane.
Jack hit Katie such a crack
He drove her teeth right through her back,
But Katie got a hammer and erased Poor Jack
Down White's Lane.

Chorus

Down White's Lane there are married men and ladies fair

Dancing mad in the midnight air.

There are ten or eleven jawbones missing there

Down White's Lane.

A policeman came and struck Muldoon

Down White's Lane.

Says Muldoon "there will be a funeral soon

Down White's Lane".

Muldoon and the peeler fought it out,

And when Muldoon came from the ground,

A policeman's whiskers is all they found

Down White's Lane.

Chorus

Down White's Lane if you don't believe me

Come and see.

They will present you with a pair of black eyes free,

Ah'Tis then you will shout for liberty

Down White's Lane.

Old Monaghan never gets his rent

Down White's Lane,

No one ever pays a cent

Down White's Lane.

Old Monaghan says he will call again.

He will be back tonight with the bailiffs at ten.

Ah sure there will be umpteen houses let by then, Down White's Lane.

Chorus

Down White's Lane there are married men and ladies fair

Dancing mad in the midnight air

There are ten or eleven jawbones missing there
Down White's Lane.

The jewman does a roaring trade
Down White's Lane.

We all have bought but few have paid
Down White's Lane.

And when they come around for pay
We pay our debts in the quickest way,
There are three or four jewmen erased each day
Down White's Lane.

Chorus

Down White's Lane if you don't believe me
Come and see.

They will present you with a pair of black eyes free,
And 'tis then you will shout for liberty
Down White's Lane.

The Salvation Army came last night
Down White's Lane.

Just to teach all the tenants what was right
Down White's Lane.

The sisters they began to moan.

The captain spoke in a snuffling tone,

He was struck on the head with a stale backbone
Down White's Lane.

Down White's Lane they are killed before
they have time to moan,

And over their heads we place no stone.

We have opened up a graveyard of our own
Down White's Lane.

White's Lane was situated between Parnell Street and Dominic Street

John Patrick Mangan
Postman

From 1933 to 1965

VOLUNTEER FOR THE SPANISH CIVIL WAR

Civil war erupted in Spain in July 1936 when Generals Emileo Mola and Francisco Franco, rebelled against the Republican government. Spain had been a Monarchy up to 1931, when the King was forced to abdicate, and a Republic was proclaimed. From then until the outbreak of the war, the country was in a constant state of political turmoil .One of the causes of this unrest was-the new Spanish Constitution of October 1931 which was aimed at the separation of the church and state. So when the war began, it was portrayed in some of the newspapers, in Ireland, as a struggle between Christianity and the forces of the Godless republic.

Eoin O' Duffy, a former General in the Irish army called for volunteers to fight on the side of Mola and Franco. At least forty-eight men from the Limerick area, city and county answered his call. One of the volunteers was John Mangan, who was an employee at the G.P.O. in Limerick. John applied for a passport and it was issued to him in November 1936. One of the countries that he was not supposed to travel to, because of the war, was Spain. This was due to Irish Government adherence to the British-Franco polices of non- intervention. While the majority of O'Duffys volunteers sailed from Galway (on a German ship) to Spain in December, 1936, John, and around 100 other volunteers travelled via Liverpool, where they boarded the SS Ardeola, which sailed for Lisbon in Portugal. From there they made their way across the border into Spain. Their training base was in the town of Caceres, where they received intensive training in the use of weapons. In Spain they were known as the "15th Bandera (battalion) Irelandes" and as such were part of the Spanish Foreign Legion. Apparently. O'Duffy had an agreement with Franco that they would serve for six months, irrespective of whether the war was over or not and also that the Irish battalion would not have to fight against the catholic Basques. On February 6th, 1937, General Franco reviewed the battalion and was impressed with the men's military appearance It was around that time that O'Duffy received orders that the battalion was to move up to the front lines, to the little town of Ciempozuelos, which was about 15 miles from Madrid. About a mile from the town they came across some Francois soldiers from the Canary Islands. The Islanders, hearing foreign speaking voices, mistook O'Duffy's men for members of the International Brigades who were fighting for the Republicans and opened fire on them. Two of O'Duffy's men and two of his Spanish liaison officers and a number of the islanders were killed in the exchange of gun-fire. On March 13th, the battalion took part in an attack on the republican held town of Titulcia .At 5.00am, O'Duffy's men made their way to the jumping off point. The artillery on both sides had already opened fire as a squadron of François Moorish cavalry galloped across an open plain in front of the battalion. Heavy republican artillery fire forced the Moors to retreat, leaving some of their men and horses, dead on the battlefield. The battalion advanced slowly across the open ground but were pinned down by the murderous artillery fire. As well as that, an armoured train came out the railway line, from Madrid, and machine-gunned the Irish positions. The attack collapsed. It was nightfall, and raining heavily as the men made their way back to Ciempozuelos. After a hot meal they made their way back to their water-filled trenches. A few hours later the battalion were ordered onto the offensive again, O'Duffy fearing the worst, set off for the Spanish field H.Q. and got permission to call off the attack on Titulcia. After that the battalion was moved to La Maranosa, which was about six miles from Madrid. By that time disillusionment was setting in and it was decided that the battalion would return home.

On June 21st, 1937, the battalion boarded the "Mozambique "in Lisbon .and arrived at the Alexander basin, in Dublin, the following day. It is believed that John Mangan had a problem getting his old job back, at the G.P.O., and when he did get it back, it was said that his time abroad affected his pension rights in later years.

Some time later the volunteers received a coloured certificate, showing the Irish and Spanish flags, with a space for the recipient's name.

Des Ryan, Historian and Old Limerick Journal.

John Patrick Mangan, Certificate of Service.

Jack Leddin

D.O.B. 28-12-1889.

Boy Messenger 1904 to 1907, Acting Postman 1908 to 1914.

Postman 1914 to 1935, Postal Sorter 1935 to 1954.

Retired 28-12 1954.

Here is Mr. Jack Leddin, Catherine St. Limerick one of the old- stagers of Limerick's G.P.O. who retired last week after 51 years' service. He was one of the most popular men in the service and when he sorted his last letter into a pigeon hole last week, all the staff turned up to wish him luck,

Jack, as he was known by his fellow-workers, joined the service as a messenger. At that time there was only one bicycle available, and the boys had to walk with most of the messages. They received a halfpenny pay for each message delivered. They were compelled to walk from four to five miles a day and their average weekly earnings were five shillings.

The facilities now available, were not at the G.P.O. in those days. For instance, the spacious yard was in the course of construction, and the messengers' quarters were in a small yard at the back of the G.P.O. lane. He was appointed a postman in 1908 and continued in that capacity up to 1938 when he was promoted to the rank of sorter. Many of the people living in the N.C.R. will remember him because he was delivering letters there for twenty-two years. In those days, postmen's wages were 19/- per week, and they were compelled to work on Sundays and on Christmas Day. Jack was very prominent in the Trades Union Movement. He was eight years a member of the P.O. Workers' Union, and is a past Chairman of the Outdoor Branch of the Union. He was also President of the Postal Sorters' Section. In addition to being on the city delivery, Jack often had to go as far distant as

Ballyneety, Crecora, Clonlara and Sheehan's Cross, and was one of the men instrumental in bringing to Limerick the late James Connolly, who addressed a meeting in Bank Place in 1914. Jack was also prominent in sporting circles and was a member of the P.O. rugby, hockey and hurling teams which took part in local competitions in the city in those days. While playing in a rugby game against 'Abbey in 1923, Jack caused a sensation by taking off his football boots in the middle of the game and continuing in his stocking feet.

Although he has gone from the GPO, he still has connections there, having three sons in the Service. His eldest son Father Anthony Leddin. O.S.A. is at present in North Queensland.

By Gerry Leddin.

Protest Meeting in Limerick, 1953.
Names that are known - Jimmy Curran & Frank O'Connor.

POWU Annual Conference Monsey 10th June 1953

Frederick A. Hourigan *(Feardorcha A. Ó Hodhragáin.)*

In June 1941, a few weeks before my tenth birthday we went to live in the Apartment over the G.P.O. in Henry St. where my Father had been appointed Cleaner / Caretaker.

On 10th July 1948 I entered the Department of Posts and Telegraphs as a boy messenger (later renamed Junior Postman). My starting wage was £1-8s-6d. I acted as a postman for the Christmas Period. This duty involved two Deliveries each day including Christmas Eve.

On the 14th March 1949 I was appointed a learner clerk; my wages then dropped to £1-7s. I lost 1s-6d Cycle Cleaning allowance. In those days it took two years training to become a P.O.C. (Post Office Clerk) The training included learning to send and read Morse.

On the 2nd April 1951 I was appointed P.O.C. Grade B, The duties in the P.O.C.B. grade mostly consisted of late sorting office 6 days a week and Telegraph work. In 1960 I was promoted to P.O.C. Grade A. At first as a P.O.C.A. you covered the Counter Duties, Sorting Office, Airmail, Late Letter + Parcel Office, Night Letter + Parcel Office and Early Morning Locker. You later progressed to the writing duties which included Accounts, Wages, Customs, R.L.B. (Returned Letter Branch) Claims, Radio and later Television Licence, Uniform Duty.

On 14th March 1980 exactly 31 years to the day I became a learner, I was promoted Overseer and was back on shift work. Duties included Enquiry Office, Counter Stocks, and Remittance work, Early Sorting Office and Late Counter + Sorting Office.

1st June 1987 saw me promoted to Superintendent II. There were four Superintendents, one in charge of the Counter, one early and one late Sorting Office and the other Establishment.

On the 2nd December 1991 I was promoted Head Postmaster in Ennis; I had previously spent 5 weeks Acting Superintendent II there in the early eighties. So when I arrived as Postmaster I knew most of the Staff. I spent 10 months there and I enjoyed my time. On the night I left, every member of the Staff turned up for a presentation to me.

On 14th September 1992 I was promoted as Head Postmaster in Limerick. On that date there was a Head Postmasters' Conference in the Hotel Greenhills. I took up my post the following day. I remember walking up the stairs and saying to myself "Welcome home". The biggest change during my period as HPM was the introduction of the Rail to Road.

In my last year the sudden tragic deaths on duty, of Eric Quinn, Overseer and Joe Bennis, Postman will never be forgotten. In all my service this had never happened before.

On the 26th July 1996 I retired after a service of 48 years and 16 days.

I was not the only member of my Family to join the P&T. My Father, as already stated, was Caretaker / Cleaner. My Brother Gerry was a Postman in Limerick. My other brother Tom retired as Superintendent II Dun Laoghaire and my sister Pat retired as Chief Supervisor Telephone Exchange, Limerick.

Fred Hourigan.

Eric Quinn

Joe Bennis

Record Christmas Traffic at Limerick G.P.O.

Though authentic-figures will not be available for a day or two, it is authoritatively stated that the traffic this Christmas in the Limerick G.P.O. was the heaviest on record.

During the three days preceding the festival, the staff, which had been increased by one hundred temporary hands was overwhelmed with what appeared to be avalanches of letters.

An official stated that during these 3 days posting in the city, apart altogether from posting in the 102 sub-offices affiliated to Limerick, totalled 320,000 items, representing seven items for each member of the population. Postings for the whole area connected with Limerick amounted to approximately 1,000,000 items, all of which were cleared despite late postings.

Parcels to Great Britain, though fewer turkeys went out, were above the average. Inward parcels numbered over 14,000.

Money remittances from the United States were to the value of £25,000. Air mail items to pass through Limerick numbered over 500,000. To deal with the air mail a special dispatch service had to be organised daily.

Limerick Leader 25-12-1954

Great Christmas Rush in the G.P.O.

Inquiries by our representative at the G.P.O. elicited that the Christmas postal traffic this year was generally well above the level of-previous years.

Parcels for Great Britain were approximately of the same pro-portions as last year, though there was a noticeable decline in the number of turkeys exported by post. Inward parcel traffic from Great Britain was, however, in excess of last year's high standard. There was a slight increase volume of "home" parcels and packets dealt with.

Christmas greeting cards showed a very substantial increase. The figures recorded on the automatic stamping machine were considerably in excess of previous years. Well over half a million letters passed through the machine during the six days prior to Christmas. During the three days prior to Christmas some 350,000 items were for the city alone, representing about six items for each of' the population. In addition to this abnormally heavy posting, the staff had to deal with deliveries from over one hundred sub-post offices attached to Limerick G.P.O.

In this connection it was mentioned that the public did not, post as early as usual, this Christmas with the, result that the staff was called upon to handle, at short notice, items that could have been posted a week earlier. Air mail traffic from the U.S. this year was as heavy as last year, but outward airmail to the U.S. created an all time record of almost 400.000 items.

Remittances from U.S. were above last year's high level. Advices for above £26,000 for residents in the Counties Limerick, Kerry, Clare, and parts of Tipperary passed through the G.P.O. during Christmas week.

The telegraph and telephone Department were heavily taxed to cope with the Christmas traffic and an augmented staff had to be employed to a late hour on Christmas Eve to effect a clearance.

Continuous telephone service was provided during the whole of the Christmas period. A large number of temporary postmen were engaged through the local Employment Exchange and the sum paid out in wages provided a welcome income to many homes.

Limerick Leader 29-12-1954

Two Ministers at Post Office Workers Function

The members of the Limerick Branch of the Post Office Workers' Union held their annual social in Cruise's Hotel last night. . The guests included Mr. W. Norton, Minister for Industry and Commerce, and Mr. M. J. Keyes, Minister for Posts and Telegraphs.

An incident occurred during the proceedings arising out of the use of a tape recorder as a medium for supplying music. A deputation of the Federation of Musicians attended and protested against the use of the recorder, maintaining that a regular band should have been engaged.

Officials of the Union explained they were not aware that the Federation had banned the use of recorders. If they had been so aware they would have engaged a small band, as had been done formerly. It was also felt that as the function was private, there being no admission charge, there was no need to engage a regular band.

The Federation however, placed a picket on duty outside the hotel the members of which carried notices saying "Trade Dispute on Here" The picket continued to parade until the function had concluded.

Mr. Michael Casey, Branch Chairman presided. The guests in addition to the two Ministers included the Mayor G.E. Russell, Mr. P. Lynch Postmaster Limerick. Mr. W. Bell. Deputy General Secretary of the Post Office Workers Union and Dr. A.

Crehan M.O. to the Limerick Branch. Over one hundred members of the Union attended. The Minister for Post and Telegraphs, proposing a toast of the Union, said that he was very glad to learn that the Union, which very ably conducted was growing in strength. He was aware that the Post Office workers were endeavouring to have many grievance removed and he could assure them that so far as he could he would co-operate to the fullest extent possible in securing better conditions.

The Minister proceeded to say that the Post Office service was being efficiently administered by first class officials and it was only right and proper that public servants should enjoy conditions in keeping with their status and in relation to modern conditions.

Mr. Bell, responding, thanked the Minister for his tribute to the Union and his promise of co-operation. At present, he continued, important negotiations were proceeding between the Union and the Department, but as these were sub judice he did not want to elaborate on them. He hoped, however that as a result of these negotiations important developments for Post Office would follow.

Mr. James Hanrahan in a happy speech proposed the toast of the guests and said that it gave the members very great pleasure to be honoured by the presence of two Minsters of State and the civic head of the city.

The Minister for Industry and Commerce responding, spoke of the pleasure and joy it gave to him to be amongst old friends in the Trades Union movement. The Post Office Worker's Union' was founded to protect the interests of men and women, silent workers, who, if unorganised, would be powerless to do anything for themselves. Trade Unions were a powerful force for good for many reasons but especially in the field of collective bargaining.

The Mayor said that Post Office workers were noted for their calm efficiency and for a willing desire to be most co-operative with the public in the carrying out of many varied tasks that called for patience and ability of a high order.

The Postmaster, who also responded, said that he was amazed at the manner in which the Limerick staff handled the Christmas traffic. Having come to Limerick from a smaller centre, it was his first experience of Christmas traffic in a big office. At first he had a nervous feeling that the staff could not cope with the avalanche of letters, packets, parcels and mail of all kinds but he was soon to find his composure in the realisation that he had under him a first class staff.

A most enjoyable private dance followed.

Limerick Leader 24-1-1955

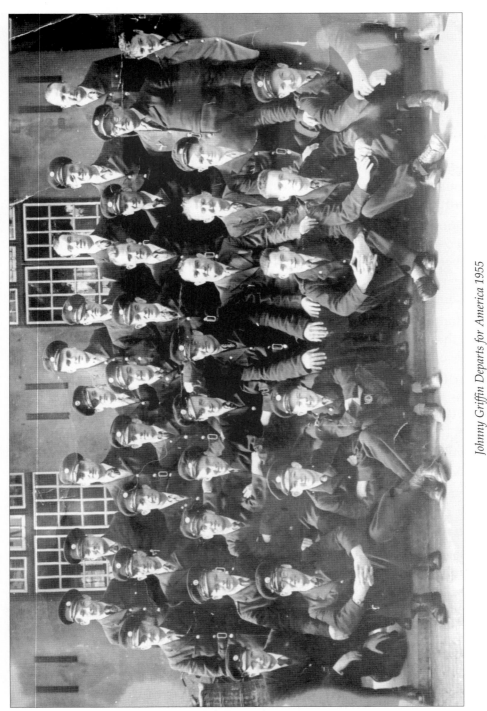

Johnny Griffin Departs for America 1955

Back Row: P. Kiely, J. McMahon, M. Ryan, P Moran, J. Gillane, J. Mangan, G. Leddin, D. Henn, C. Bartlett.
Second Row: B. Barry, J. Collins M. Costello, G. Sheehan, J. Lacey, C. Casey, J. Jackman, P. Mitchell, J. Jackman J. Hayes.
Third Row: T. Moloney, J. Hogan, T. Roche, C. McDonnell, D. O'Brien, J. Griffin, J. O'Connell S. Malone, T. Kenny.
Front Row: J. Curran. S. Liston, P. O'Halloran, P. Bennis, J. Ryan, M. Kennedy.

DÁIL EIREANN
BAILE ATHA CLIATH
(Dublin)
6 November 1957.

The Private Secretary
to the Minister' for Posts and Telegraphs,
General Post Office,
Dublin.

Dear Flo,

I have been approached by the residents of St. Mary's Park, Limerick, who point out that, although there are four shops in the area, there is nowhere to purchase stamps or to cash Money Orders such as Children's' Allowance, Widows' and Orphans' Pensions, etc.

This is a highly populated area and I should be greatly obliged if the Minister could see his way to giving this facility to these people. Should he so desire, I would be in a position, of course, to make a recommendation as to the most suitable applicant in my opinion.

Yours sincerely,

P. 23530/57

Representations by D. O'Malley for establishment of a Sub Office at St. Mary's Park, Limerick City.

An tAire,

A rough sketch of the area concerned is attached.

St. Mary's Park is a purely residential area comprising a slum clearance scheme of 454 houses, which was completed in 1936. The population is estimated at 1,800.

Castle Barracks' letterbox is 200 yards from the proposed site for the Sub Office. Bridge St. and Thomondgate Town Sub Offices are each only half mile away. The former is on the direct road from St. Mary's Park to the city centre. The majority of the residents work in the city and transact their business at Bridge St. T.S.O. which they must pass travelling to and from work.

There are 10 occupied shops but, having regard to the class of residents in the area, it is considered doubtful if a suitable and financially sound candidate would be forthcoming for the position of Sub Postmaster if it were decided to establish an office.

A return for the period of four weeks ended 30.11.1957 showed that an average of only 5 Money Orders per week at Thomondgate T.S.O. and 7 weekly at Bridge St. T.S.O.

It is considered that existing facilities are adequate as far as the St. Mary's Park area is concerned and it is recommended, therefore, that the application be refused.

The question of issuing a Stamp License to one of the shops would be favorably considered if application were made to the Postmaster Limerick.

18 Nollaig, 1957

Runai,

Noted by an tAire and reply sent.

Runai Aire,
20/12/57

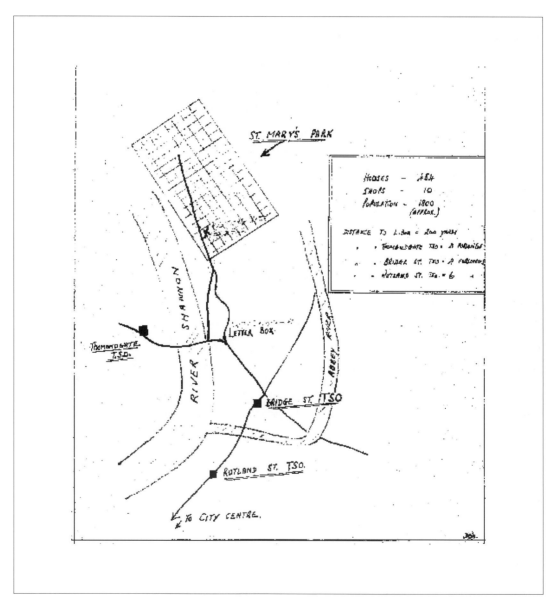

Sketch of St. Marys Park.

June 1958
Delegates attending the Annual Conference of the Post Office Workers Union in the Royal George Hotel, Limerick.

Sean Kiely

Boy Messenger, Postman, Postal Sorter, Inspector.

From 1942 – 1988

Sean joined the Post Office staff as a temporary Boy messenger on the 15 August 1942. His weekly wage was 11 shillings and 5 pence for a six day a week, or one shilling and eleven pence for an eight hour day. At that time there were twenty one boy messengers employed delivering telegrams and T.M.Os (telegraph money orders) in Limerick City and the surrounding area. Any overtime worked was paid at 3 pence an hour and 4 pence an hour on Sundays.

He sat his Civil Service Commission exam in 1944 and was appointed a Civil Servant in September 1944 at the age of 16 years. At the age of 19 years he had passed the oral Irish test and was appointed postman in 1947.

After passing his driving test he was put on a driver's panel and substituted for annual leave, sick leave etc. While on this panel he performed all the walking, cycling and driving duties in the Limerick district.

In 1950 he qualified by virtue of seniority for his own permanent duty and served in the Corbally - St. Mary's Park area until he got his own driving duty. He served on the Pallasgreen feeder service and City centre parcel delivery until he was appointed Postal Sorter.

Sean soon discovered that the majority of sorter's duties finished after 9.30pm at night and for that reason he went on the acting Inspector's panel.

When the soldiers in the Irish Army were demobbed after the emergency (Second World War) a number of them were given appointments in the Post Office but Sean had been appointed postman before they took up their appointments. This meant that even though he was senior to them, some of them were much older then him and so he was promoted fairly quickly. He served as Inspector 2 for a number of years and when James (Jimmy) Curran R.I.P. retired he was appointed Inspector I.

Having been trained in Phibsboro in Dublin and in Cork H.O. he quickly realised that the Limerick Office was years behind the times. He found himself making up wages, dealing with the public and supervising the preparation and dispatch of a delivery at the same time and there was no security in the Limerick office at that time.

It was decided that he would do a complete revision of the duties and it was agreed that the postmens' office would be out-housed in Spaight's Shopping Centre (Shannon St - Henry St) until the G.P.O. sorting office would be changed and extended. This was the first time that the Inspectors in Limerick had an office where they had a filing cabinet, a telephone and a door to lock while he was preparing the wages and dealing with public. Sean refused to accept the old antiquated furniture from the old office and a complete set of new furniture (sorting benches, chairs stools etc.) was provided. When the new sorting office at the G.P.O. was finished, the new furniture from Spaight's was put in place including a new fully equipped Inspectors 1 office and a new office for Inspectors 2's.

At this stage An Post had taken over and Sean quickly realised that big changes were about to happen. He had worked hard to improve the service to the public and to make the job of postmen more tolerable. He succeeded in improving working conditions such as showers, drying rooms, new retiring rooms, new lockers, improved heating etc, but it soon became obvious to him that the job and the service to the public was changing fast.

After long and careful consideration Sean decided to call it a day and retired on his birthday 23 June 1988.

Sean Kiely was a member of the National Executive of the Post Office Workers Union for 3 years.

Sean Kiely

ST. MARY'S CATHEDRAL, LIMERICK,
Was built between the years 1168-1172 by Donal Mor O'Brien, King of Thomond, on the site of his own Palace.

PAPAL VISIT TO IRELAND
Pope John Paul II. On Saturday, 29th September, 1979. The stamp design by Peter Byrne.

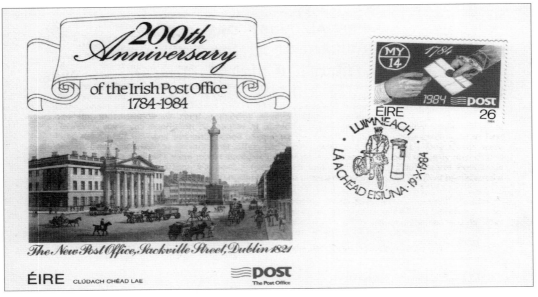

IRISH POST OFFICE 1784-1984
The Irish Post Office commemorate the 200th Anniversary of its foundation.
The stamp was designed. By Brendan Donegan, and the illustrator was Christiaan Vis.

BICENTENARY OF THE MAIL COACH IN IRELAND
The stamp was designed by Katie O'Sullivan. The first day cover was designed by Noel Mooney.

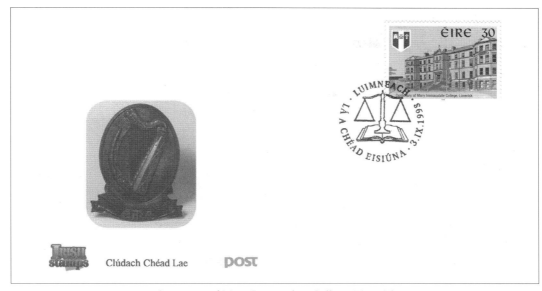

Centenary of Mary Immaculate College, Limerick
Mary Immaculate College was founded in 1898 by Dr Edward Dwyer, Bishop of Limerick, in collaboration
with the Sisters of Mercy, Limerick. Designer - Eric Patton Printer Irish Security Stamp Printing Ltd

The Battle of Fontenoy

The Battle of Fontenoy

Cath Fontenoy
Cuimhnigh ar Luimneach

On May 15, 1995 the postal administrations of Ireland and Belgium released together a postage stamp in remembrance of the Battle of Fontenoy, one of many episodes in the "Succession of Austria war". Fontenoy is a small village in the province of Hainault, attached to the town of Antoing since the communes joined together. It is situated 2 kilometres to the east of Antoing and 8 kilometres to the south east of Tournai.

On the 11th of May 1745, the village lent its name to a bloody battle, the outcome of which was that the French army commanded by King Louis XV and the Marechal Maurice of Saxe defeated the armies led by the Prince of Waldeck and the Duke of Cumberland. The courageous comportment of the Dillon Irish regiment that fought at the sides of the King of France certainly contributed in a large measure to this victory. If one goes to the trouble of researching the origin of the battle cry, "Remember Limerick", one rapidly finds the reason why the Irish were fighting on the French side.

As a result of a fund-raising drive in Ireland, a Celtic cross was erected at the beginning of this century on the village square of Fontenoy. The composition of the postage stamp, an allegory, was created by Belgian artist Eric Daniels.

First Day Covers Courtesy of Dermot O'Brien.

WILLIAMITE WARS 1690

These stamps mark two important battles of the "Williamite Wars" in Ireland, "The Battle of the Boyne" and "Siege of Limerick 1690." The first day cover design is based on the bookplate of the Royal Hospital, Kilmainham, Dublin. The stamps and first day cover were designed by Stephen Conlin and printed by Irish Security Stamp Printing Limited. First day Cover Courtesy of Dermot O'Brien.

TREATY OF LIMERICK, 1691, SIEGE OF ATHLONE

These stamps commemorate two significant events in the war between William of Orange and James II for the English Throne. The "Treaty" design features portraits of Sarsfield and Ginkel, the signatories of the treaty. The "Athlone" design features a view of the town, and shows the bridge over the River Shannon, which was the focal point of the battle. The first day cover portrays a trophy of arms, and is based on the bookplate of the Royal Hospital, Kilmainham, Dublin. The stamps and first day cover were designed by Stephen Conlin, and printed by Irish Security Stamp Printing Ltd. First Day Cover Courtesy of Frank O'Connor.

Did You Know

Limerick woman, Eleanor McGhie, on 21 May 1873, to her niece Mary Mossop in Philadelphia, the letter she wrote used both sides of one sheet of paper, and having filled the second side, she turned to the first page again, rotating it by ninety degrees and writing over the initial writing. This method of writing was known as 'cross writing' and was common practice during the Victorian era, when postage was still charged by the page and writing paper was expensive. Occasionally letters were even re-crossed, which entailed writing the third and fourth pages in the crossed style and then returning to pages one/ three, turning it forty-five degrees and cross writing once more. In this fashion six pages could be written onto one sheet, although in many cases this would render the letter almost illegible. Although

Eleanor McGhie's letter, which was a folded sheet, filled three pages in straight writing and one in crossed, it was still quite clear and concise.

Extract from The Old Limerick winter 2006 by Sharon Clancy.

1843 saw the 'Birth' of the first Christmas card. This was the brainchild of the Englishman Sir Henry Cole.

Cole, a busy businessman, wanted to save time in writing his Christmas letters and also to encourage the expansion of the young postal system. The card cost one shilling each to produce and a 1,000 were printed on the occasion.

With the advent of cheaper printing methods in the late 1860s, the production of cards accelerated. Soon after, the post office introduced a half penny stamp for the sending of the cards.

In Christmas 1937, the Austrian Postal Authorities issued the first commemorative Christmas stamp.

Alfred Nolan

50 years service

I entered the Department of Post and Telegraphs on the 10 October 1946 as a Boy Messenger. In those days a messenger's main function was to deliver telegrams and what was then known as TMO'S or Telegraph Money Orders. This period, 1946 was immediately after the Second World War, which ended in 1945. Thousands of Irish people were working in the United Kingdom at that time and on Thursdays, Fridays and Saturdays, TMO'S were sent by telegraph to be delivered to various families in Limerick City and rural areas. It would not have been unusual for a messenger to have a batch of 20-30 telegrams for delivery. The city was divided into 3 divisions for delivery purposes i.e. Uptown from the GPO and all areas North, Downtown from the GPO and areas South, and Garryowen from the GPO and all areas East. The rural areas in the various divisions were included as appropriate. At one stage there were 18 messengers employed at the GPO. Boy Messengers also worked on Switchboards and distributed Telegrams in the Telegraph Office to the various positions both Morse and Teleprinter.

In the early 1950's Boy Messengers were employed in Shannon Airport. Their duties were delivering telegrams to the many Airlines, PAN AM, TWA, AOA, Sabina, Air Italia, Swissair etc and taking outgoing mail to the bus for dispatch to both Limerick and Dublin. I recall being called from my lunch to be photographed receiving the first airmail dispatch from Boston. Unfortunately I was never given a copy of the photograph. I remember the wooden control tower in Shannon going up in a blaze and the then overseer Mr. Sean McCarthy handing me a "green bag" with the entire stock of Shannon P.O. in it and being told very forcefully not to leave it out of my sight and needless to say, I did as I was instructed. My messenger days were happy days and I enjoyed them very much. In 1946 I competed in the confined examination for promotion to Learner grade, more or less a trainee clerk and I was successful in gaining a place.

The Learner Grade was an apprenticeship for the Clerk Grade and usually the duration of the training was 18 months. The training was very comprehensive and was under the control of a very senior clerk who taught the class Morse code, Teleprinter Operating, counter work, sorting office work and register locker work etc. Senior Telephonists usually gave Telephone Exchange training. The training was pretty intensive and you were given tests in all subjects to show your proficiency and if unsuccessful, you had to repeat them later. Eventually when you came up to the required standard, which you proved by passing your various tests, you were promoted to Post Office Clerk Grade B.

At this stage of your career you were assigned to some Post Office where there was a vacancy and off you went, hoping to return to Limerick some day. I was lucky I was appointed to GPO Limerick and spent the rest of my working Life in Limerick. I will always remember our Morse code training. You were paired off with another Learner- one would "send" and the other "receive". The training Officer would hand the sender a page of the newspaper of the Stock Exchange quotations and you "received" stocks and shares for the next 30 minutes. No opportunity of guessing what was being sent unless you were a financial wizard. It certainly took the guesswork out of your half-hour practice!

Things changed dramatically when you were appointed Post Office Clerk Grade B (POCB). You were on the rota and rotated on various duties- counter, sorting office, and telegraphs. The various duties on the Grade B rota had most unsociable hours and most of them were split duties. You worked from 10am to 2pm but you were free in the afternoon and did not finish duty until 9.32pm, yes 9.32pm. The reason for this unusual finishing time was a mystery to everyone except Post Office staff. At that time you worked 51 'A minutes in every hour from 8pm to 6am the following morning. Later this ludicrous and cheap labour tactic was replaced with Night Duty allowance (NDA).

The Post Office in Shannon Airport was staffed from Limerick H.O. and it provided a 365day and 24 hour service. You worked long, long hours there. For example, working on the evening duty you travelled to Shannon on the 3.15pm bus to commence work at 4pm.and finished at 12 midnight. During that time you worked on the counter or sent foreign telegrams on the Teleprinter. You arrived back in Limerick at 1am having taken the 12.15am bus from the airport. You did that for 7 days. Night duty began on the following Sunday when you took the 11.15pm bus to commence work at 12 midnight arriving back in Limerick at 10.30am the following morning. It was hard going but you had plenty of that curse of the Post Office worker, O.T. (overtime)!

Around 1958 I was promoted to POCA and continued doing counter and register locker work for about 5 to 6 years. In the 1960's 1 was taken off these duties and worked as a writing clerk. This work was very varied and interesting and I enjoyed it very much. I did wages duties and prepared Superannuation Papers for all grades. You must remember that GPO Staff serviced all Telephone Exchange Staff (now Eircom). If my memory serves me correctly I would say that we catered for up to 600 staff (of all grades) in the wages and other sections. My seniority and service entitled me to promotion but I opted to remain a POC and never applied for promotion.

I eventually found myself in charge of Income Tax and all that type of work, which I found very interesting. I remained looking after Income Tax and Superannuations for the rest of my service.

The Civil Service did not come into the PAYE system of tax collection until April 1976. I was asked by the then Head Postmaster, Mr. Thomas Haughey, to go to Dublin concerning Income Tax systems. I was actually going there for the introduction of computerisation and PAYE into the Department of Post and Telegraphs. We eventually ended up in IBM Burlington Road. The object of the visit was transferring the full wages and accounts systems to" floppy discs" or computers. Post Office Clerks from Cork, Galway, Waterford and myself were in the pilot scheme for the transfer. We met for the first time in November 1975. Our objective was to have the frill system up and running for the beginning of the new Income Tax year on April 6th 1976 and I say in all modesty that it was introduced without a hitch.

We were told afterwards that it was one of the best schemes introduced. The reason, we contended, was that all the people involved were "grassroots" clerks who actually did the various jobs themselves. We were all well acquainted with the work and had the essential practical experience.

I hope that I have thrown some light on the conditions and work of POC's during my service —1946-1996.

I must admit that on the whole I enjoyed my time in both the Dept. of P&T and An Post.

Alfred Nolan
Post Office Clerk at Limerick GPO (retired)

Paddy Hayes.
Christmas at the Limerick G.P.O. in the 40s and 50s.

Christmas in the G.P.O. Henry St was far different in the 40s and 50s than it is to-day. At that time you had no fax, and no e-mail to send your Christmas greeting to friends or family. The only way to send your Greeting was by Post. Some however, had the luxury of phones.

The amount of cards posted, was far heavier then it is to-day. Most of the Christmas pressure covered a period of 8 days prior to Christmas Day. Sorting space at the G.P.O. would be at a premium for Letters and Parcels and it wasn't unusual to see 3 or 4 Postal Sorters and Clerks sorting on the same bench trying to clear for the night mail dispatch at 9:30pm. This included all mail for England and also air mail for U.S.A. for dispatch to Shannon Airport. The wire skips used for parcels during the rest of the year were now filled with sub office mail and the sorting of these would commence immediately after the night mail dispatch.

The incoming mail due at Limerick Railway Station now known as Colbert Station at 1:40am, was now arriving between 1 to 2 hours late. This meant the sub offices mails were now been dispatched between 9am and 10am instead of normal dispatch time of 6:30am. Postmen waiting for the mail for their respective delivers were now receiving it late. This included a huge amount of extra mail. On the Whitegate run which include Mountshannon, postmen would be seen starting their deliveries in the dark with their carriers on the front of bicycles full of parcels. On the Tarbert run, Newtownsandes and Athea were suffering the same fate.

The hours of attendance for postmen at head office was from 5am to 11pm. There had to be two deliveries. Each day each postman had a helper and they were known as "slacks". They started for duty at 8am and worked until the second delivery was completed. They helped the postman to sort his delivery if they could find a vacant space and it wasn't unusual to see some of them sorting letters on the floor in the confined cramped conditions. Many of those helpers had no Protective Clothing and on wet days would been seen returning to the office after the deliveries, wet and soaked. The same helpers would be seen on night duty each Christmas.

There are stories that come to mind about helpers at Christmas time. One such story relates to a gentleman known as the poet Ryan; he was there so many Christmases he would have been nearly entitled to a pension. He was a regular customer at the White House pub, located at 52 O'Connell St., a great poetry Pub. One evening a Sorter who thought he knew him told him so. The poet Ryan replied, *"I don't know you but we will soon find out. Did I ever ask you to buy me a pint"* *"You did not"*, was the answer. *"Well, did I ask you for a loan of a half crown"*. *"You did not"*, was the sorters reply. *"Well then I never met you"*, the poet Ryan replied.

Another character, John, surname unknown, from St. Mary's Park was working on the Landing Stage all day taking mail to the parcel office, opening table and the register locker. He told us one morning that he woke up in the middle of the night and pulled the pillow from under the wife's head. She roared, *"where are you going with the pillow"*, and he roared back, *"I'm going to the bag opening table"*.

Paddy Hayes Postal Sorter Retired

Savoy Bedford Row 1951
Mick Galvin, George Ryan, Ger Sheehan. far left Jim Jackman.

Savoy Bedford Row 1952 - George Ryan, Rita Logan

Back Row. Mick Ryan, Eamon O'Brien, Eddie Lee, Jimmy Curran.
Front Row. Tony Kenny, John Ryan, Jim Jackman, Paddy Mitchell, Charlie Bartlett. 1952.

Back Row. Paddy Mitchell, Ger Sheehan, Jim Jackman, Dermot O'Brien Mick Ryan.
Front Row. Gerry Leddin Jimmy Curran, Paddy Hayes. 1955

Redemptorist Retreat, 1956

Michael McNamara also known as 'Old Stock' 1956

ostal sorters at work prior to Christmas, 1958. Standing from left, Joe Clohessy, Tom Hehir, Benny O'Callaghan, Eddie
tzgerald, Sean O'Kelly, Tom O'Sullivan, Tom Scanlan, fred Hourigan, Martin Daly. At the back are Tom Ward and

1958
L to R Joe Clohessy, Tom Hehir, Benny O'Callaghan, Eddie Fitzgerald, Sean O'Kelly,
Tom O'Sullivan, Tom Scanlan, Fred Hourigan, Martin Daly, at the back Tom Ward.

AN ROINN P01ST AGUS TELEGRAFA

TREORACHA D'OGANAIGH P0IST

INSTRUCTIONS

FOR

JUNIOR POSTMEN

1962

Rg.3.

CONTENTS

Rules

INTRODUCTION - GENERAL RULES:

DELIVERY OF TELEGRAMS:

EXPRESS DELIVERY:

INTRODUCTION

The Department of Posts and Telegraphs, of which you are now a member, is an important public department. Its main function is to provide an efficient telegraph, postal and telephone service. As a junior Postman, you will probably be connected mainly with the telegraph service, e.g., the delivery of telegrams, but you may also be employed on indoor duties. Your job is a responsible one and it is important that you should do it well. This booklet will tell you how the Department wants you to do it. Read it carefully so that you will fit yourself to perform your duties well and thus become a useful member of the staff.

Keep the book carefully and refer to it if in difficulty on any point. If you are in doubt about the meaning of any of the rules, do not hesitate to consult your superior officer. Be always able to produce the book whenever requested to do so by your superior officer. If you lose or damage the book you may be called upon to replace it at your own expense. You should return the book when you leave the Junior Postman grade.

1

NOTE.—The rules contained in "Staff Rules" also apply to Junior Postmen and you should read them carefully. Junior Postmen employed on cycling or motor-cycling duties should also be thoroughly acquainted with the contents of "Cyclists' Handbook" or "General Instructions for Motor Drivers" as the case may be.

GENERAL RULES

1. Attendance and Punctuality. You must come on duty punctually and report immediately to your superior officer. You must not absent yourself, without permission, during your hours of duty; neither must you go off before your duty finishes, without (a) special permission, and (b) reporting to your superior officer. Any breach of this rule will result in disciplinary action.

Although you may have a fixed attendance each day, you must, if called upon, be ready to attend as long as your services are required.

If you arrive late on duty you must report immediately to your superior officer. A record of late attendances is kept and special notice is taken of repeated unpunctuality.

You will be required, in turn with other Junior Postmen, to perform duty on Sundays and Public Holidays, but work done on those days is paid for specially.

2. Attendance at Educational Classes. It is in your interests to continue your education, and if you attend approved educational classes in your own time, you may have all or portion of your fees refunded by the Department. Under the terms of the Vocational Education Act, 1930, Junior Postmen at Cork, Limerick, and Waterford are obliged to attend continuation educational classes until they reach 16 years of age.

3. Uniform—Articles Supplied. The following articles of uniform will be supplied to you when employed on outdoor duties, viz., a coat, pair of trousers, cap, overcoat, waterproof cape, waist belt, pouch, 3 permanent badges (for cap, coat and overcoat), boots and overall leggings. The boots, waterproof cape and overall leggings will he supplied only if you spend at least 4 hours a day on average on outdoor duties. The waterproof cape and overall leggings are usually supplied for the joint use of two or more Junior Postmen using a particular cycle.

If you are employed on motor-cycle driving duties you will, in addition to the ordinary uniform, be supplied with the following articles of protective clothing waterproof coat (instead of cape), leather jerkin, goggles, gloves, crash helmet, and special leggings and overcoat instead of the ordinary type. The crash helmet must be worn at all times when on motor-cycling duties. Under no circumstances should you ride an official motor-cycle without wearing your crash helmet.

If you are regularly employed on indoor duties you will only be supplied with a coat, trousers and the necessary uniform badges, but if these duties entail some outdoor work you will also be supplied with a cap and overcoat. You should attach the badges to the uniform to the satisfaction of your superior officer, and you may remove the badges only when you are wearing another coat temporarily or when a new coat or cap is supplied. If your uniform or your boots do not fit you properly, you should return them at once for exchange.

Uniform will not be supplied to you if you are leaving the Service or taking up other employment in the Post Office within six weeks after the date at which the issue would in ordinary course become due.

4. Uniform— Wearing of. You must at all times appear on duty in uniform (except when your uniform is under repair and you find it necessary to wear some part of your ordinary clothing). You should wear a collar and tie with your uniform. During the winter months you should wear your overcoat when you are employed on outdoor duties. Bring your waterproof cape to the office each day so that it will be available when you require it. When you leave your overcoat, overall leggings or waterproof cape in the office, you must keep them in the place provided for the purpose. During the summer months you may, if you wish, leave off your tie provided that a collar- attached shirt is worn. When a collar-attached shirt is worn only the top button or stud of the shirt may be left unfastened.

5. Pouch. Wear your pouch only when you are on duty. You should wear it on the left side and slightly to the front.

6. Uniform—-Care of: Cleanliness. Wearing of Private Badges, etc.—(a) you are not to exchange or lend any part of your uniform. Any loss or damage to your uniform while you are in the Service will have to be made good by you.

(b) When you receive new uniform you must keep the old one in its entirety for use as a change when you require it. You should remove the buttons from the last issue but one and return them to your superior officer; failure to do so will render you liable to disciplinary action.

(c) On receipt of new uniform you should remove the cap and breast badges from the old articles and affix them to the new. You should at all times keep yourself clean, and your uniform in good repair, neat and well brushed. Buckles, buttons, and straps for overall leggings and cloth for repairs will be supplied when necessary. Your boots, which must be black, must be well cleaned, properly laced and kept in good repair; your belt blackened, and the buckle and badges burnished. The standard instructions which are displayed in the office, regarding the waterproof articles of uniform, should be carefully observed. You must not wear your uniform except when on duty.

(d) You are forbidden to wear your cap on the back or side of the head, or to change its shape, e.g., by bending the peak. The chin-strap of the cap should be used in stormy weather. You must keep your hair cut short and neatly brushed. **(e)** You are not allowed to wear any private badge, medal, etc., on your uniform, but you may wear the badge of your staff association (if it is officially recognized), the badge of the Pioneer Total Abstinence Association, an Fainne, Eochair-Sciath na Gaeilge, or such other badges as may from time to time be authorized. You may also wear Shamrock on St. Patrick's Day.

(f) When you leave the Service you may purchase articles of your uniform clothing. The purchase price of each item can be ascertained from your superior officer. All items of your last uniform which have not been purchased are to be returned to your superior officer without delay, and if you fail to return all the articles (including the cap and breast badges) in proper condition, you will have to make good their value.

7. Conduct in Office. You must always take off your cap when in the office and he attentive and courteous in your manner. Practical joking is strictly forbidden.

You must obey orders given you by a superior officer failure to do so will result in disciplinary action.

8 Conduct Outside Office.—(a} You must always be courteous to members of the public. When you are in uniform the public know you are in the service of the Post Office, and unruly conduct or slovenly habits bring discredit upon the Department and on yourself. (b)
You are specially cautioned against attempting to travel in any lift not intended for passenger traffic.

9. Conduct while Cycling. Safeguarding of Bicycle, etc.—(a) You should always ride with care, and, as a rule, not faster than eight miles an hour. (For general rules for cyclists see "Cyclists' Handbook" (Rg.116).

(b) You must on no account ride on a footpath, and you must not race. You must not ride in company with other Junior Postmen and you must not ride one bicycle while leading another; neither must you carry a "passenger" nor ill-use the bicycle in any way. Furthermore, your general conduct should not cause annoyance to pedestrians or other road users.

(c) Safeguarding of Bicycle. You should, as far as possible, keep the bicycle in sight when you have to leave it to deliver a message and you should place it in such a position that it will not be an obstruction to pedestrians or lie damaged by passing traffic.

(d) Parts Broken or Lost. If any part of the bicycle or any cycle appliance is broken or lost, you must report the circumstances to your superior officer without delay.

10. Loitering. You must not loiter when you are engaged in delivering telegrams, or in the discharge of your other duties, and you must always proceed and return on your own. You must not read books or papers while out on delivery or when returning to the office.

11. Smoking. You are strictly forbidden to smoke in or about the office at any time or in the streets when you are in uniform.

12. Public Houses. You must not enter a public house except in the course of your duty.

13. Junior Postmen's Room. You are expected to play your part in keeping the Junior Postmen's room clean and tidy. Wilful damage done either to the room or its contents will have to be made good at the expense of the Junior Postmen, including yourself.

14. Christmas Boxes. Gratuities from the Public. You are forbidden under penalty of dismissal to ask for Christmas boxes or gratuities from the public.

15. Letters for Junior Postmen. You are not allowed to have letters addressed to you at the office where you are employed.

16. Suspicion of Dishonesty on the part of Post Office Officials or others. If you have knowledge or suspicion of dishonesty or other criminal conduct on the part of any Post Office official (if, for example, you suspect another Junior Postman of opening or allowing an unauthorised person to open a telegram, or of destroying a telegram, or of not handing in at the office a reply telegram, or of dealing irregularly with an express letter), you must at once report the matter confidentially to your superior officer.

If you have knowledge or suspicion of dishonesty or other criminal conduct affecting the Post Office on the part of a person who is not a Post Office official, you must follow the same course.

17. Divulgence of Information.—(a) You must not divulge any information which you may acquire in your official capacity as Junior Postman. If any person should try to persuade you to do so, you must report the fact to your superior officer without delay.

All officers, including Junior Postmen, are bound by the Official Secrets Acts and any officer offending under the Acts renders himself liable not only to dismissal, but to prosecution as well **(see Rule 42 " Staff Rules ")**.

(b) If any person, whether a Post Office official or not, tries to persuade you to act contrary to your duty (for example, if you are asked to reveal the contents of a telegram or to allow any person to open a telegram or express letter before it is delivered) you must refuse. When you return to the office you must at once tell your superior officer, but no one else, what the person said to you, all you can remember as to his appearance, and anything else which will help towards identifying him.

(c) Should a stranger try to make your acquaintance while you are on duty you should be cautious of his purpose, and not delay with him. On return to the matter to the office you must at once report your superior officer.

18. Social Welfare Insurance. On reaching the age of 16 you become insurable under the Social Welfare Acts and the employee' 5 contributions will be deducted from your wages. On appointment to an established post you will he insurable in respect of Widows' and Orphans' Pensions only.

19. Notification of Illness. Furnishing of Medical Certificate. If you are prevented by illness from attending for duty, your superior officer should be informed without delay, if possible before the hour at which your turn of duty commences. A note from a parent or guardian will suffice in respect of the first two days of absence, but if the absence extends beyond two days it will be necessary to furnish a medical certificate. An absence extending from Saturday.. to Monday, inclusive, must be covered by a medical certificate. See also Rules 133-442, "Staff Rules.") If sick absences are frequent, the question of your fitness for service in the Department will arise. **(For Sick Pay Rates see Rules 143—147 "Staff Rules.")**

DELIVERY OF TELEGRAMS

20. Telegrams not to be Opened, Delayed, Destroyed, or Transferred to another Junior Postman. You are forbidden, in any circumstances, to open an envelope in which a telegram is enclosed, and having received a telegram for delivery, you are strictly forbidden to give it to another Junior Postman.

If you open, delay, or permit anyone else to open or delay, or if you destroy, any telegram, you render yourself liable not only to dismissal, but to prosecution as well. If you see another Junior Postman open or destroy a. telegram you must report the matter to your superior officer without delay.

21. Expeditious Delivery. On receiving telegram you should start immediately and deliver it as quickly as you can; alter which you should return to the office and report to your superior officer. You must not go off duty after the delivery of your last telegram, without returning to the

office for the purpose of having your pouch examined by your superior officer and of having your time of leaving recorded in the attendance book, unless you have special permission to act otherwise.

22. Telegram bearing Unknown Address. If you should receive a telegram of which the address is unknown to you) you must ask your superior officer for guidance.

23. Two or more Telegrams on One Journey. If you have two or more telegrams, you are to deliver each in its turn, that is, at the nearest address first, and the furthest address last, but if from any cause there is difficulty in delivering one of them, you are to hasten on with the others, after which you are to return to the neighborhood and make enquiries respecting the telegram you could not deliver in the first instance. Try to deliver it before returning to the office. If you have two or more telegrams and one of them is marked "Urgent" you must deliver that one first and then proceed as described above. If your superior officer instructs you to deliver several telegrams in a particular order, you must then strictly in that order.

24. Delivery to Addressee. The addressee is person or firm whose name appears on the envelope.

You are at all times to deliver your telegrams, if possible, to the addressee in person, or if not, to someone employed on the addressee's premises. You should not give a telegram to any other person even if you are asked for it, unless you know that the person asking for the telegram is entitled to receive it. A telegram should not be given to a child.

When delivery is made to the addressee before his premises are reached no charge should be made for porterage where so assessed, unless the place at which delivery is made is beyond the free delivery limits, when a charge of sixpence should be collected for every mile or part of a mile beyond the free delivery limits.

A telegram for a railway passenger must be delivered to the Station-master whether so addressed or not.

25. Refusal to Pay Porterage, etc. Should the addressee of a telegram refuse to pay porterage or other charges, you are to deliver the telegram and report the refusal on your return to the office.

26. Delivery of Telegrams.—(a) At Business Premises:

If premises are closed.

You should knock or ring twice and allow a reasonable time to elapse between each knock or ring

If no answer.

Make certain that the name and address are correct. If so, drop the telegram into the letter- box and place a despatch notice (Form T.35), suitably filled in, under the door.

If there is a letter-box but no means of leaving the form T.35, for example, where letter-box is fitted to a gate.

Leave the telegram in the letter-box and fill up a form T.35. This should be handed to your superior officer on return to the office.

If there is no letter-box.

You must fill up form T.35 and, if possible, place it under the door, but, in no circumstances, must the telegram be placed under the door.

If you are not certain that the name and address are correct.

You must fill up and leave a form T.35, if possible. The telegram should be taken back to the office and handed to your superior officer. Note the time of your arrival at the address on the envelope.

Do not use a letterbox unless it bears the name of the addressee and do not put a telegram into any box marked "Competitions," "Statements,' "Invoices " or into a letter-box in or by the side of an open door.

Telegrams addressed " Stationmaster."

Do not place in a letter-box if the Station- master's office is closed, but deliver to the Station Inspector on duty.

(b) At Residential Flats and Private Houses. When attention cannot be gained at a private house or residential flat you must satisfy yourself by enquiry at one of the next houses or flats that the address on the envelope is correct, and ascertain, if possible, whether the occupier is expected to return the same day.

(1) *If the address is correct and the addressee is likely to return the same day.*

Leave the telegram in the letter-box and place a form T.35 (suitably filled in) under the door.

(ii) *If the address is correct and the addressee is like/v to return the same day, bid there is no letter-box at the address.*

Place a form T.35 under the door and bring the telegram back to the office. **(iii)** *If the address is incorrect, or if you learn that the addressee is not returning the same day.*

You must take the telegram back to the office. A form T.35 should not be left.

(iv) *If definite information cannot be obtained that the address is correct.*

You must fill up and leave a form T.35 and take the telegram back to the office, reporting the circumstances to your superior officer.

Telegrams for residential flats, when the outer door of the building is closed, are to be treated in the same way as those for private houses, but enquiry need not be made at neighboring residences.

27. Addressee gone to New Address. If you find that the addressee has moved to a new address, and that address is close by, or so situated that you call, without delay, all there on the way back to the office, you must deliver the telegram at the new address before returning to the office. Otherwise, you must take it back to the office and give it to your superior officer. Whenever you deliver a telegram at an address different from that written on the envelope, you must report the circumstances immediately on your return to the office. If you are told that the addressee has moved, you must try to obtain his new address, and you should ask whether the redirection fee can be prepaid.

28. Undelivered Telegrams. Immediately you return to the office with an undelivered telegram, you must enter the time and write a short statement on the envelope as to the cause of non-delivery and hand the telegram to your superior officer.

These rules apply also in the case of the delivery of telephone express letters.

29. Reply Telegrams. - (a)When you have delivered a telegram you may accept the following kinds of telegrams from any person at the address of the delivered telegram

(i) a telegram on a "reply address (see Rule **30**);

(ii) an Inland telegram, i.e., telegram addressed to any place within the State, Great Britain or the Six Counties (see Rule **31** (ii))

(iii) a Foreign telegram, i.e., a telegram addressed to a place abroad, or a Radio-telegram, i.e., a telegram addressed to a ship at sea, but only if the sender has a telegram account with the Post Office or if you are specially instructed to do so by your superior officer (see Rule **31** (i));

(iv) a telegram to be repeated (see Rule **32**);

(v) a re-directed telegram (see Rule **33**).

(b) Except as shown in para. (a) above, you must not accept a telegram from any person anywhere (e.g., a person in the street) unless instructed to do so by your superior officer.

30. Reply Paid Telegrams. It a telegram is "reply paid" you must ask if there is a reply and, if you have no other telegrams to deliver, you may wait ten minutes for the reply, if required, but not longer. If you have other telegrams to deliver you must not wait but must call for the reply telegram on your way back to the office alter you have delivered the remaining telegrams. The reply should he read over by you, unless the sender objects to your doing so, or unless you have special instructions not to do so from your superior officer.

You must calculate the charge for a reply telegram as follows:

(i) if addressed to a place within the State—at the rate of **three shillings** for the first twelve words, address included, and **threepence** for each additional word;

(ii) if addressed to a place in Great Britain or the Six Counties—at the rate of **three shillings and sixpence** for the first twelve words, address included, and threepence for each additional word.

On **Sundays, Good Friday** and **Public Holidays,** you are to charge in addition, a fee of one shilling. If the total charge calculated in this manner exceeds the amount prepaid as shown on the back of the reply paid" telegram form you must collect the excess.

If the reply is to a place abroad or to a ship at sea you should explain courteously to the sender that you do not know the rate, and cannot guarantee that the number of words in the "reply paid" telegram corresponds with the charge prepaid; but that if the telegram is given to you, it will be duly despatched, any supplementary charge being collected later.

31. Telegrams to which a Reply has not been Prepaid. When delivering in country areas you should always ask if there is a reply telegram; in town areas you need not enquire, but if asked to wait for a reply you should do so. You should enquire as to its destination and act as follows:

(i) *Reply telegram for a place abroad or ship at sea.*

Ask the sender if he has a telegram account with the Post Office; if he has, you may you should ask for the telegram you delivered to be handed back to you, with **the word or words to be repeated underlined.**

No charge is made for this repetition.

On your return to the office you should at once inform your superior officer of the request for repetition.

33. Re-directed Telegrams.—(a) You are forbidden to take a telegram to another address after having received money for its re-direction. Such a telegram must be brought back to the office and handed to your superior officer, together with the money received for re-direction.

(b) The charge for re-direction of a telegram is ordinarily the full rate specified in Rule **30**.

If, however, a telegram is re-directed, without being opened, to an address in the same town, the charge is three shillings only, irrespective of the length of the message. Telegrams from places within the State, Great Britain or the Six Counties addressed to visitors at hotels or boarding houses are not re-directed unless the charges are prepaid. Persons making a request that such telegrams be re-directed should be informed of this rule. In the event of the fee not being paid the new address should be obtained for the purpose of advising the office of origin, and the telegram taken back to the office. Telegrams re-directed on **Sundays, Good Friday** and **Public Holidays** are charged one shilling in addition to the ordinary charges for re-direction.

If the telegram has been opened at the address before being re-directed the person by whom it has been re-directed should be asked to write out a fresh message. In the event of a refusal to do so the telegram should be accepted on prepayment of the full rate, the words Opened at first address" being charged for in addition. If prepayment be refused, the re-directed message should, nevertheless, be accepted, and the matter explained on your return to the office.

34. Acceptance of Reply Telegrams when Post Office is Closed.—(a) If your office is closed and you are asked to take a reply telegram, whether prepaid or not, you must politely inform the sender that your office is closed for the night and that it will, therefore, be necessary for him to make his own arrangements for the despatch of the telegram. In no case must you incur expense in traveling or overtime for the conveyance of such replies. If, however, after the circumstances have been explained, the sender specially requests you to take a reply message, and offers to pay your expenses, you may do so, but you must make it clear that the arrangement is quite apart from your official duty, and that it is entirely a private one.

(b) When it is possible to return with a reply telegram to your office before it closes, the reply should be taken, even though you may be detained on duty after your proper time.

35. Money Unexpended. You must hand to your superior officer any money you have received for reply, or re-directed telegrams, or for porterage or other charges, or money which has been given to you to pay taxi or bus fares and has not been expended.

36. Pouch Examination. You must not leave an undelivered or a reply telegram in your pouch and the pouch must be shown to your superior officer before going off duty.

37. Telegrams not to be written for Senders. You must not, under any circumstances, write out a telegram for another person.

38. Irregular Conveyance or Delivery of Messages. You must inform your superior officer if any attempt is made to persuade you to receive, convey, or deliver as a telegram a message which it is not your duty to receive, convey, or deliver as a telegram.

EXPRESS DELIVERY

39. Definition. An Express Delivery Service is the delivery of a letter or parcel by special messenger.

40. Delivery Instructions. Before leaving the office with an Express packet you will receive instructions regarding delivery and collection of any charges.

41. Acceptance of Telegrams when delivering Express Packet. On delivering an Express packet you may, if requested, take back an Inland telegram for transmission. No Express fee is charged for this service.

42. Verbal messages between members of the Public not to be Conveyed. When on duty you must not convey or undertake to convey verbal messages between members of the public.

43. Acceptance of Express Packets. You should not accept a packet intended for Express delivery from a member of the public.

44. Delivery Receipts. No acknowledgment for an Express packet is required from an addressee unless it is registered, in which case you will be handed a green receipt form to obtain the signature of the person to whom you deliver the packet.
45. Delivery from other Offices. You may be required to deliver Express packets from neighboring sub-offices. In such cases you will receive the necessary instructions at the office to which you are attached and at the office from which the Express packet is to be delivered.

46. Non-delivery. If you cannot deliver an Express packet to a responsible person at the address you should do as follows

(i) Provided that the packet is unregistered and that there are no fees to be collected you should place the packet in the letter-box, if practicable, and place an advice form T.35 under the door.

(ii) If there is no letter-box put an advice form T.35 under the door and hand in the packet at the nearest Post Office. If the packet is registered, or if there are charges to be collected, place a form T.35 under the door and take the packet back to the office at which you received it. (See also Rule 26.)

47. Delivery arrangements at Dublin. At Dublin there are special arrangements as regards the delivery of Express packets. Junior Postmen attached to Dublin will receive special instructions from the officers despatching them on Express delivery in those cases in which the foregoing rules are not applicable.

48. Supervising Officer to be consulted in cases of Doubt. When in doubt about any matter relating to the Express Delivery Service consult your superior officer.

MOTOR-CYCLE DELIVERY

49. Selection and Training of Motor-Cyclists. Motor-cycles are in use at some delivery offices. Junior Postmen of 16 years of age and over who are serving at such offices may be selected for training in motor-cycling duties. The training includes instruction in the care and operation of a motor-cycle, behavior in traffic, and, in general, all essential points which would help the trainees to become careful and efficient motor-cyclists. At the end of training the trainees are given a competency test and, if they pass that test, they are placed on motor-cycling duties.

D. O'Brien, W. Coffey, P. Rowan, J. Ryan, S. Spillane (Dasher), circa 1960

POWU Killarney 1961 - Dermot O'Brien, Joe Jackman, Sean Kiely.

Dermot O'Brien. At Kilpeacon Cross 1964

1965
Back Row. Joe Jackman Tom Sullivan, Mick Casey, Bart Cleary, Dave Clancy, Charlie Bartlett,
Jack (Horse) Mc Carthy, Sean Kiely, Mick Keyes, Dermot O'Brien.
Front Row: Christy Casey, Tony Finn, Terry Quinlan, Maurice Cosgrave, Jim Jackman,
Tom Haughey, John Ryan, Gerry Sheehan.

Richard (Dick) O'Neill Overseer 1965

Fred Hourigan as Junior Clerk 1967

Sean Real as a Telegram Boy 1968

Jim Rael, Mick Keyes, Joe O'Sullivan. 1969

Thomas O'Connell
CHRISTMAS 1966

I remember that evening when Macker had said
"Tom would you go to Mungret, poor John is since dead"?
So I took on a duty that I did'nt know
Here and there an old friend I had met long ago.
There was Molly complaining of ashes from fags,
And Tileman's bulldozer arriving in bags.
That Christmas in Mungret I'll never forget
Though I was on the dry, I was never so wet.
The way into Larkin's, a flooded bohreen
And the water four feet at the foot of Camheen,
Don't mention the Island, 'twas flowing down the line
And O'Hanlon's brave forecast, tomorrow'l be fine,
The very next morning was gone by the board,
For the rain just lashed down and a Sou'wester roared.
I rang Macker, he said, "I'd have sent you Jim Lyons,
But sure Finn is bogged down between Pallas and Foynes
The best you could hope for, he might give a call
If he ever succeeds getting Finn out at all:"
So I swam it, I pedalled, I pushed and I swore
In the boxes, the windows or under the door
'Til I came to the last one, where thousands had been
And I made midnight mass in good time at Raheen

Then the Dean, he came out and he started to speak
Half the things he'd to say, would have done me next week!
I saw Dora regaled in her best at the rear
Though a word from the pulpit she never could hear.
Well I knew the Lord's coming was really worthwhile,
Though it gives us a cross He once bore with a smile,
And a prayer I remembered to say there that night
Was that Finn and Jim Lyons would get back in alright.
Then I came out from mass and I hit for the "Well",
And I felt every Christmas works postmen to Hell.
Later on then that night it came starlight and fine
I said "Lord, why'd you change all that water to wine"?

Thomas O'Connell

The late Tommy O'Connell, a native of Patrickswell, worked as a postman in the G.P.O. in Limerick. Inspired by the Maigue poets his writings dealt, to a large extent, with the beauty of the Croom—Patrickswell landscape and it's people. His poetry was published in a wide selection of broadsheets which included The Limerick Weekly Echo (now defunct), The Limerick Leader, The Limerick Chronicle, The Cork Examiner and The Holly Bough. The attached work is unusual in that it deals with his occupation, an area that he seldom if ever referred to in his literary output. Nevertheless this poem conjures an image of what Christmas meant to postmen in the days when resources were scarce and rural areas were still being serviced by men on bikes.

In this poem the man referred to as 'Macker' is Tom McMahon the Inspector of postmen in the G.P.O. in Limerick. Tommy O'Connell will be remembered for his unique talent and his colorful outlook on life which endeared him to all those who had the privilege to have known him.

Joe Spearin

Michael Ryan
Richmond RFC, Munster Junior and Transfield Cup 1935-36

1951

Back Row P. Kiely, D. O'Brien, P. Neville, B. Power, J. Hanley, G. Ryan, S. Healy.
Front row B. Cleary, D. Hayes, J. Lowe, D. Meade, A. Cooney.

1952

Back Row: Ger Hanley, Bunny Power, Dick Meade, Tom Hourigan, Sean Healy, Paddy Neville,
Gerry Sheehan, George Ryan.
Front Row: Donie Hayes, Tony Cleary, Bart Cleary, Dermot O'Brien, Jim Lowe, Albert Kinsella,
Jack Lacey, Paul Kiely, Tony Cooney.

Killarney 1961
Back Row: D. O'Brien, P. Rowan, J. Jackman, Eric Costello, G. Canty, W. Coffey, T. McMahon, T. Moore, M. Bennis, G, Bennis, P.Carroll, O' Barry, B. Flannery.
Front Row: B. Cleary, Sam Brown, M. Kelly, John Cahill, P. O'Brien, J. Lowe, P. Bennis.

1963
Back Row; J Lyons, P O'Carroll C. Moane, E. Costello, M. Griffin, G. Bennis, T. Mc Mahon, J. Cahill
Front Row; B Cleary, P. Bennis, G O'Brien, M. Kelly, D O'Brien, P. O'Halloran, B. Barrett.

Inter Firm 1963
Back Row. D. Linane, P. Madigan, T. Crowley, M. Byrnes, T. Punch, B. Hourigan.
Front Row. B. Cleary, L. Hanley, S. O'Donoghue, H. Byrnes, G. O'Brien, T. Quinn.

1965
Back Row. Noel Moran, Paddy Carroll, B. Carey.
Front Row. Dermot O'Brien, M. Kelly, John Hannon, P. O'Halloran.

1977 Cup Final Limerick/ Dundalk 0-2

Names that are known Wayne Brazil, J. Ryan, G. Foley, B. Whyte, D. Rowan, S. O'Brien, E. Madigan, J. Whelan, J. Manning, D. O'Dwyer, J. Barron, G. Tuohy, V. Jennings. B. Downey, D Baggett, C. Conway, B. Fennell, J. Collopy, G. Devito, F. Renihan.

1986

Back Row: Stan Rodgers, J.J. Hurley, Tom Buckley, Tony Power, Camen Waterstone, Eric Quinn
Front Row: Liam Hanley, Joe O'Sullivan, Philip White, Tom McElligott, Garry Collins.

18-7-1991 Inter-Firm

Back Row D. Hayes, R. McMahon, L. Hayes, E. Cussen, S. Barry, M. Redden, M. Blake, D. Henn, J. Kelly
Front Row R. Neville, T. Keane, J.J. Hurley, S. Rodgers, D. Leddin, A. Lipper.

William Norton

William Norton (1900-1963), Irish politician, Labour Party leader (1932-1960). William Norton was born in Dublin in 1900. He joined the postal service in 1916. By 1920 he was a prominent member in the trade union movement in Ireland. From 1924 to 1948 he served as secretary of the Post Office Workers' Union. He became a TD for County Dublin in 1926. He represented Kildare from 1932 until his death. In 1932 he became leader of the Labour Party. In the first inter-party government, (1948-1951), Norton became Tánaiste and Minister for Social Welfare. In the second inter-party government, (1954-1957), Norton served as Tánaiste and Minister for Industry and Commerce. William Norton died in Dublin in 1963.

Norton Cup
The Norton Cup was donated by Mr. E.T. O'Sullivan Superintendent and played for annually in Soccer by outdoor staff against the indoor clerical grades.

Norton Cup Winners 1965 Postmen
Back Row L to R. Gerry O'Brien, Tom Bourke, Billy Coffey, Jim Lyons, Dermot O'Brien, Barry O'Sullivan.
Front Row. L to R. Paddy O'Halloran, (res), Tom Hanafin, Tony Fleming, Bart Cleary (Captain),
Tom O'Connor, Jim O'Shaughnessy

Norton Cup 1973 Clerks (Barrack Field)
Back Row L to R. Eric Quinn, Donie Collins, Tom McElligott, Mick Burns, Paddy Burns, Jimmy Harrold.
Front Row L to R Garry Collins, Liam Hanley, Des Horgan, (Captain) Ger O'Neill, Tadhg Crowley.

1978
Back Row. N. Ryan, G. Flaherty, B. Scanlan, S. O'Brien, M. McKeon, E. Madigan, E. Lowe, V. Phelan.
Front Row. G. Tracy, L. Hayes, G. O'Flynn, G. Hunt, M. Blake.

1978
Back Row. L. O'Brien, J. Cleary, E. Banville, G. O'Brien, T. Crowley, D. Horgan, G. Molyneaux.
Front Row. J. Harrold, L. Hanley, T. O'Connor. G. O'Neill, J. Sullivan, E. Quinn. (Morgan Crowley)

1979
Back row Tom O'Flynn, Ger Flaherty, Eric Lowe, Liam Hayes, Ger Foley, Eugene Madigan, Sean O'Brien.
Front row Noel Ryan, Ger O'Flynn, Joe Collopy, Michael Blake, Johnny Barron

1979
Back Row. Eric Quinn, Timmy O'Connor, Eddie Banville, Jimmy Harrold, Tadhg Crowley,
Tom McElligott, Liam O'Brien, D Ronan.
Front Row. (Morgan Crowley) Liam Hanley, Gerry O'Brien, Ger O'Neill, Joe O'Sullivan, Bart Cleary

1981
Back Row; Eric Quinn, Timmy O'Connor, Dermot Small Gerry O'Brien Eddie Banville, Tom Sears,
Tadhg Crowley, Colm O'Connor, Liam O'Brien, John Cleary, Bobby Downey, John Cahillane.
Front Row; D. J. O'Sullivan, Garry Collins, Jimmy Harrold, Bart Cleary, Alan Browne,
Morgan Crowley, Paddy Browne, Liam Hanley

1981
Back Row: D. Henn, M. Blake, S. O'Brien, M. McKeown, S. Rogers, E. Lowe, P. Hayes.
Front Row: G. Tracey, M. Reddan, T. Curtin, T. Keane, G. Flatherty.

1982
Back Row: T. Crowley, G. Molyneaux, S. Rogers, J.J. Hurley, E. Banville, T. Sears, L. O'Brien,
E. Quinn, C. O'Connor.
Front Row: T. McElligott, L. Hanley, G. O'Brien, J. O'Sullivan, T. O'Connor, G. O'Neill.

Norton Cup 1982
Back Row: N. Whyte, S. O'Brien, S. Fitzgerald, L. Hayes, M. McKeown, J. Dillon, J. Barron.
Front Row: G. Tracey, D. O'Connor, G. Flatherty, G. Hunt, E. Lowe.

Paddy Hayes

During my early days in the G.P.O as a telegram boy we had 4 appointed and 4 temporary boys. After the second world war hundreds of Limerick unemployed went to work on the building sites in England. The number of telegram boys was increased to deal with the large numbers of telegraph money-orders arriving from England each day. The temporary boys were let go when they reached their 16th birthday but there was always a list of names of those waiting to be recalled. The boys came in on the open civil service exam birthday if a vacancy for postman arose at the G.P.O.

If there was no vacancy at Head Office you could be appointed postman at another office and we all dreaded this as wages were so small you barely had enough to covers yours digs. However the Dept. did it's best to get you back as soon as possible. Once appointed you went on an incremental scale until your max at 27 years of age. We always had 4 or 5 temporary postmen at H.O and they could be working continuously during the summer holidays but the rest of the year they had to wait to be called for work. I remember one such temporary man, John Hanrahan, O' Curry Place and when someone went sick he was sent for at 6am in the morning. Unfortunately the postman sent to call him didn't know his address and he called to the Garda barracks in O' Curry Street to enquire if they know any Hanrahan's in O'Curry Street and they told him the only Hanrahan they knew was Mr. Hanrahan the harbour master. Our friend went to the harbour master's door, knocked and when the harbour master, Mr. Hanrahan, put his head out his bedroom window, he was told to report to the G.P.O immediately. A few minutes later he arrived down at H.O to be told the wrong man had been called and you can be assured he wasn't too happy at first but later saw the funny side.

Overtime was very scarce at this time apart from Christmas and monetary allowance for shift work and night duty was unheard of. However, between the hours of 10pm and 6am we only worked 52 minutes instead of 60. They continued as telegram boys until they were 19 or perhaps be appointed postmen before their 19th Birthday.

By Paddy Hayes

Donal Hayes 1910

Son, Paddy Hayes First Day 10-5-1940

Liam Hayes, Grandson, 2001

Donal Hayes, Grandson, 2003

Jimmy Harrold, Eric Quinn, Ennis 1971

1973
Back Row: Mick Keyes, Billy Coffey, Tony Finn, Brendan Hourigan, Billy Whyte,
Paddy Rowan, Bart Cleary, Dermot O'Brien, Gerry O'Brien, Joe Jackman, and John Ryan.
Front Row: Eamon O'Brien, Jim Jackman, Maurice Cosgrave, Sean McCarthy, Thomas Haughey.
(Postmaster)

Austin O'Regan. 1974

Back Row: T. Scanlan, J. O'Sullivan, J. McCarthy, J. Curran, E. O'Brien, J. Ryan
Front Row: T. Haughey PM., M. Keyes, D. O'Neill, J. Clohessy. 1975

JOINT COUNCILS CONCILIATION

Joint Conciliation Councils are now in existence at 14 centers in the Department. In Dublin, they operate in Dublin Postal District, Central Telephone Exchange. Central Telegraph Office. Stores Branch, Headquarters Offices and Dublin City Engineering District. Outside Dublin, there are separate Councils for the Postal and Engineering staffs in Cork and Limerick and Councils for the Engineering Districts of Waterford, Sligo and Portlaoise. There is also a council for Draughtsmen, covering Dublin and the provinces. The first Council was set up in 1969 in the Dublin Postal District on an experimental basis. The establishment of the D.P.D. Council followed acceptance of a recommendation of a sub-committee of the Departmental Council that had been set up to examine how communication' between management and staff could be improved. The Departmental Council's sub-committee recommendation that a Joint Conciliation Council should be established in the Dublin Postal District was made only after a very detailed examination of systems of communications and consultation in large undertakings, an investigation of schemes in operation in various European countries and a study of several documents published by the International Labour Organisation. On the recommendation of the Departmental Council, the other 13 Councils subsequently came into being.

The main objective of the Councils as set out in their constitutions is to provide a regular means of prior consultation between management and staff on matters of mutual interest with a view to improving relationships and providing the best possible standard of service. The Councils are also intended to enable the staff to take an active interest in the operations of their district or office. The primary functions of the Councils are to encourage and promote general co—operation and mutual trust between management and staff, to promote job satisfaction to enable management and staff to convey their points of view to each other, to discuss and effect settlement of local problems concerning working conditions, welfare, health, safe measures, and to examine how the efficiency of the services provided could be improved.

The Councils consist of a Chairman, who is generally the top Departmental Official in the immediate work area, management representatives nominated by the Department and staff representatives nominated by the recognised staff organisation in the area. The secretaries of the various Councils are nominated by the staff organisations concerned.

The constitution of each Council sets out in general terms how the Council should operate but obviously, the way in which they do so depends very much on the Councils themselves. The intention is that every Council should function as a unit and that members would not regard themselves as representatives of either management or staff, but simply as members of a Council dedicated to promoting the objectives of the body of which they are members.

The various Councils established to date have discussed a wide range of topics of local interest and have undoubtedly served a very useful function. This is not to say that improvements might not be effected or that changes might not be usefully made. Indeed, in recommending the setting up of the Councils both the staff and management sides of the Departmental Council were conscious of the fact that it would be surprising if they worked perfectly from the outset. It was agreed, therefore, that the functioning of the Councils would be kept under review by the Departmental Council. Accordingly, the sub-committee of the Department Council (on whose recommendation the Councils were originally established) are now engaged in a review of their operations with the object of recommending how they might be improved, whether they should be extended to other centres etc. It is expected that this review will be completed within the next few months.

It is the intention from time to time to publish in this magazine comments on aspects of the Department's operations which dealt with various Councils.

1973
Members of the Limerick Consultation Council,
From L to R Mr. M. P. O'Cathasaigh, P.O.C.A. (and Secretary), T. Ó'hEochaidh,
M. Poist, Denis O'Neill Supt, E. C. O'Brien, Inspector, M. G. Keyes, Assistant Superintendent,
J. P. Jackman, Postman, Sean Leddin P.O.C.A. P. O'Brien, M.N.T., Margaret Dwan, Chief Supervisor,
Telephone Exchange, Miss. Mary Lillis, Telephonist, Gerard Leddin, Postal Sorter.

F. Hourigan, M. Keyes, M. Sheehan. M. Kelly. On the Facing table E. Lowe, S Griffin. 1975

TV Section 1975
G O'Brien, T. O'Connor, J.Cahillane, P. Brown, E. Banville, J. O'Sullivan, and Tom Dillon on the Phones.

Tommy O'Connell, Clem Sheehan, Eamon Meaney, Sean O'Brien. 1975

PO Conference 1976, T. Sullivan NE, W. Coffey, J. Lyons, G. Leddin,
S. Ryan NE, C. Costello Kilmallock, D. O'Brien, S. Walsh Dublin.

Gerry O'Brien, Dermot O'Brien 1976.   *Jack Sheehan Cleaner 1977*

Jimmy Kennedy, Timmy Sheehan, Cyril Conway. 1977

Brendan Fennell, Gerry Leddin, Paddy Mitchell, Willie Coffey, John Manning,
Sean O'Brien, Noel Ryan. 1977

Mr. Tim Leddin, on behalf of the clerical staff, G.P.O., presenting a silver tea set to Mr. Joe Clohessy overseer, to mark the occasion of his retirement from the service.

1977

The Rickshaw

It was that time of year again when I was taken off my delivery for a couple of weeks to help "Chester", Timmy Sheehan to deliver Telephone Directories. At that time, summer of 1977 we would load up the "Rickshaw" as it was called by members of the postal staff; it was a two wheeled large basket that was used for delivering parcels around the town before the introduction of vans. Then somebody had the bright idea to get Frank and Chester to use it to deliver Telephone Directories around the Town.

We delivered the Telephone books in O'Connell St, Farranshone, The Crescent, Ennis Rd etc. We had also to sign cards for each book delivered. Each card had the customer's name. It took a lot of time checking the name with the right address. There were quite a few telephones in some estates but not everybody had a phone so we had to get the name right with the house address. We were not familiar with some areas and that was a nightmare. We were in Farranshone having a hard time matching house names and addresses, when Chester came up with a great idea to save some time on the delivering these large heavy books. *"Frank we will follow the wires from the telephones poles to the houses and we will know exactly which house has a telephone."*

It was a very warm day when we were delivering in the Long Ave, South Circular Rd, and Henry St area. Chester and I were feeling the heat so we decided to take a rest outside the Redemptorist Church (The Fathers) when a car pulled up near us. A tall gentleman approached us and in a strong American accent asked, *"Can you tell us the way to Killarney."* After we gave him directions, we asked him for his autograph because we had recognised him from such films as "All the Kings Men, the TV series King of Diamonds". The gentleman's name was "Broderick Crawford".

Frank O'Connor

Timmy Sheehan   *Parcel Basket*

1978
Left to Right S. Kiely (Inspector), T. O'Connor, W. Coffey, E. Madigan, W. Jackson,
D. O'Brien, E. Meaney, C. Scanlon, A. Lipper, P O'Halloran.

Jim Lyons, John Considine. 1978

John Hannon.1978

John Devine, Sean O'Brien, Brendan Hourigan. 1978

1978 Willie Jackson, Dermot Sheehan, Tony Fleming, Sean Kiely.

Tommy Moloney, Gerry Leddin, Paddy Mitchell. 1978

1978
L. Hayes, D. Sheehan, J. Cotter, M. Gallahue, E. Madigan, J. Sexton, T. Sexton
B. Whyte, G. McGrath, N. Whyte, J. Hackett.

Retirement of John Ryan with Timmy Leddin. 1978

Tommy O'Connell Postman and Poet. 1978

Brendan Fennell, Eugene Madigan, Dermot Sheehan, Johnny Barron, Henry Byrnes. 1978

Tom O'Flynn, Paddy Mitchell, Gerry Leddin, Standing Mick Cunningham. 1978

Believe it or Not.

By Patrick J. McNamara.

Over the years Limerick GPO had more than its fair share of 'characters'. One who springs to mind was most unusual, to say the least. For the sake of anonymity and to save embarrassment, we will call him 'John'.

John was a night supervisor and on one occasion during the American Mail', it was Christmas time as far as I can remember, he had occasion to visit the postmen's restroom in order to check-up on the staff to make sure that they were complying with 'tea-break' rules and regulations. On this occasion however, he was in error. Apparently the time allotted to the rest period had recently been altered, an arrangement that had not been passed down to his exalted position. When the new time arrangements were pointed out to him, John replied that it didn't matter, they had exceeded the time allotted. He continued to assert his position saying that he was the boss and the buck stopped with him. A certain member of staff took exception to his attitude and decided to report the matter to the Union as an act of 'excessive supervision'. The matter would have rested there except for one thing. John was also the Branch Secretary of the Union! Now, an unusual situation presented itself. It placed 'John' in the envious position of reporting himself! This situation was not lost on a particular member of staff, who, at the monthly meeting of the Branch, directed that a paper be sent to 'John' the supervisor, by 'John' the Branch Secretary, admonishing him for his attitude on the occasion with the added rider that he should note and return the paper to himself. This in fact culminated in 'John' reporting himself to himself, a most unusual occurrence, you will agree. None the less it was done. The story afterwards travelled the length and breadth of the country.

John has since gone to his eternal reward, but it must be stated that he was a great member of staff, one of the old school.

Another famous character comes to mind. I will refer to him as 'Dirty Harry', no, not the Clint Eastwood character, but a more intelligent man, who roamed the corridors of power in Cecil Street for more years than I care to remember. Before the division of the Post Office into An Post and Telecom, I worked in the telex room in Cecil St. Every working morning without fail, 'Harry' frequented the office to 'chew the fat' and read the Irish Times. This sojourn ended every time with 'Harry' drinking a glass of water and afterwards opening the window and saying 'this is the best water in Limerick'. With that he left the office and continued with his duties. This ritual continued for a long time. 'Harry' it would appear had beaten Ballygowen to the water market. As luck would have it, the GPO was scheduled for a visit by the Minister. This visit was to be the catalyst that explained 'Dirty Harry's' meaning of 'the best water in Limerick' Up to then I always thought it was the OLO mineral water company in the city.

Those of you who recall the 'old days' may remember the Board of Works workshop and the late and great Joe McGarry, Joe, in is own way was another famous character, but that's another story. Just before the Ministerial visit, Joe called me and told me that I should clean up outside my window, it was a disgrace. This suggestion had me perplexed, what did he mean? Further investigation gave the answer. Lined up in the window ledge in near military fashion, was a collection of empty 'baby Power' bottles. What 'Dirty Harry' had been doing was after having his daily ration of 'Holy Water' he was disposing of the empties on the window ledge with the intention of disposing of them when the office was vacant, or when the opportunity presented itself, but on this occasion he either forgot or time beat him to it.

The job I had of persuading my boss that I was not the culprit took some doing, but as I have written elsewhere, that was another story.

The stories about the postmen, sorters etc were legion but I'm afraid neither time nor space permit the telling of such fabulous stories.

Patrick J. McNamara MHSI

1979
In the yard Dermot Sheehan, Willie English, boy not known. In the window, Billy Whyte, Brendan Fennell.

1979
Christy Bromell, Gerry Moylneaux

Dermot Sheehan, Eddie McNally, Noel Ryan, Gerry Leddin. 1980

Frank O'Connor on Delivery in Fitzgerald Place Rosbrien. 1980

Gerry Leddin, Paddy Mitchell on the phone to the U.S. 1980.

Mary Barry, Christy Coonihan. 1980

S. Fitzgerald, P. Rowan, W. Coffey, B. Cleary, E. McNally, D. Healy and M. Sheehan. 1980

P. Hayes, M. Downey, L. O'Brien, D. Clancy, P. Rowan, B. Cleary, G. Molyneaux , D. Barry. 1980

Facing Table Christmas. 1980

Margret O'Flynn, Jim Crew. 1980

Inspectors Eamon O'Brien, John Ryan. 1980

Liam Hanley, Michael Cunningham. 1980

Jimmy Laffan. 1980

Joe O'Sullivan, Eric Quinn, Paddy Rowan. 1980

Joe Spairen & Jerry O'Brien

Ann Hogan. 1980

Sean Kiely Inspector 1980

*L to R. J. Collopy, W. Coffey, E. Meany, P. Browne, D. Healy, B. Cleary, E. Mc Nally,
back to the Camera C Bromell.1980*

Sorting Office 1980

Sorting Office 1980

Christmas Rush in the 80's Henry St.
L to R Stan Rodgers, Ger O'Neill, Ollie Naughton, Christy Bromell, Colm O'Connor, John Hannon, (Supervisor).

Mick Ryan retirement 1-10-1980
Joe Collopy, Tommy Maloney, Jack Sexton, Paddy Mitchell, Jim Lyons, Gerry Leddin, Willey Coffey,
Sean O'Brien, Mick Ryan, John O'Sullivan, Paddy Hayes, Eamon Meaney, Paddy O'Halloran,
Brendan Fennel, Roger Sheehan.

LIMERICK POST OFFICE

(A personal memoir)

By Pat Bolster.

As a child growing up in Mallow, I was reasonably well acquainted with Cork city. I knew Glanmire Railway Station, Oliver Plunkett Street and Patrick Street. But this 'knowing' of a city was not very helpful when at the age of sixteen years and five months I came to live in Limerick – a completely different city. I quickly overcame the obstacles of being a stranger and a Corkman, and soon, became very much 'at home' in Limerick. To put the change into proportion, Limerick then was 12 to 15 times larger in population than Mallow. One aspect of the change that appealed to me was that I was now anonymous – no longer did I know "almost everyone", as I did in Mallow - population 4000. More importantly, "almost everyone" didn't know me! I revelled in this feeling of anonymity.

Starting work on December 13th, 1946, almost in the height of the Christmas Rush, was chaotic. Within days, I was sorting at Sub-office sorting tables and gaining a 'training-by-doing' baptism. Normal training in Morse telegraphy and Counter Regulations began in January, when the Christmas Rush had ended. "Learners" was the name given to trainee clerks. At that time, Learners spent much of the day in the Telegraph Office under the tutelage of Miss Peg Barry who was at that time "Mother Hen" to all Learners. The Telegraph Office was under the supervision of Assistant Superintendent, Mr Jack Anderson, ably assisted by Miss Annie Clancy, who was described as the Matron. Here I learned most of what would be required for me to become a Post Office Clerk having served an 18 month apprenticeship. I acquired sufficient ability with the Morse Sounder Key and with the Teleprinter – both used in the transmission of Telegrams – to become eligible for eventual promotion to Clerk Grade B.

My fellow learners from the December 1945, Learners Examination, were Seamus Hanrahan, Brian Gleeson, Tessie Fitzgerald, Sheila O'Brien, Eddie Lynch, and John Jameson. I was 7th in the successful list.

Over the course of the next 12 years, my life development took place in the context of Limerick Post Office – it provided my work, my acquaintances, my friends and my social contacts; I had however one other point of contact in this new environment and that was my digs (lodgings). My first was in the home of the Lipper family in the Fairgreen; others followed over the years.

After 18 months training, I was appointed a Grade B clerk and soon after, I was promoted to Grade A clerk. This sudden rise was in no way due to me – it arose because of the increase in clerical staffing necessitated by the opening of Shannon Airport Postoffice, which created 6 new vacancies. These, plus those created by normal wastage, were responsible for my quick up grading.

The hierarchy of the office was an essential part of the social structure with the (seemingly) all-powerful Postmaster at the top. Postmasters tended to come and go. Limerick was the second biggest provincial postoffice (Cork being the largest). The men who were promoted to the post tended to be coming towards the end of their service. However, in the normal scheme of things, a Postmaster and junior clerks rarely met – he was like a minor god in his remote office.

I don't know if Limerick was unique in the number of Post Office families who served in various ranks and sections of the office. Foremost among these names were - Hourigan, Guina, Kelly, Leddin and Lewin* - with members among all sections of the job – Clerical, Postal and Telephone Exchange.

I do believe however, that Limerick was unique in the degree of camaraderie and friendship that existed among all sections and members of staff. There were social gatherings yearly – generally under the auspices of the Union Branches – and these provided opportunities for socialising among the staff outside the office. There was quite a bit of socialising within the office also and from this, quite a number of marriages took place between staff members. The female side of many these unions was provided from among the Telephone Exchange day staff. Because of the size of the city and the growth of telephone traffic, the "Exchange" was - if not haunted by the prospective husbands – certainly visited, on as many occasions as possible, on the most flimsy of excuses. In my own group, Tessie Fitzgerald and Sheila O'Brien both married Clerks. In the group of learners after my set was a young, Lady Hannah Anslow. She subsequently became Mrs Pat Bolster.

In my personal life, through my association with Limerick Post Office, I met two men with whom I became most friendly. For both I have the highest regard. They were Eddie Lynch, who left the job after the sudden death of his father and joined the Redemptorist Order. Although his path and mine separated then, our friendship continues to this day – even though our separate occupations, Redemptorist Missionary Priest in Eddie's case and husband of Hannah and father of 5 children didn't afford many opportunities for socialising. The second was the late Michael Casey. He and my wife Hannah, joined the service in 1948 and almost from the start, I found a fellow traveller in Michael. Our friendship survived my transfer to Dublin in 1959 and continued until his sudden death in 1990. His wife Roseleen and I have retained the friendship and we meet quite frequently for a social meal. I feel proud to.

I was transferred to Dublin in 1959. Because of family ties, we kept up contact frequent visits and through holidays. I returned in 1974 in an official capacity and renewed my association with Limerick and Limerick Post office. I retired in 1988 but my contact with Limerick Post office continues. Almost every Wednesday morning I join a group of retirees for coffee. These include Fred Hourigan, Pat Carroll, John Hannon, John Ryan and Paraic Uas. O'Dalaigh

*If I have left out any family, I apologise. I can only offer the excuse of Old Age and declining powers of recollection!

1998
Limerick Post Offrice old Boys
Jim Jackman, Michael Guerin, Jim Lowe, Michael Treacy, Joe Finucane, Gerry O'Halloran, Michael O'Brien

Tommy Moloney Retirement 16-12-1981
Back Row. J Sullivan, P. Mitchell, S. Fitzgerald, G. Leddin, S. O'Brien, B. Fennell.
Front Row. C. Sheehan, Tommy Moloney, Paddy Hayes, E. Meaney, J. Collopy.

1981
Mary Gallahue, Michael Blake, Gerry Flynn, Moylan Ryan, Terry Long.
At the back Charlie Smith.

Noel Ryan (Tipp) Murty Madden, Jim O'Dwyer. 1981

Christmas 1981. Henry Byrnes and John Considine.

Memories of Service in the Post Office Limerick....

I am a native of Templemore Co Tipperary. I sat for the open Civil Service examination and I was appointed in October 1948 as a Learner to Sligo Post Office. I remember having a good view from Sligo GPO of the funeral procession of W B Yeats whose remains were brought back from France. I applied for a transfer to Limerick because it was nearer home and I was transferred there in the following spring.

My earliest memories of Limerick Post Office related to our Training Course in the Old Telegraph Office, which was situated above the Sorting Office. Our Tutor at the time was a Miss Peg Barry. We had to learn Morse code because all the telegrams were transmitted by this method. The Telegraph Office was under the Supervision of a Miss Annie Clancy. We were also given Training on counter duties, Considerable emphasis was placed the Rules governing work in the Telegraph and Sorting Offices and Counter services. I recollect while on Counter work there was a significant level of Telegraph Money Orders (T.M.Os) from Britain to support families in Limerick. There was a noticeable level also, of British Army pensions to veterans of the First World War. On my appointment as a Grade B clerk in 1956 I was sent to Nenagh Post Office but returned to Limerick two years later.

In 1955, I decided to sit for the confined CS examination for Clerical officers. I was appointed to the Post Office Engineering Office in Dublin. However, a vacancy arose in the Limerick office later that year and I again returned to Limerick. I was the first clerk in the Post Office to use the confined CO outlet and in the following years, a number of my colleagues availed of the same career move. Other colleagues took the Telephone Officer promotional route I subsequently was successful in the confined Executive Officer examinations and was posted to airport Management at Shannon Airport.

During my years in Limerick Post Office, I became friends with a number of my contemporaries and this friendship has continued to the present time. I have good memories of my time in Limerick GPO and particularly of the assignment every few months to the Shannon Airport Branch Office. It was an exciting time with so many US and European airlines using the airport. The Teleprinter at Shannon for telegram and Presswork was a great advancement on the Morse code. We had to work seven-day shifts of consecutive days, evenings and night duties. Despite this, it was much sought after because of the additional overtime payments. Certain aspects of the job did not appeal to me particularly broken shifts night duties and weekend work. It is likely that these were the main reasons for my decision to avail of the confined Clerical Officer examination.

Michael Guerin

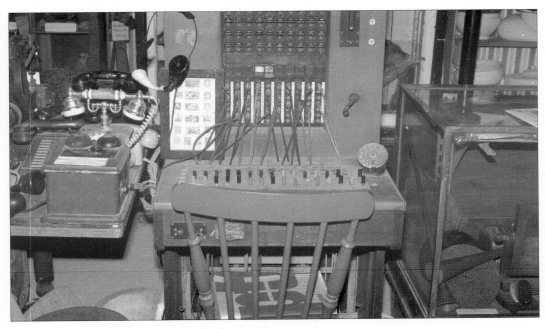

Telephone switchboard, Bennetsbridge Museum, Co. Kilkenny.

John Manning having a rest after a double tap. 1981

1981 Paddy Mitchell, John Divine, Jimmy Laffan, Rodger Sheehan, Joe Collopy.

1981 Cyril Conway, Billy Whyte, Rodger Sheehan, Bobby Downey.

Gerry Leddin, Joe Collopy, Clem Sheehan. 1982

Sean Real in Garryowen. 1982

Tops of the Town Gaiety Dublin 1982 Post Office V Jacobs
Jimmy Harrold, Eugene Madigan.

Jack Sexton (Cleaner) 1982

Holmes and Watson Enquire Office Henry St 1982
Back Row L to R Des Horgan, Carmel Collins, Catherine O'Riordan, Dave Clancy.
Front Row L to R Tony Finn, Jimmy Harrold.

Bobby Harrington in the Customs. 1982

Denis Moloney. 1982

Mary O'Sullivan, Tom O'Sullivan on his retirement, with Maurice Fitzgerald. 1982.

Cruises Hotel 1982
Presentation to E. T. O'Sullivan Superintendent on his retirement.

1983 Chapel Lane from William St on the left Canty Bean an Ti.
Right 8 to 2: No8 Wallace's Shoemaker, No7 O'Kanes Sweet Shop,
No6 McMahon's Vegetables, No5 Darcy Milk Shop Only, No4 Hannon, Barber,
No3 Grimes later Daly's Jeweller, No2 O'Brien's and St. Michaels Church.

Robert Street 1983

Patricia Dollard

First Postwoman

RESIDENTS of the Ennis Road side of Limerick had a surprise this week when their mail was delivered by a smiling young female, Miss Patricia Dollard, who can lay claim to fame in that she is Limerick's first Postwoman.

Patricia, 18, a former pupil of Presentation Convent in Sexton Street, took up a post in the telegrams office at the Post Office last year and when the job of postman was advertised, specifying that it was open to both sexes, she decided to try her luck:

Interview

She was called for interview, undertook an examination and was later informed that she was to go into the history books.

"After only one week in my new position, I am absolutely delighted," said a tired looking Patricia at 2 p.m. this Thursday, just after she had finished her second run for the day.

Her daily routine commences at 6 am., which means that she is out of bed one hour earlier. 'If we have a busy period at work, then I may not finish until 12 hours later." grinned Patricia, described by her supervisor, Mr. Sean Kiely, as an outstanding worker.

Dogs

It doesn't bother Limerick's first Postwoman that she has to carry an average of 35 lbs. of mail each time she sets out on her rounds "And there might be occasions when I will be expected to carry 60 lbs. weight" smiled Patricia, whose only interests outside of her work are going to dances and to films.

When she took up her appointment she was warned by her colleagues to beware of dogs. "Well, they were the first that I made friends with," continued Patricia, who is now on first name terms with people in her postal district.

She said that the postmen at the GPO had given her every encouragement—"and they offer a little help whenever I need it"

One of a family of five, she is daughter of Mr. and Mrs. Pat Dollard, 41 Galvone Road, Kennedy Park. Limerick. On an average day she estimates that she walks about 20 miles. And she has yet to suffer from sore feet.

Limerick Leader 4th August 1979

1983
Back Row J Hackett, E. Banville, D. Barry, P. Hayes, E. Meaney, F. Hourigan,
W. Coffey. E. McNally, N. Whyte, T. Sayers, Timmy. O'Connor.
Front Row Tom O'Connor, G. O'Neill, B. Fennell, P. White, B. Whyte. P. Scannell, in front D. Linnane.

Rapid Delivery of Irish Letter in U.S.

The mystery of how a letter posted in Limerick at 3.15 p.m. on Monday could have been delivered in Knoxville, Tennessee, in the deep south of the United States nearly 5,000 miles away, at 2.45 p.m. (7.45 p.m. G.M.T) next day was solved by a 'Leader' reporter in Limerick yesterday. Altogether, there are three despatches of airmail from Limerick to Shannon Airport daily, at 4.30 p.m... 9 p.m. and 10.30 p.m, I so happened that the letter in question was posted in time to catch the first collection.

WENT BY JET

A the mail van was arriving at Shannon after the 15 miles journey from Limerick, a Swissair D.C.8 jet was landing, The mail, in a small bag marked "Washington," left Shannon at 5.40 p.m. on the Swiss jet and arrived In New York at 12.12 am. (Irish time), nine hours after it was dropped into the G.P.O. in Limerick.

There was a flight leaving for Washington immediately, which caught a connection to Knoxville right after it had been sorted; and the recipient, Mrs. Wm, Bigelow, had it in the afternoon delivery.

A spokesman for Mr. Patrick Lynch Postmaster, Limerick, said: "We have no knowledge of the internal service in the United States, but it was probably a chance in a million, although all mail is handled with the greatest possible speed."

Limerick Leader. January 1961

Post without haste: letter arrives 13 years later

A LETTER posted in Ballingarry 13 years ago finally arrived at its destination in Limerick city within the past few days. The writer of the letter has been dead for three years.

It was addressed to Mrs. Mary McLoughlin, who at the time lived in 19 Ballykeeffe Estate. The family moved to Raheen two years ago. But the new occupant of the Ballykeeffe house delivered the letter to her. The date on the letter was Saturday. July 23 1966 and the tattered envelope was post marked in 1966.

It was sent from Ballingarry by an aunt of Mrs. McLaughlin, a Sr. Mary Bernadette, who was in the Convent of Mercy there, Mrs. McLoughlin explained that her aunt died about three years ago. The family were naturally surprised to get the letter. She said the incident led to the family praying for their deceased relative.'

Limerick Leader 21 July 1979

Back Row. Johnny Conlon, Tadhg Crowley, Liam Hanley, Tom Dillon, Alfie Nolan, Dan Mullane.
Front Row. Paddy Moran, Walter Hurley, Stan O'Neill, Garry Collins, Tom McElligott.
Seated. Maurice Fitzgerald, Dermot Small. 1984

Vesting day 1 January 1984

Postal service was taken over by the Department of Posts and Telegraphs in 1922, which administered the system until the establishment of An Post in 1984. Back Row Left to Right. M. Folan, E. McNally, J. Lyons, J. Jackman, T. Quinlan, J. Lynch, M. Sheehan, C. O'Connor, Sean Lavelle RPM, S. Kiely Inspector 1, J. Sheehan, T. Gloster, G. Leddin, P. McCormack, Louis Byrne M. Collins, P. O'Dalaigh, B. Flannery, M. Finucane, B. Banville, M. Bartlett.

Seated S. O'Moran, P. Nolan, G.E. Harvey, Terry Kelly (Mayoress), E. Delaney, M. Fitzgerald, J. Dunleavy, F. Hourigan.

Munster Senior Cup won by Young Munster 1984
Tom McElligott, Michael Cunningham.

Munster Junior and Senior Cups Won by Young Munster 1984
Hugo McGrath, Jimmy Harrold, Donie Baggott.

St. Munchin's House 1984
Back Row L to R P. Moran, J Connellan, D. Mullane, W. Hurley, T. O'Connor,
A. Nolan, J. Harrold, T. McElligott, T. Dillon.
Seated L to R Michael Cunningham, Pádraig O'Dalaigh, and Garry Collins.

St. Munchin's House 1984
Johnny Connellan, Dan Mullane, Bobby Downey, John Hannon.
Seated Des Horgan.

Maurice Downing, Pat O'Donoghue, Joe O'Sullivan, Stan O'Neill, Mary Barry. 1984

1984
Back Row, M. Ryan, C. Sheehan, J Collopy, E. Meaney, E. McNally, D. Sheehan, N. Ryan, J. Devine, Not Known.
Middle Row S. Kiely, G. Leddin, P. Hayes, M. Blake, J. Sullivan, B. Fennell, D. Linnane, J. Tobin, G. Flaherty.
Front Row. T. Moloney, C. Bartlett, J. Real, J. Ryan, P. Mitchell, P. O'Halloran.

1984
Paddy Hayes, Jim Real, Gerry Leddin, Charlie Bartlett, Sean Kiely, John Ryan,
Paddy Mitchell, Tommy Moloney, John Sullivan

Presentation to Mick Mac Eoin and Mick Sheehan on their retirement, 1984
L to R C. O'Connor, M. Mac Eoin, B. Marnane Postmaster, M Sheehan, J. Ryan.

Ken Kiely, Tony Cronin, Frank O'Connor, Gay Hunt. Seated Tom Sparling. 1985

Bobby Harrington, Stacie Curtin, Patsy Heffernan. 1985

Raymond Flynn. 1985

Maurice Marshall, Jim Lyons, Joe Jackman, Dermot O'Brien.
C.W.U. AGM Glentworth Hotel. 1985

Henry Byrnes, Jimmy Harrold in London. 1985

Bobby Harrington. 1985

Paddy Hayes. 1986

Des Henn Inspector. 1986

1987 Paul Dwane, Ger Cunneen.

1987 Dan Quin.

1987   Brendan Hourigan, Tom Hannon.

Bobby Downey retirement 1987

Back Row: Barman Philip Ryan, M. Cunningham, K. Cunningham, T. O'Connor, E. Quinn. Standing: M. Collins, G. Bennis, S. Rogers, J.J. Hurley, M. Lynch, C. O'Connor, J. Cahillane, D. Horgan, J. Croave, J. O'Brien. M. Treacy, Barman Mike Buckley.
Seated: P. Neville, Bobby Downey, Timmy Leddin, P. Rowan. Photograph taken outside Tom and Jerry's Bar Glentworth St by G. O'Brien.

Paddy Rowan, Timmy Leddin (Mayor) Eric Quinn. 1987

Sean Mullarkey Postmaster. 1987

GPO 1988

1988
During the GPO Renovations the Counter moved to Spaight's Shopping Centre.

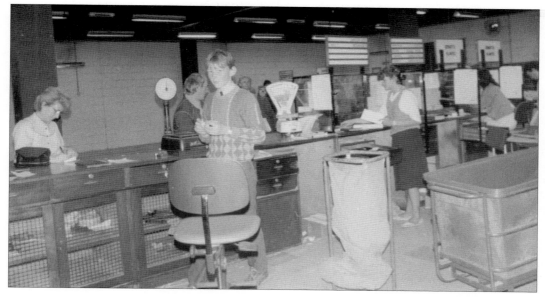

At the Counter in Spaight's Fergus O'Brien. 1988

1988
Patrick McKeown, Ger Nolan, Liam Gleeson, Liam Hayes.

October 1988
Joe Jackman & John Colfer.
Sean Real in background

October 1988
Sean Real, John Considine.

J. Hannon, E. Meaney, S. Griffin, B. Fennel,
D. Sheehan, M. Blake. G. Leddin. Christmas 1990

Tony Fleming (Doc) Delivering to J.J. Kennelly's
Wickham St. 1990

Head Postmaster's Conference 1989

1990
Peggy McCormack, Paddy Moran, Tom McElligott, Tadhg Crowley, Dan Mullane, Catherine Bourke.

Michael Tracy, Liam Gleeson, Mill Rd Corbally. 1990

Jimmy Shaughnessy, Joe Dillon, Henry Byrnes. 1991

Billy Purcell, Dennis Crean. 1991

Paul Dwane. 1991

Willie Jackson. 1991

Pat Keane, Dermot Leddin. 1991

Martin Sheridan, Sean Fitzgerald. 1991

Dermot O'Brien, Noel Ryan, Billy Whyte, Timmy O'Connor.
All Ireland Quiz 1991

Limerick Head Office – Postal Management Team 12-11-1993
Standing L to R. P. O'Halloran, J. Harrold, J. Conlan, M. Collins, M. Cunningham,
S. Fitzgerald, W. Coffey, D. Small, L. Hanley, T. McElligott, E. Quinn, D. Barry, J. Hannon.
Seated L to R. J. Ryan, C. O'Connor, B. Marnane, F. Hourigan, PM. D. Horgan, P. Carroll.

17 March 1993
Tony Cronin, Paddy Carroll, Paddy O'Connor, John Hackett Willie Jackson, Jim Rael.
Marie Ryan, Dermot O'Brien, Patricia Barry.

Des Horgan, Billy Whyte. 1993

The Brothers Noel and Billy Whyte. 1993

Celine Marsh

SHE never really yearned for an outdoor job when she was a schoolgirl in County Clare, but now says Celine Marsh from Broadford, "I couldn't even imagine myself working indoors all day. You get used to the fresh air. You do your own thing in your own time. -It's great." Celine is one of a growing number of women now being employed on postal deliveries in the city. "There are about five of us," says Celine. "We're still outnumbered." But whatever about numbers, the day of the postman could be over. "I think I'm supposed to be called a postperson, but I'd prefer to be called a Postwoman," said Celine.

She has been working for the postal service for two years, and has been full time since last October. Her route is Ballynanty and Woodview, covering 1200 homes a day, a task that sounds quite daunting to an onlooker. But Celine takes it all in her stride, or should we say, on her bike.

Sometimes, when deliveries are particularly heavy, such as at Christmas time, she has help from temporary staff but mostly she is on her own. Valentine's Day, however, turned out to be a bit of a damp squib. There was no great avalanche of cards to be delivered "Actually it was a bit dead this year, she said.

Sometimes too, she is called upon to help out in other areas, and that is much more difficult because she mightn't be as familiar with the area in question. There are other down- sides to the job of course. The weather for one thing, and cross dogs for another. "The rain is the worst. Although I'm out in all kinds of weather," she says, "and nearly every house on the route has a dog, what do I do when I'm confronted with a dog barking in the driveway? Well, sometimes I shout at them, but mostly I try to ignore them. I have never been bitten or attacked, thank God."

Celine lives in Dooradoyle, and her day starts at 6am each morning when she arrives at the sorting office on the Dock Road. She sorts her own mail, which is then carried by Van to the different stations along the route. Any addresses which are indecipherable are sent to the supervisor for clarification.

Then she sets off on her bike, usually before 9am. Her day finishes just after 2pm, although sometimes when post is heavy she could be out until late in the evening. "It's not easy getting up so early in the winter, but you do get used to it," she said.

When the weather is good, she loves the cycling. It helps her to keep fit, but she wouldn't even dream of cycling for leisure, she says, because she gets enough of it at work. She grew up with the postal service. Her dad, Tony, is the postmaster in Broadford, and while she toyed with the idea of working in the service herself when she was younger, she never thought of working as a city Postwoman. The benefits of the job, she says, are that she gets to meet lot of different people. Despite all the dread of bills coming through the letterbox, most people actually do look forward to the arrival of the post. Hope springs eternal... As well as that it's a healthy life. "I've never been fitter in my life," she says. "City Postwoman! It's a very responsible job, one that has to be taken very seriously". She is very conscious of the fact that people's lives and livelihoods can often depend on the promptness of the service. A letter can bring great happiness or terrible sadness, but that is something over which she has no control. Her earnest wish, however, would be that the news is always good when the recipient opens the envelope.

Limerick Leader 11 March 2000

Celine in the sorting office at the Dock Road.

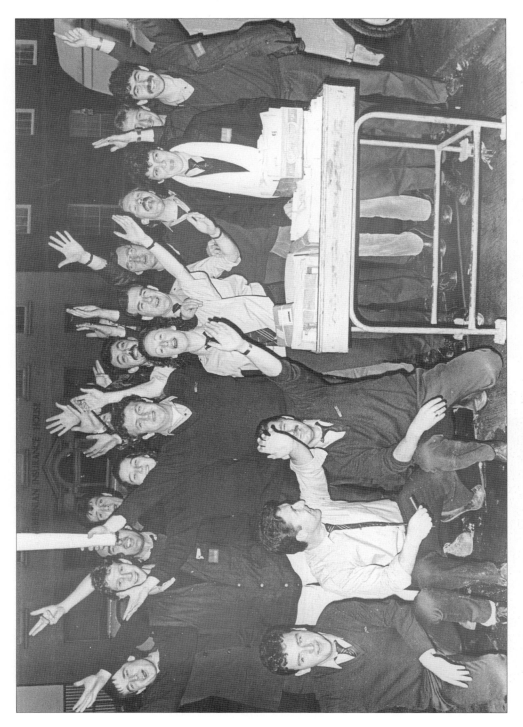

Christmas 1990 Carol Singing for Milford Hospice.

Carol Singing for Milford Hospice

Milford Hospice December 1988
Persia Barry, Billy Whyte, Willie Russell and Stasia Curtin.

December 1988
Ger Foley, Dan Quinn, John Hannon, Eric Quinn.

Sean Barry & Jimmy Hartigan, December 1989

Willie Coffey, December 1989

December 1990, Alex Murphy.

December 1993 - Patsy Heffernan, John Hannon & Marie Ryan.

Post Office Staff Cycle for Charity

When Mr. Fred Hourigan was promoted to Postmaster in Ennis he stepped down as Chairman of the Sport and Recreation Club in Limerick. I was elected Chairman of An Post S. and R. Club at the A.G.M. in March of 1992. I was the first post person to hold this position for many years. I thought about introducing something new and after plenty of deliberation with other members of the committee we decided to hold a Charity cycle from Limerick to Kilkee for the Share a Dream Foundation for sick children. The cycle took place on the 16th of June 1992. Permits were granted from the Limerick and Clare Garda Siochana. With Ger Cunneen (postman) as our coach, former Irish champion cyclist, we started our training schedule every Sunday morning with a few brave and well motivated post office staff. We began our training slowly by covering short distances at first, increasing gradually; we covered between ten and 40 miles each weekend.

An Post and SDS had given us permission to use three of their vans for the day, Musgrave's Cash and Carry supplied us with chocolate bars, Mathew Richardson with bananas and O'Brien's shop, 96 Henry Street with bars of chocolates. Statoil on the Ennis road supplied us with petrol and diesel for the vans. Willie Coffey was nominated to be in charge of the collectors and Mary Rogers was in charge of the distribution of the food and water for the cyclists on the route from Limerick to Ennis. Eric Quinn was invited by Clare F.M. radio station to discuss and comment about the cycle and the charity involved. I also had been invited by Limerick 95 F.M. radio station to do likewise. The Limerick Leader newspaper gave us plenty of publicity and also took numerous photographs; An Post and SDS presented us with T shirts and hats as did Share a Dream Foundation. Before the cycle took place we had to make some rules and regulations because we did not want any heroes. On the day of the cycle all cyclists had to stay behind the lead van.

On Saturday, the 16th of June 1992 there was a great buzz of excitement at the GPO that morning as we all geared up for the day ahead. The weather was overcast and drizzly. Mr. Fred Hourigan got us under starters orders in Henry Street and we were off. Billy Whyte and Liam Hayes were seen regularly getting in and out of the back of various vans to help us to arrive at our destination.

We arrived in Kilkee at approximately 03:00 and were greeted by lots of holidaymakers from Limerick. Saint Mary's Fife and Drum Band greeted us at our final destination with some lively tunes. We cycled around Kilkee while our collectors went through the town and on to the beach. Saint Senan's school provided us with changing rooms and shower facilities. Everybody had a most enjoyable day.

A sum of £4500 pounds was presented to Share a Dream Foundation later that year.

By Sean Real.

Dermot O'Brien

Cycling for Charity

Billy Whyte overtaking 1992

Henry Byrnes (Bunty) 1993

Charity Cycle 1993

Cycle through Kilkee 1993

1993
Keeping the road clear Tony Curtin, Ger Kearns, John Ryan.

Kilkee 1993

1993
Having a rest Liam Hayes.

Limerick Marine Search and Rescue 1996 - Fred Hourigan, Sean Real.

1996
Rodger Sheehan.

1996
Martin Quinn Marine Search and Rescue Sean Real, Dan Quinn. An Post.

1996 Marine Search and Rescue
An Post Staff with Sponsors of Cycle Supermacs Staff

The Official File

"An enquiry, a report, with reference to", or something of the sort,
"I am directed", so, with words like these it runs unto the end "Submitted, please".
Another step. A slightly higher mind peruses it to see what he can find.
He reads it through, returns it with "Please state". or better still, perhaps,
"Elucidate".
Again, it mounts with slowly phrased reply.
This time it pleases the superior eye.

Now all is well, the inferior has been twitted, the document is grudgingly
transmitted.
Again a higher being reads it through and adds, as higher beings always do,
a string of queries, "Will you please explain a, b, c, d,?", and sends it back again.
Once more, it travels downward to the source.
The queries are all answered and of course,
it goes to him to whom it first had gone again to be transmitted further on.
And so by easy stages up it goes until it reaches heaven only knows
what dizzy heights of Departmental power but all does not happen in an hour.

The document is changing all the while; it was a letter now it is a file.
With every motion, with each fall and rise it managed to acquire a greater size.
Its very thickness brings it to the top it goes into a basket,
there to stop for many days, perhaps for many weeks until the August
one gives tongue and speaks the great decision waited for below-
the magic word, "Agreed", or "Yes", or "No".

Then from its basket out is pulled the sheaf with codicils attached beyond belief and then, yes, in the end, it comments to descend. It goes to Mr. G. to see and thence to Mr. C., to note, to the registry of files. To please peruse, to temporary under secretary, to check, to typist, Clerk, a dozen more or so.

All those many intermediate stops no is allowed, no sudden hops for all must add initials, pass it on, with records that will last when they are gone.

Upon the table where it first appeared, (the low official now has grown a beard) it comes to rest for all things must at last. Even Official files which move so fast.

By, Michael Casey.

1981
Group Photograph of the 5A Side Teams

Eddie Banville, Dermot Sheehan, Willie Coffey, Noel Ryan, Tom McElligott. 1981

Colm O'Connor, Gerry O'Neill, Henry Byrnes, Christy Counihan, Ger Foley. 1981

1981 Stan Rogers, Tom Kirby, Eric Lowe.
Ger Cunneen, Terry Keane.

1981 Ollie Naughton, Sean O'Brien, Noel Whyte
Christy Kelly, Caimin Waterstone.

1981
Paddy Hayes presenting Noel Whyte
With 5 A side Cup

1981
Billy Whyte, George Tracy, Rodger Sheehan,
With the 5 A side Cup

1982
Tom McElligott receives 5 A side cup from
Fred Hourigan.

1980
Paddy Hayes presents his son Liam
with 5 A side cup.
In the background M. McKeon and M. Ryan

Bobby Harrington Memorial Shield 1994
Sports Club Awards Pike Anglers - Billy Reeves, Dave Reeves, Sean Real (Chairman),
Paddy Carroll , Joe Bennis 1st, Michelle Bennis, Tom Kirby, Bertie Flannery, Paddy Bennis.

Angling Awards Christmas 1994 - Joe Bennis, Tom Kirby.

Doon Lake 1997
Niall Bennis (Weight master), Dave Reeves, Sean Real
In the background Tom Kirby.

Bobby Harrington Memorial Shield Doon Lake 1998
Paddy Bennis, Alan Bennis, Sean Real, Billy Reeves, Tom Kirby.

GPO SPORTS and SOCIAL CLUB

Des Horgan is presented with the Sportsman of the Year trophy
by Senator G.E. Russell, Mayor of Limerick.

The Annual Social of the club took place at the Glentworth Hotel towards the end of last year when staff prize winners for 1976 were presented with their trophies.

The soccer team, beaten in the final by a single goal, was presented with runner-up medals by the Chairman of the Inter-firm Board. Captain of the team, Des Horgan, was selected Sportsman of the Year by the board and was the recipient of a beautiful trophy.

Jim Harrold, captain of the clerks' team, became the proud holder of the Norton Cup for a year having beaten the postmen in the final on penalties after what had been a thrilling game. Mr. E.T. O'Sullivan, donor of the cup, made the presentation of the cup and trophies.

Mick Burns took home the Gerry Hourigan Cup in the seven-a-side having beaten the Liam Hayes team in extra time in the final. Fred Hourigan, brother of the late founder member Gerry, made the presentations in this competition.

Prizes won at the Sports Meeting, which had been held at the P.Y.M.A. Grounds in June, were also presented and the lucky winners here were:

100 yards: Liam O'Brien, Eric Lowe. Half mile: Paud McKenna, Liam O'Brien.

440 yards: Liam O'Brien, Eric Lowe. Mile: Liam Hayes, Liam O'Brien.

Relay—Clerks: M. Bums, G. Collins, K. O'Connor, L. O'Brien. Wheel barrow: P. Rowan and G. Collins. Sack race: D. Linnane, P .Carroll.

Long puck: Liam O'Brien, Jim Lyons. Long puck over 40: Paddy Hayes, J. Hannon. Mothers' race: Mrs. M. Costello, Mrs. P. O'Halloran. —

Husband and wife race: Mr. Mrs. T. Crowley, Mr. Mrs. M. Burns.

Walking race over 40: M. Costello, Des Henn.

Finally, the presentations for the Annual Pitch and Putt Competition were made to the following winners:

Overall Nett for Perpetual Shield and Replica: Brendan Fennell.

Overall gross: Paddy Hayes. 18 Nett: Eamon Meaney, Sean Kiely, D. O'Brien.

18 gross: Tom O'Sullivan, Billy Coffey, John Fitzgerald.

9 Nett: Paddy O'Halloran, Connie Scanlon, Gerry Collins.

9 gross: Sean O'Connell, Liam Hanley, Jack Joyce.

Oifige an Phoist PagusT Summer 1977

Limerick Outdoor Branch 1st June 1994

Front Row (seated), N. Tobin, M. Long, S. Curtin, B. Ryan, M. Cahill, L. Hayes, D. O'Connor, D. Quinn H. Byrne, E Cussen, K Guerrini, P O'Connor, E McMahon and N Supple.

Second Row (seated), A. Fleming, P. Dwane, T. O'Connor, A. Murphy, D. O'Brien, P. O'Halloran, W. Whyte, E. O'Neill, W. O'Connor, E. Lowe, C. Conway, J. O'Shaughnessy F. O'Connor and T. Keane.

Third Row (standing), M. Ryan, S. Fitzgerald, M. Kierce , M. Treacy, L. Gleeson, J. Ryan, N. Walsh, A. Cronin, S. Real, S. Sheehy, M. Marshall, P. Bennis, J. Hannon, D. O'Flynn, J. Conway, G. Foley, M. Reddan and J. Hartigan.

Back Row (standing), C. Scanlon, M. O'Leary, P. Heffernan, P. Corner, E. Madigan, S. Griffin, C. Grimes, N. Whyte, J. Kiely and P. McCarthy.

Photograph by Keith Alec Wiseman.

22-4-1995
Presentation from CWU to Brendan Hourigan and Gerry Leddin on their retirement.
L to R. T. O'Connor, M. Marshall, B. Hourigan, G. Nolan, N. Ryan, S. Real,
M. Hannigan, J. Condon (Dublin), F. Hourigan, J. Hackett, G. Leddin, T. O'Connor,
D. O'Brien, J. Lyons, C. Sheehan, M. Lynch, G. O'Brien.

1995 AGM Limerick.
Maurice Hannigan, Dermot O'Brien, Jim Lyons, David Begg. Union HQ

The last Telegram boys. September 1997 Kevin McCarthy, Paul Ryan, Joe Kelly, Liam Fitzsimons.

1985
Gerard Harvey, Chief Executive An Post, unveiling a Plaque to Hanging Gardens.
GPO Henry Street.

Christy Grimes. 1997

Eamon Meaney receiving Service Certificate from Paddy Carroll Postmaster. 1997

Frank O'Connor Henry St 1997

Opening of LFO - 1997

Sandra O'Connor, Maryse O'Connor, Gearoid O'Connor, Jim Hayes.

Veer Kennedy, Tom Kirby.

Carmel McKenna, Paddy Carroll. PM.

Billy Whyte, Eugene Madigan, John Hackett, Johnny Barron, Ger Purcell.

Paddy Carroll Postmaster

Sean Fitzgerald, Liam O'Brien, Paddy O'Connor

Ger McMahon, Tom O'Flynn.

Ger Clancy, Ger Collopy, Des Henn.

In 1973 I joined the post office as a junior postman this was a new name for a Telegram boy. It was the same year that Limerick won their last Senior Hurling All-Ireland final against Kilkenny.

As a junior postman, I spent my time delivering telegrams all over the city and was a very welcome sight to many people on a Friday or Saturday as we used to deliver TMO's (Telegraph Money Orders). This was a service by which people working in England could send money home to their families. In 1975, I became a Postman and my first delivery that I was trained on was No 6 the old Corbally that was being done by the late Henry (Bunty) Byrnes. Eventually I got my own duty, which was No 9 Henry stand part of the S C Rd. In 1978 I became the youngest Postal Sorter or Brothers as they were known in Limerick in the country at 21 Both Sean O'Brien and I were appointed to this grade on the same day. In those day's we worked long hours as at the time the wages were not great and this came to a head in 1979 with the longest National strike in the history of the post office which lasted nearly 6 months. I have seen many changes in my 32 years working in the post office. In 1984 it began with the post office going semi-state and this brought huge changes over the following years to present times.

I have worked with some of the best people and characters that one could ever ask for, they made life easy and I broke their heart (Management) as they never knew what I would get up to. Going to the railway station for the mail on night duty and everybody mucking in to get the vans loaded and brought back to sorting office so we could get home early as most times we would be back on overtime later in the day The late Jim Lyons name comes to mind as he was the man that was an icon on the night shift.

I have to say that I miss the camaraderie of the post office. Through good times and bad times, we all pulled together and tried to make life a little easier for each other and that made my decision to leave it after 32 years a lot harder in 2005. Work had changed so much and the job had got so impersonal not that it was the staffs fault but the whole tone of the company. The skills that I acquired in my years in the Post Office have stood to me on the outside. On a personal note, I would like to take this opportunity to thank Gerry Leddin for the kindness that he show me both inside and outside the post office. Thank you for being a great friend. To the remaining staff and retired staff of An Post I wish ye will.

Joe Collopy.

Dermot O'Brien and Jim Lyons Retirements 1998

Christmas 2000
Ger Foley, Joe Kiely, Eugene Hannon, Mary Tierney, Mick Mullane.

Christmas 2000
Robert O'Flynn, Con Scanlan, Sean Real Liam O'Donoghue, Tony Fleming, Ger Clancy.

Bertie Flannery December 2000

306

Dave Barry, Gerry O'Brien December 2000

Docklands December 2000

Preparing for the Euro coin Introduction at GPO Limerick December 2001.
L to R Johnny Connellan, Paddy O'Donoghue, Colm O'Connor.

Con Scanlan, Paddy O'Connor, Liam Hayes, Eddie O'Neill, Ger Foley, 2003

Cyril Conway been presented with CWU certificate from Donal Hayes Secretary CWU Limerick 2003

Liam Hanley Manager, with Jimmy Tobin on his Retirement 2004

Christy Bromell, Donal Hayes, Jimmy Tobin, Noel Ryan 2004

Paddy Rowan 2004

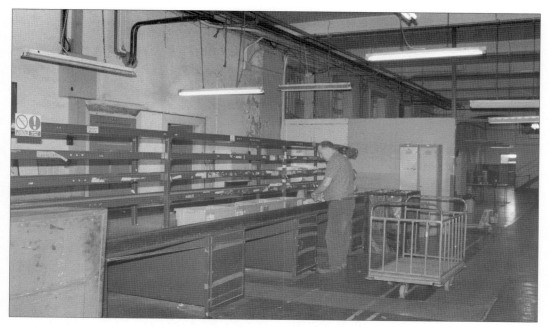

At the Facing table on a Saturday Tony Kennedy 2004

On Security Ken Kiely and Michael Tobin 2004

*Willie Jackson with Edward VII Wall Box
removed from outside St. Johns Hospital 2004*

*Patricia Cassidy, Tony Kennedy
with Edward VII wall Box 2004*

Philip White, Eddie McNally Christmas 2004

Michael Blake, John Cahillane - Christmas 2004

2004
Presentation to Larry O'Connell from An Post Staff Limerick on his retirement

2004
Brendan Fennell receiving last bill from Larry O'Connell

Gay Hunt, Adrian Lipper, Ray Neville Christmas 2004

Christmas 2004
L to R Ger Riordan, Martin Kiely, Helen Fleming, Des Henn, Mike Mullane, Jim Conway, Alec Murphy,
Eric Lowe, Paddy Comber, Paddy O'Connor, Liam Hayes.

Christmas 2004
L to R Ger Foley, Mike Neville, John Mulcair, Joe Kiely, Brian Farragher, Patricia Barry,
Eugene Madigan, Liam O'Donoghue, Mike Hayes, Eddie O'Neill.

The Last Sunday Staff 28 August 2005
J. O' Brien J. Harrold J. Conway, G. O'Neill, E. McNally, T. O' Connor, D. Henn J. Costello
John Ryan (Sonny), C. Tuite, F. O'Connor, P. O'Connor, G. O'Sullivan, J. Hackett.

Closure of LFO - 2nd September 2005

Johnny Barron With the last Air Mail Despatch to Shannon 2005

John Manning, Tony Cronin Last Despatch of Dell packets 2005

Gerry O'Sullivan, Paddy Bennis. 2005

J. Hayes, M. Thomson, G. Hunt, S. O'Brien, A. Lipper, D. Reeves, N. Ryan.

Declan O'Mara.

Ian Guerrini, Gavin Spearin, Pat McNamara.

Sean O'Brien, Noel Ryan, Donal Hayes.
2nd September 2005

Night Staff 22-5-2006

A. Lipper, S. O'Brien, N. Tobin, M Murphy, J. Manning, C. Ryan, E. Noonan, N. McGowan, L. Butler, O. O'Flynn, D. Cosgrave,
D. O'Connor, P. Crean, C. O'Connor, M. O'Connor, T. Kennedy, B. Fennell, C. Hickey, I. Guerrini, G. O'Sullivan, P. Hanrahan,
A. McAuliffe, M. Cantillon, M. Collins, B. Madigan, G. O'Connor, J. Morrison, H. O'Sullivan, P. Dorothy, M. Treacy, J. O'Brien,
B. Meaney, P. White, G. Hunt, J. Hayes, D. Barry.

Day Staff 31-5-2006

GPO Counter Staff 1-6-2006
L to R Manager Michael Cunningham, Johnny Connellan, Oliver Naughton, Barry O'Connor,
Margaret McCoy, Pat Cassidy, Aidan Curtin, Brenda Leslie, Catherine Mc Dermott,
Rodger McMahon, Margaret Conway, Jim Jackman, Patrick O'Donoghue.

TV License Section 1-6-2006 - Tom Buckley, Mick Lynch, Gerry Kelly.

An Post Area Office Staff 15-12-2006

Back row Alan Brown, Robert O'Leary, Tom McElligott, Tony Corr, Eamon Lenihan, Garry Collins, Pat Howard.
Front row Catherine Bourke, Mary Rogers, Gerry O'Brien, Carmel Treacy, Patricia Nealon.

County Limerick Postmasters 1983

Kilmallock Post Office opened in 1803

POSTMASTERS KILMALLOCK SINCE 1824

Mc Connell H.	1824
Harris G.A.	1870
Harris J.W.A.	1890 to 1900
Senior E.M.	1900 to 1902
Clayton W	1902 to 1908
Freeman T	1909 to 1916
Gallagher M.J.	1916 to 1918
Bleech P.J.	1920 to 1921

Abernethy A. 1923 to 1928

Kehoe E.J. 1934 to 1940

Fanning J.J. 1940 to 1946

John Dynes 1946 to 1952

Cornelius O'Regan 1952 to 1958

Charles J. Stone   1958 to 1967

Breandán Mac Gearailt 1967 to1969

Patrick O'Leary 1970 to 1973

Michael Quirke 1973 to 1974

Michael Baker 1974 to 1975

Patrick Landers 1975 to 1980

Joseph Wingfield 1980to1982

Tony Conroy 1983 to 1983

Joseph Lonergan 1983 to 1984

Donal Hayes 1984 to 2000

The Post Office in General; Kilmallock

By
Tim O'Donovan

Before the Post Office became a semi-state body a few years ago its services were controlled and operated by the Department of Posts and Telegraphs. Under Departmental regulations, the Minister for Posts and Telegraphs, by virtue of various Post Office Acts, had the exclusive privilege (with certain exceptions) of carrying letters from one place to another and performing all incidental services such as collecting and delivering the letters.

 Similarly, the Minister for Posts and Telegraphs, by virtue of the Telegraph Acts, had the exclusive rights of transmitting telegrams within the State and to any part of Northern Ireland and Great Britain. Other services provided by the Post Office included the issue of television licenses and dog licenses. The sale of a wide variety of Inland Revenue stamps was also the sole right of the Post Office, as was the sale, up to the introduction of the P.R.S.l. system, of several denominations of Social Insurance stamps.

The telephone service, which included the installation of telephones, and the provision of telephone exchange working, was also the function of the Post Office until transferred to Telecom Éireann in the mid 1960's. The payment of various pensions such as Old Age Pensions, Widows' Pensions, Widowers' Pensions, Retirement Pensions, etc., and Children's Allowances, was another of the functions of the Post Office. Other Social Welfare benefits, for example, Unemployment Benefit and Unemployment Assistance, were payable at a large number of post offices.

The issue and payment of postal orders and money orders was still another sole function of the Post Office. As regards the payment of money orders, it is worth mentioning that during the years 1939 to 1945 mail services between Ireland and England were very uncertain due to war restrictions. This was a period during which a large number of Irish workers emigrated to England, and these found that the best way of sending home money to their Families was by the Telegraph Money Order (T.M.O.) services.

These T.M.Os were transmitted by the Morse code system, and it was nothing unusual for Kilmallock Post Office to receive two or three hundred T.M.Os over any weekend period during the years in question. The amount of money transmitted varied considerably from one T.M.O. to the next, but was usually from £3 to £10. The money order was issued on receipt of the T.M.O... and was delivered by hand immediately.

An interesting point worth referring to is the way things have changed in the Post Office service over the years. Up to the mid 1940s the cost of postage of an ordinary letter was two old pence. The present postage rate is now, in the year 2000, thirty new pence, which is the equivalent of six shillings of the old money. The postage rates in the old days were one penny for a postcard and a halfpenny for printed paper.

Up to less than twenty years ago all mails to and from Kilmallock were conveyed by rail. The bulk of the mail arrived into the post office between 11.30p.m. and 1:00a.m. The mail was sorted immediately, and was ready for despatch and delivery by 6.00am. The mails were despatched to a number of sub-offices such as Kilfinane, Bruff and Croom Up to early 1952 the conveyance of the mails to and from Kilmallock railway station was by donkey and cart, and the despatches to the sub-offices was by Pony and cart. In 1952 these services were replaced by motor transport.

The local delivery of mails in the period mentioned above commenced at 7:30 am. The means of delivery was either by bicycle or on foot. It is interesting to note that in the old days most of the Post Office bicycles were manufactured by Pierces of Wexford, the well known manufacturers of farm machinery.

Up to the mid1940s many rural offices had only three day delivery of mail - a Postman delivered to a particular area on Monday, Wednesday and Friday, and to a different area on Tuesday, Thursday and Saturday. In 1952 a six day delivery was extended to all areas. This however has since been reduced to a five day delivery there now being none on Saturdays.

One of the earliest records of the Post Office in Kilmallock goes back to the 19th Century. It was located in Sarsfield Street, in what was known later as Crotty's Licensed Premises which is now part of the Old Oak premises As far as can be ascertained the post office was operated by the Harris family. Some time in the 1870s the office was moved to its present location in Lord Edward Street, the new premises there having been built by the Harris family.

Kilmallock Post Office became a head office in 1902. The large Kilmallock Head Office District as it is known today, was finally established in the early 1920's. It embraced 42 sub offices, and still covers a large part of Co. Limerick and an extensive portion of North Cork. It extends from a point half way between Freemount and Kanturk to a Point near Ballyneery (between Bruff and Limerick city), and from a Point a few miles from Mitchelstown to within a short distance of Newcastle West. It is estimated that, in all, it covers an area of approximately 1500 square miles.

Tim Donovan started with the Department of P&T in 1935 as a Clerk in Kilmallock PO and went on to become Postmaster in Charleville where he retired in 1981.

KILMALLOCK

There was a big attendance at the Annual General Meeting which was held in the People's Hall, on Sunday the 10th October, 1954. The programme was heavy but all matters were dealt with satisfactorily and in the minimum of time.

Christmas arrangements were the chief topic of discussion and the Committee decided to submit to An Maistir Poist suggestions, which if put into operation this Christmas will undoubtedly ease the hardship which was experienced in previous years.

Wage Claim

The circular received from Headquarters setting out the position on the wage claim was read to the members. Disappointment was voiced at the delay experienced in bringing the claim to a conclusion but all were satisfied with the efforts of the National Executive in the matter and the hope was expressed that good results would shortly be forthcoming.

Welcome

We extend a hearty welcome to Donie Hayes, P.O.C.B., who has come to us from Athenry.

The Postal Worker November 1954

November 2004
Paddy Gubbins on his retirement with Noreen Lynch Manager Kilmallock PO

Paddy Gubbins with Tom McElligott. 2004

Paddy Gubbins with his Colleagues on his last day of service 2004

Hospital Co. Limerick. Circa 1890

MOUNTCOLLINS

THE POST OFFICE WHERE THE THREE COUNTIES MEET!

Mount Collins is located where the three counties of Cork, Kerry and Limerick meet. Serving customers from three counties required special diplomatic skills to maintain good business relations. One had to appear neutral, particularly when the All Ireland Championship started every year! Having a choice of teams to follow, you could change to another team when your favorites were beaten. You can imagine having three chances of success in both hurling and football. A dream for many fans!

Good old-fashioned country practices applied in that place and a remarkable thing like a man keeping his pension book on his head (under his cap!) was accepted behaviour. Likewise, a farmer buying a bull license for five shillings in the Post Office, while the inspector of animals was examining the bull outside the front door!

The history of Mount Collins Post Office can be traced back to when daily deliveries of mail were made by post boys on horseback and only delivered to the authorities' and 'people of importance.' The 1886 Postal Directory of Munster lists a woman named Mrs. Leahy as a grocer in Mount Collins and we know that she was also the postmistress. Known locally as 'Mama Leahy', she was born in 1830 and married Maurice Leahy from Knocknagoshel. They had a daughter, Hannah, and when Denis Naughton from Roscommon came as a member of the R.I.C. (Royal Irish Constabulary) to Mount Collins in 1891, he met and married her. As members of the R.I.C. were forbidden to have family connections in the area of their station, the newly married couple had to move to Tipperary. They returned in 1910 when Mama Leahy's failing health warranted full-time family support. This forced Denis to retire from the R.I.C. and he then became postmaster of Mount Collins until 1926.

An old character, Jackie-Jack Tom Lenihan, remembers collecting his grandfather's pension at the P.O. from Hannah Leahy He also remembers the big grocery shop and buying a half- quarter (two ounces) of Clarke's Perfect Plug tobacco for his grandfather at one shilling and three pence. Jackie also mentions the two postmen in the early twentieth century - Paddy 'The Post' Brosnan and Jack Murt Sheehan. Paddy collected the post at Brosna and brought it on foot to Mount Collins where a group of people usually waited for letters, especially from

America. Paddy 'The Post' progressed to a bike after some years walking and once fell off it and had to be brought to hospital in Newcastlewest on an ambulance known as a 'buggy,' which was drawn by a horse.

Denis and Hannah Naughton had a son Maurice, a tailor, and he married the red haired Joan Keane from Brosna in 1929. Maurice was Postmaster from 1926 until he died suddenly in 1953. Then his widow managed until she died suddenly in 1960. Their son Patrick took over the reins and ran the post office for over forty years. Patrick married Noreen Keane (another redhead) and they have a family of four - the fifth generation to grow up in Mount Collins PO.

One Children's Allowance morning, Patrick and Noreen were checking the newly arrived money remittance in the kitchen. With them was their little grandson and their very small dog. Suddenly two men with masks ran in with a gun, demanding the money. Reaction from the residents was very slow and Noreen even told them to "give it over" as their physique resembled two neighbours and she thought they were playing a trick on her! The little dog barked cheekily, adding more ridicule to the situation. Then when the little boy started to cry, Noreen told him not to he afraid because the gun was only a toy. Seemingly this was the last straw for one of the robbers because with a loud bang he fired a shot towards the doorway. They then grabbed some money and made off.

Later when detectives were examining the scene, they came across the bullet lodged in the frame of the door and nearby on the ground found the spent brass shell. Despite Noreen's best efforts to turn the situation into a pantomime - the robbers and the gun had been real!

Mike Hackett. Youghal / Postnews June/July 2004

Denis and Hannah Leahy Naughton 1911

Patrick and Noreen Naughton 2004
Photograph taken by Colm O'Connor

Charles Phipps

01 .06.05 — 25.06.93

(Entered) Cork Post Office 25th March 1924

Cahir Post Office 6th July 1924

Cork Post Office 23rd Aug 1924

Killarney Post Office 22nd June 1925

Thurles Post Office 15th July 1925

Cork Post Office 12th Oct 1925

Thurles Post Office 25th Oct 1925

Kilmallock Post Office 5th June 1926

Appointed "Grade B" 7th June 1926

Appointed "Grade A" 7th Oct 1936

Appointed "Overseer" 8th Feb 1952

Retired on Pension 1st June 1965

41 years 3 months service in Post Office.

Charles Phipps as a Telegraphist

CO. LIMERICK POST OFFICES

Adare P.O.

Abbeyfeale P.O.

Ballagh P.O.

Ballyagran P.O.

Castletown P.O.

Drumcollogher P.O.

Milford P.O.

Newcastlewest P.O.

Bruff P.O.

Frank O'Connor

Tullylease P.O.

Rathkeale P.O.

P.O. Photographs courtesy of Michael Rupp.

POST OFFICE SURVEYORS MILESTONES

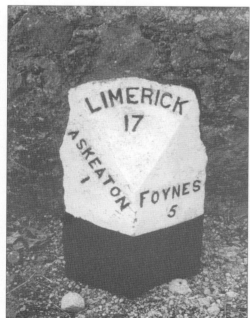

Courtesy of Brian Warren.

LETTER FROM GLIN DELIVERED AFTER SIX YEARS!

We have received from our correspondent at Glin, Co. Limerick (says the Irish Times) an item of news which begins:-

Field Marshal Viscount Kitchener, who was been motoring in his native Kerry, has brought his tour to a close, and before leaving the 'kingdom' paid a visit to Tarbert six miles from where his lordship was born 60 years ago. The paragraph suggests at first sight, either that Lord Kitchener is ubiquitous or that our correspondent is in error. The simple explanation, however, is that this item was fresh and accurate when it was posted in Glin on July 12th 1910. It was delivered at the 'Irish Times 'office in March 1916. The Post Office informs us that the letter slipped behind a partition in the Sorting Office of the General Post Office, where it lay for six years, and was only discovered during the present reconstructions in that department. It may be added that our correspondent had taken care to mark his envelope'New – Immediate.'

Kitchener

The above newspaper article appeared in the Limerick Leader, 13th March 1916, just a short time before Herbert Kitchener death. (1850-1916)

Post Office, Foynes.   Co. Limerick.

Post Office, Foynes. Co. Limerick

In 1935 by the Montreal Agreement, the governments of the USA, the UK, Canada and the Irish Free State ruled that all transatlantic aircraft would land at an Irish airport when travelling east or west. Foynes is today, as it was then, a small town on the south side of the Shannon estuary on the road from Limerick to Tralee. Its geographical position on the west coast of Ireland, its sheltered harbour with a long stretch of calm water and its railway connection to Limerick and beyond, which had existed since 1858, were all important factors which resulted in the announcement in the Irish Times, on 16 December 1935, that Foynes would be the European terminal for transatlantic services.

At that time, crossing the 3,000 miles of the North Atlantic with a worthwhile load of passengers or freight, and the large quantity of fuel required, represented a huge technical challenge.

Moreover there were few, if any, airports with runways suitable for the large and heavy machines envisaged. Therefore flying boats were the preferred option. By 1936, wireless telegraphy stations were under construction at Rineanna (now Shannon Airport) and Foynes.

Later that year, on 28 October, the first experimental radio messages were sent from Ballygirreen (near Rineanna) for the Gander in Newfoundland.

Imperial Airways "Mayo Composite". Composed of a short S20 on back of a short S21. This was a most unusual aircraft. On the 19 July 1938, 'Mercury' arrived under the command of Captain Donald Bennett. Shortly after the 'Maia' arrived flown by Captain A.S. Wilcockson. The crews were received by Lord Monteagle. The inventor of the 'Pick–a-Back' aircraft arrived as a passenger on Mercury. Shortly after arrival both aircraft were locked into one. The following day, 20th July 1938, the 'Mayo Composite' left Foynes with the first commercial transatlantic mail load. It set a new transatlantic record reaching the Newfoundland coast in 13hrs 29mins, and Montreal in 20hrs 20mins. It then continued to New York. The mail for this record flight was brought from the GPO in Limerick to Foynes, by Charlie Bartlett and Des Mulhall postmen.

Yankee Clipper

Spurred on by Juan Trippe, the dynamic owner of Pan Am, the Boeing Airplane Company had come up with a true transatlantic, commercially viable flying boat, the stunningly beautiful B.314 Clipper. On 11 April 1939 the first Boeing B.314 Yankee Clipper NC18603, flown by Capt Harold Gray, landed at Foynes. Just as Glenn Miller or Artie Shaw seemed more modern than the British dance band, leaders Henry Hall or Geraldo, so the streamlined Boeing seemed to epitomise the future rather than the more rounded shape of the Empire boats.

A romantic and nostalgic swansong or two remained. Charles Blair, having become famous not only as the husband of Maureen O'Hara but also as the owner of Short Sandringham Southern Cross N158C and of the last Sunderland ML814, returned to Foynes in Southern Cross in 1976 and 1977. While owned by Edward Hulton, the ML814 Sunderland made the trip to Foynes in 1989, renamed Spirit of Foynes.

THE IRISH PRESS, THURSDAY, JUNE 29, 1939.

CLIPPER'S PIONEER TRIP TO FOYNES

Taoiseach Welcomes U.S.-Ireland Mail Service

(IRISH PRESS Special Reporter.)

FOYNES, Wednesday.

THE first mail 'to be carried by air from the United States to Ireland arrived at Foynes at 2.54 this afternoon, when the Pan-American Airways' Yankee Clipper completed its first regular flight between the two countries on the North Atlantic Route.

An Taoiseach, Mr. de Valera travelled to Foynes to welcome the Clipper. Greetings and good wishes from President Roosevelt to him were conveyed by the oldest passenger, Judge Walton Moore, Councillor of the Washington State Department, who is 81.

Mr. de Valera was shown over the seaplane by Mr. Juan Trippe, President and General Manager of Pan-4merican Airways, who explained the .working of the Clipper. With him were Mr. Oscar Traynor, Minister for Posts and Telegraphs; Mr. J. Walshe, Secretary to the Department of External Affairs: Mr. an Leydon, Secretary to the Department of Industry and Commerce; Mr. T. J. Monaghan, Engineer-in-Chief to the Department of Posts and Telegraphs, and other Irish Government officials.

Mr. de Valera was also accompanied by his daughter, Maureen; Miss Kathleen O'Connell, his personal Secretary; and Capt. Sean Brennan, A.D.C.

GPO LIMERICK SORTING OFFICE DIARY

13. 6. 39 Notification received from an Riúnaí that the New York - Foynes Air Mail Service had been arranged to commence with a departure from New York by the Pan American Airways Clipper on June 24th. Mails due to reach Foynes about 6.30am on Sunday June 25th. Mails to be collected at Foynes by official van and forwarded to Dublin by first available train.

The first flight west-bound via Foynes will be made up in Dublin for despatch by the 9.30am train on Wednesday June 28th. The Clipper is timed to leave Foynes about 4.30pm on that date.

Future arrivals to be forwarded to Dublin by first available train, and P. ch. B. advised by wire.

Ppo. F. 11658/39.

23. 6. 39 Mr. J. Jackson Headquarter Staff arrives, and proceeds to Foynes to await Clipper arrival, and keep us advised regarding flights.

24. 6. 39 Foynes phones " Clipper held up
9. 20pm and not crossing owing to unfavourable weather.

11. opm. Foynes confirms crossing postponed for 24 hours.

25. 6. 39 Foynes reports " unfavourable weather
Sunday conditions at the dinae continue.
Noon. Further report at 11. opm "

25. 6. 39 Sunday 11. 0pm	Foynes confirms flight again postponed for 24 hours.
26. 6. 39. 6. 0pm.	Foynes reports. Postponement again probable. Further report 11. 0pm
11. 0pm.	Postponed further 24 hours.
27. 6. 39. 6. 0pm.	Foynes. reports "Clipper will probably leave tonight on Crossing"
10. 40pm.	Foynes reports Clipper has arrived at Botwood. from Shediac at 10. 5 pm Irish time.
28. 6. 39. 1. 45 am	Foynes reports Clipper left Botwood for Foynes at 1. 30 am Irish time.
7. 0am.	Foynes reports Clipper due at Foynes about 2. 30pm.
12 Noon	Foynes reports Clipper will arrive at Foynes. 2. 55 pm.
2. 56 pm.	Foynes reports Clipper arrived at 2. 56 pm.
	Mails met by official in charge of Mr. J.H. Anderson Asst. Supt.
	Owing to reception of visitors etc. mails not transferred to van until 3. 50pm. when van left for Limerick to catch 4.35pm train at Limerick for Dublin
	14 bags of air mail addressed Dublin.
4. 35pm	Mails despatched to Dublin

LIMERICK CHRONICLE, TUESDAY, JUNE 27, 1939
STILL NO NEWS
Yankee Clipper's Arrival
Has Not Left Botwood

Another postponement for twenty-four hours in the first east-bound mail flight of the Pan-American Airways flying boat, has caused a breakdown in the arrangements already made for the shipping of Irish mail on the first return flight of the Clipper, which was to have been made from Foynes on Wednesday night.

News of the further postponement was received at Foynes shortly after 8 o'clock last night by radio from Port Botwood, Newfoundland. The Clipper is still at Shediac, New Brunswick, which it reached after leaving New York on Saturday afternoon. Shediac is only 400 miles from Port Botwood. Fog is stated to be the cause of the delay. In a message received last night, however, the time of departure from Shediac was fixed at 3 p.m. (B.S.T.) to-day. This means that the Clipper should reach Botwood about 3 hours later, and spend only a short time there re-fuelling in preparation for the transatlantic crossing, which, according to the thrice-revised schedule of what is officially known as "Trip Number One," will be made to-night, Foynes being reached between 6 and 8 a.m. on Wednesday. According to the original schedule, the Clipper should have reached here on Sunday, and flown on to Southampton later in the day, returning to Foynes on Wednesday to pick up mails for the return flight to America.

NO DATE FOR RETURN FLIGHT.

In view of the postponements of the eastbound journey, it will now be possible for the mail to be despatched by the flying-boat on Wednesday. No official return date for the flying boat has been fixed, but the mail already posted for the flight will be held until it is ready to make the journey. Mr. States Meade, the operations manager for Pan-American Airways at Foynes, who has personal knowledge of the weather conditions at Shediac and Botwood, stated that he believed that the fog which has been holding up the flight since Saturday, will definitely clear within the next twenty-four hours, and allow the Clipper to start on its Transocean journey.

Mr. de Valera, Mr. Oscar Traynor, Mr. Sean Leydon and Mr. S. P Walshe have returned to Dublin, but are ready to come to Foynes again immediately the message announcing the Clipper's! Departure from Port. Botwood is received. The Army Air Corps 'Walrus" Amphibean also has returned to Baldonnel; but the Dublin caterers who were brought to Foynes to prepare the official Government breakfast to the crew and distinguished passengers of the Clipper are still standing by It was learned in Foynes this afternoon that no word had been received regarding the departure of the Clipper, which is due in the morning from Botwood.

S20 Mercury on the back of S21 Maia

GPO LIMERICK SORTING OFFICE DIARY

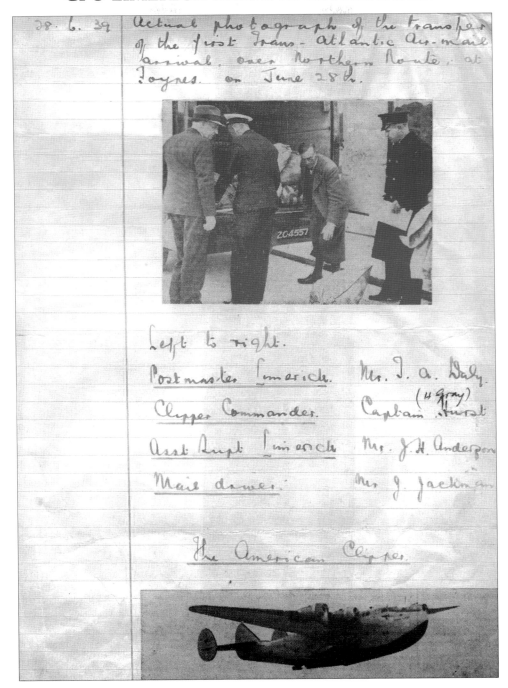

28. 6. 39   Actual photograph of the transfer of the first Trans-Atlantic Air-mail arrival, over Northern Route, at Foynes. on June 28th.

Left to right.

Postmaster Limerick. Mr. T. A. Daly.

(H Gray)
Clipper Commander. Captain Hurst

Asst Supt Limerick Mr. J. H. Anderson

Mail drawer. Mr. J. Jackman

The American Clipper.

7. 7. 39. Second Mail Crossing.
Notified by Radio Foynes that Yankee
Clipper would leave Botwood for Foynes
at 22 hrs. G.m.T. 8. 7. 39.

Mail will be met at Foynes on Sunday
morning the 9. 7. 39 at 11. o am
approx by Messrs Anderson & Looney

9. 7. 39 Clipper arrived Foynes 12.55 mm. mails (3 sacks) handed
over at Pier 1.55 mm. and despatched in one sealed bag
to Ra.Clinik at 2.0 by road. Drive J Jackman.
Foching Office advised by Service message.
Mr Jackman returned to Limerick 11.30 mm after
delivering Airs Mail at Rase H.S.O.

12. 7. 39. Clipper return journey arrived Foynes 6.10 pm and
left for Botwood at 8.30 pm. 3 sacks of mail
(one each for Newyork. S.Johns & Botwood) transferred
by Mr J.J. McCarthy — Drive J. Jackman.

23. 7. 39 Clipper arrived Foynes at 12.15 pm
mails handed over at 2 20 pm.
Pch B advised of arrival + disposal
of mails.
Four bags of Air Mails received.
Newyork Mail No 3 — IV.   29 lbs 12 ozs.
Moncton   do   454 grams
     do   Red Label   383 grams
Botwood N.2   7½ ozs.
Four bags of mails ex Yanka Clipper
opened + contents disposed of as per
instructions. Su to An Ceannasai
Pch B Dublin.
Two Way Bills four Letter Bills + two
special Regd Lists, bag & labels shewing
weight of each bag under cover with
appropriate correspondence for Dublin
                                        hence.

5.8.39 contd. Mails handed over at 6.45 pm

6.8.39 Radio Foynes wires at 7.30am — Anticipate arrival
of Clipper at Foynes approximately 9.30am B. S. T
today.
Mr Elliott POC A & Mr Mulhall driver left
for Foynes at 10am + returned 12.15pm -
3 bags Air Mails to Dn 12.45pm train

LIMERICK CHRONICLE AUGUST 8, 1939
"WE HAD A HARD TRIP."

Delayed By Winds

Atlantic Air Mail Service
Inaugurated

The Imperial Airways' 231/2-ton flying boat Caribou, inaugurating Britain's first air mail service, arrived at Port Washington at 9.27 p.m. (New York time) on Monday, having completed the 3,500 mile flight from Southampton in 36 hours 14 minutes. Delayed by head winds between Botwood, Newfoundland, and Montreal, she was two and a half hours behind schedule.

A graphic account of his flight, battling against a 41 miles an hour head wind—almost gale force—was given by Capt. J. C. Kelly Rogers, commandant of the Caribou, on his arrival at Boucherville. "We had a hard trip," he said. "We probably had the longest trip any transatlantic flying ship has made. We actually took 191/2 hours from Foynes to Botwood. That means we had only 891/2 knot average."

On the journey to Botwood the Caribou was flying completely blind in heavy rain for nine hours. It had to journey through for seven and a half hours.

Fine weather from Botwood to Montreal sliced nearly an hour off the flying time. The Caribou arrived 52 minutes earlier than was first expected, The reason was that Capt. Rogers cut across Maine, crossing the international boundary at Littleton and Caribou, the flying boat's namesake.

Mr. Howes, Canadian! Minister of Transport, and officials of Trans-Canada Air Lines, were at Boucherville to welcome the Caribou.

The Caribou's actual flying time for the complete trip was 31 hours 33 mins. Captain S G. Long, chief officer, said the flight was uneventful. Caribou flew for three-quarters of the way at a height of 1,000 feet, though once she went up to 12,000 feet to take bearings on the stars.

Caribou's landing after dark is believed to have been the first night landing by a trans-Atlantic commercial plane. She was guided by two rows of lighted buoys and two large floodlights.

19th July 1938
Crew of the Mayo Composite with its inventor Major R.H. Mayo.
L to R: Eric Hobbs, wireless operator; Captain. B.C Frost,
Captain A.S. Wilcockson, Major Mayo,
Capt. Donald Bennett; A. J. Coster. "Mercury" was flown by Captain Bennett.
'Mata' was flown by Capt. Wilcockson.

CURRENT REVIEW

People and Events

FROM ALL PARTS

They came from all parts to Foynes on Saturday afternoon for the inauguration of Imperial Airways trans-Atlantic service. There were cars bearing Cork, Kerry, Clare, Tipperary. Limerick, and, of course, Dublin index plates. The first thing that attracted attention in the village was the Irish and British flags fluttering in the breeze side by side. Gardai were directing the traffic and holding the approach to the jetty— sacrosanct place—with the tenacity of Horatio. To my mind the pleasantest personality in the whole group of officials was Mr. Danny Corcoran, in white peak cap, looking well and wearing an engaging smile.

The Limerick mail was loaded on the Caribou under the supervision of Mr. Jack Anderson without a hitch. That is only what one would expect from the Limerick postal staff, whose reputation for efficiency is not a thing of to-day or yesterday. The crowd at Foynes on this occasion was the largest that has so far assembled for observation or service - flights. Cars were packed from the Post Office out along the estuary road for half a mile. Every young person was armed with a camera, and not a few were fortified with binoculars Head gear was generally laid aside and dress was skimpy and summery.

Imperial Airways officers, in neat uniforms, were in evidence in the city on Saturday night. They were greatly pleased with the cordiality of the welcome given Caribou at Foynes, and spoke enthusiastically of the Shannon as an air base. No finer stretch could have been chosen, was the comment of one, and so say all of us. They were having a look round the city, where their forbears fought for mastery, but never vanquished the enemy. They have now come on a more peaceful expedition, one which will bring prosperity in its train to Limerick, whose star is rising in the international air link up.

GPO LIMERICK SORTING OFFICE DIARY

9.8.39   Foynes Radio wires — Caribou expected to
depart Botwood for Foynes 2200 GMT
10/8 . arrival Foynes will be sent later

Foynes Radio wires. Departure of American
Clipper Hythe to Foynes postponed until
1500 GMT stop time of departure Foynes
Botwood will be sent later.

~~Foynes Radio wires~~

8.8.39   Foynes Radio wires — American Clipper expects
depart Hythe for Foynes 1200 9/8 + depart Foynes
for Botwood 1700 GMT 9/8

9.8.39   3 air mails bags conveyed to Foynes by
Mrs J McCarthy PBC + Mr Mulhall (driver)
Plane arrived Foynes 8.5 pm
Mails handed over at 7.45 pm
One bag each New York, Montreal + at John's

11.8.39   Imperial Airways Caribou arrived Foynes 10.10 pm from
Botwood. 6 bags air mail recd and forwarded to Dublin 4.45 pm
Davey + driver J Jackman

12.8.39   Imperial Airways Cabot arrived Foynes
4.30 pm from Hythe..   3 bags.
Mr McCarthy conveyed mails to Foynes
at 3.30 pm + handed them over at 4.45 pm
plane left at 6.30 pm —
Davies Mr Mulhall

13.8.39   American Dixie Clipper arrived Foynes
at 12.30 pm from Botwood
4 bags mails. New York 1 Moncton 2
Botwood 1.
Mr Cantillon + driver J Hourigan
Mails conveyed by Motor Van to Dublin

Envelope, Canada air mail first flight Montreal to Foynes, 10 August 1939.
Air mail envelope stamped with flying boat on maple leaf and shamrock.
Envelope courtesy of Limerick Museum

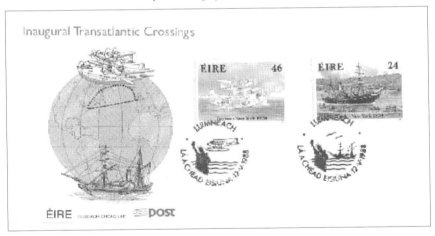

The First Day Cover Courtesy of Dermot O'Brien.
In 1838 the "Sirius" became the first steamship to cross the Atlantic. The stamp features the "Sirius" at Passage West, Co. Cork, at the outset of her historic voyage. The "Mercury" became the first airplane to cross the Atlantic on a commercial flight when it carried 1/2 ton of mail and newspapers from Foynes, on the west coast of Ireland, to New York in 1938.
Both stamps were designed by Charles Roycroft. The First Day Cover was designed by Anton Mazer.
From 1939 to 1945 Foynes, County Limerick was the centre of the aviation world, for air traffic between the United States and Europe.
Extracts from History Ireland.
The Foynes Flying Boat Museum, Foynes, Co. Limerick, The museum is open seven days a week, 10.00am to 6.00pm, between 31 March and 31 October.

Knockaderry Post Office

The Murphy's of Knockaderry sealed their last envelope this week after 126 years of providing the area's postal service.

For over 100 years, the Murphy clan have monitored all post from the west Limerick village.

On March 12, 1875, Edmund Murphy became the first postmaster of the newly opened office. He continued in the position until May 8, 1925 when his son Matthew Joseph took over the role. Thirty two years later, on July 15, 1957, the third generation of the Murphy family, Patrick J. took over as postmaster in Knockaderry Post Office. Forty four years service later, Knockaderry post office and the Murphy family have sold their final stamp...

Residents of Knockaderry have now to travel to Newcastle West, Castlemahon or Kilmeedy for postal services...

As well as the ordinary day to day postal services, the Knockaderry post office had also a telephone exchange in the past, growing from 10 to 100 lines coming into the office before it went automatic in November 1986, operating 14 hours a day, six days a week and even for a number of hours on Sunday,

One of the many highlights remembered was on February 24, 1998 when Knockaderry post office was granted the honour of having the first day cover of a stamp to commemorate Sophie Pierce, Lady Mary Heath, who was born in the parish. Lady Heath gained world acclaim throughout her life, making the first solo flight from Cape Town to London and being the first woman to make a parachute jump. This was a huge honour for a sub office. First day sales were as high as for any other commissioned stamp.

Through the years the post office has changed buildings, but only moving next door, making the switch in the early 1920's. The building they moved into was the old RIC Barracks and the post office was to remain there until the final bag of post departed.

Edmund Murphy first opened the post office doors. Later a grocery, and flour and mill store were incorporated. Edmund was a cooper by trade and continued to supply the butter boxes for the creamery across the road.

Edmund was postmaster for two months short of 50 years, and passed on his book of stamps to his son, Matthew Joseph, who continued for 32 years before Patrick took over until his own retirement in 2001.

Limerick Leader. 7th April 2001

Knockaderry's Sophie Remembered

The following story has been transcribed from an exercise book which Áine, Bean Ui Dhiolúin wrote for Teacher, Micheal Uas O'Conchubhair in the Technical School, Newcastle West in the mid 1930s, Áine is daughter of the late Joe Murphy, her source, who was present on the fateful night and Annie McEniry, Knockaderry Post Office. She is a regular contributor to the Nenagh Guardian ("Ann Dillon writes.. ") and is also a founding member of Club Ide, Nenagh's Club for older people of which she is the Secretary/Treasurer. She was also member of the National Council for the Care of the Aged for ten years.

"It was around the year 1800 that Dr. John Pierce came to Newcastle West from Tullamore on seeing an advertisement in a Dublin newspaper. At that time there was only one doctor in the town. Dr. Pierce turned out to be a very fine doctor and lived in the Square, (in the house which later became the Munster and Leinster Branch and is now the A.I.B. office)

The doctor married a daughter of a man named Locke, who was a relation of the Earl of Devon. They had a number of children, many of them doctors. Dr. Pierce died in 1860 and his son, George, took over. George married twice, first to a Miss Evans of Knockaderry and then to a Hewson girl from Ballybunion.

There were eight children from the first marriage and none from the second. Jackie, the eldest was the only boy. George's first wife died, circa 1889.

George was very strict with the girls — they were never allowed on the street. He married again, hoping his wife would help to look after the girls but that did not work out. Jackie was his only son and heir to the lands of Knockaderry, the property of his grandfather, Thomas D'Evans. He went by the name of Old Tom and he had a drink problem.

Jackie spent most of his time with Tom. He was full of tricks and pranks and his father - in the hope of civilising him - sent him to a bank in Kilrush, Co. Clare. Even here he did not settle down and the police were called in by the bank many times. In warm weather he refused to wear a collar and tie. When he appeared one day with a chain, fastened by a lock around his neck, the Bank Manager sent him home. After that he spent most of his time with his grandfather at Knockaderry House. Here he was like a clown or jester and his fun, games and antics kept the Knockaderry people entertained.

On the death of his grandfather he succeeded to Knockaderry House and Farm where he lived alone for some time. He put an advertisement for a housekeeper in a local paper. Kate Doolin from Kerry answered and got the job. She was a fine woman, thirty four or thirty five years old. Things went well for a while but Jackie was a hard man and he had trouble with his neighbours. He brought an action against his neighbour, William Power of Chesterfield, whom he accused of courting his housekeeper. Power brought a counter action against Jackie and the case went on in Dublin High Court in April 1895. Power was awarded £1,000 with costs for alleged slander. (It was William Power, Chesterfield, who with his sister Anastasia erected the high altar in Knockaderry Church 'to the glory of God in memory of their father and mother, sisters and brothers RIP').

On May 29th 1895 Jackie married Miss Doolin in a Dublin Registry Office. A baby girl, Sophie Catherine Pierce was born in November 1896.

Shortly after the birth of the child Mrs. Jackie Pierce was found dead in Knockaderry House and there was no trace of Jackie or the child. Jackie went on the run but he was eventually arrested and charged with the murder of his wife.

I often heard he could be seen with the child in a bag hanging on the handlebars of his bike. He was charged with the murder in the Day Room, Knockaderry R.I. C. Barracks (which is now the Post Office) in the presence of Sergeant Mongey, Constable Gaffney and Constable Boyle. Jackie was found guilty but insane and he spent the rest of his life in a mental institution.

Dr. George Pierce took Sophie to his home in Newcastle West and she was reared by her aunts. She was sent to St. Margaret's Hall School in Dublin and later to the College of Science where she graduated.

In early 1920 she met and married an English Army man named Elliott Lynn with whom she went to East Africa. She was very happy for a while but the marriage broke up. She turned to poetry and had many poems published in the press. She got involved in athletics and was world record holder for the high jump at four feet eleven inches. She was Vice President of the Women's Amateur Athletic Association. A book she wrote on the subject was published in 1925.

She had her first plane flight in 1925. She broke many records and a solo flight from Cape Town to London brought her world acclaim. She was also the first woman to make a parachute jump in 1926.

About this time she married Sir. James Heath, a wealthy industrialist but the marriage soon ended. She was married for a third time to Reggie Williams and they both flew to exhibitions on both sides of the Atlantic. In May 1934 she was fatally injured in a fall from a tram. Before she died she had arranged to be cremated and her ashes were to be taken in a plane and strewn over the Square in Newcastle West. The plane was to arrive at 12 noon and the ashes to be scattered over the houses especially over Pierce's house where Sophie had lived for many years.

Paddy Murphy, Knockaderry Correspondent, Limerick Leader.

Courtesy of Limerick Museum and Tom Keogh.

First Day Cover.
Courtesy of Patrick and Ann Murphy

Sophie Pierce, Lady Mary Heath

Chronology	*Event*
10 November 1896	Date of Birth
Dec 7 1897	Death of her mother, Teresa
1914 - 1918	Dispatch Rider, Royal flying Corps.
1921	Studying for B. Sc. at Trinity College Dublin (Married to Elliott Lynn)
1922	Legal Separation from Elliott Lynn
1922 - 1923	Took up Athletics, World Records, Published Book Athletics for Women and Girls
1925 - 1927	Published East African Nights (Poetry)
	Olympic Conference Prague
	First Flight London Light Aircraft
	Received Pilots A Licence
	Eighth woman to get Licence
	Instruction Alan Cobham
	Examination B Licence. Ban lifted on women (April) 1927 Her ex-husband found dead.
	June attempt altitude record with Lady Bailey 16,000 ft.
	July Flight around England
	First woman to win Open to All, Air Race
	October, second marriage to Sir James Heath, now Lady M. Heath

1928	November, sailed to Capetown with her plane in a crate
	1928 4.30 am 5th January, Capetown to London via
	Johannesburg, Pretoria, Nairobi, Cairo, Libyan Desert,
	Tripoli, Tunis, Sicily, Naples, Rome,
	Marseilles (Eight hours non-stop)
	Dijon, Paris, Le Bourget, Corydon 17 May 1928
	Women's British Sea Plane Altitude record 12,883 ft
	September return to Ireland, Renvyle, Galway
1929	Pilot with Amsterdam Airline, KL.M.
	Lecture Tour U.S.A.
	August, National Air Race at Cleveland Ohio, Crashed.
	After surgery, silver plate inserted in skull
	Divorce from Sir James Heath
	Married Reginald (Jack) Williams, fellow flyer 1933
	Returned to Ireland.
1925 - 1933	Instructor Alan Cobham performed Air Displays in
	Ireland, including Limerick in 1933

Newport PO, 1902

Left to Right, unknown, Creigh, Martin O'Donnell, John Hartnett, Martin Creighton, George Cullen, Women unknown, Burke, Paddy O'Connor, Unknown, and Women in window Mrs. Mary Humphrey's

NEWPORT POST OFFICE

Looking back on over forty years in the post office, the changes are too numerous to mention in detail.

During the war years the mail could arrive at any time, transported by a hungry horse and flat car (no one robbed the mail then). The postmen's cycles needed constant attention, tyres and tubes, in very short supply — many a swear was heard when a wheel was still flat after hours of make-shift patching and a bandage of binder twine. Christmas during and after the war years was hectic. A government permit had to be obtained to post a parcel to England. Permits were for fowl — but people admitted stuffing the inside with rashers, home cured bacon, whiskey and our native "Mountain Dew"

THE TELEPHONE: Two subscribers in '43. Ninety-seven when the telephone system went automatic in May '73. Continuous answering of the switchboard was arduous. However the late night calls were mostly for doctors. vets, priests and hospitals, and even though I got out of bed at all hours, there was a great sense of satisfaction in being able to help someone in trouble. I remember one Christmas Eve leaving the extension bell off accidentally. At 12.45 am, two repair-men were knocking to know what was wrong.... For that "slip up" I was fined £3.50. Helping out the older generation was always a delight. I got such thanks and praise for looking after a very simple problem and had many a good laugh too.

Inflation has hit the post office like every other business, and I had to be continually on my toes, reading up instructions to keep in line with the changing times,

STAFF: I had some very funny incidents two of which I will relate. Far back in the Forties, one Postman was huge, 6' 5". Two uniforms were applied for, one for the 'big" man and one for an average size. The parcel arrived one morning to find it only contained the suit for the smaller man. The big man (the seat of whose pants was wearing thin) looked over the counter and his comment was "Isn't it as easy to make a suit for a man as for half a man".

One evening after Christmas a temporary man was employed on the "four" post. He arrived back on his bicycle, wet to the skin, produced the carcass of a cooked goose wrapped in newspaper, out of his letter bag, which some kind person made him a present of for his supper. While he was leaving his bicycle down in the store, my assistant decided to hide the goose, dropping it into the mail bag. She persuaded him, that he had left the parcel on the window sill and that a dog ran off with it. While we were enjoying the joke, the mail car arrived, the bag was sealed in a hurry and the 9.58 was on its way to Limerick. No repercussions, someone else had a supper.

Many good men worked in the office — sad to say nearly all are gone to their eternal reward, some of them untimely. We were always a very happy family — treated each other as brothers and sisters, and to the few of us that are left with God's help, may we enjoy many years of health and happiness.

Newport News Publications 1984

N.H. (Nora Humphrey's)

Martin Creighton, Newport 1920

END OF AN ERA

Address of Michael Collins on occasion of retirement of Mrs. Nora Humphries from Newport Post Office, having spent 40 years as Postmistress.

The Humphrey's family have a long association with the town. Their Post Office has been a landmark in Newport for over eighty years. None of us can appreciate the amount of work which the running of a post office entails. Mrs. Humphrey was always courteous and friendly. The Post Office had that kind of atmosphere. There was always the friendly word and chat for everyone, even at peak hours on Children's Allowance and Pension Day. In the days before the telephones became automatic, it was quite common for Mrs. Humphrey's to be called from her bed at the most unseemly hours to put through an urgent call for priest, doctor or vet. This she never failed to do and she did it graciously.

There are few, if any, in this parish as well versed in the traditions and love of the locality as Mrs. Humphrey's. Her knowledge and love of local history is well known

Back in the Fifties she was the guiding light behind the Irish classes, which were held in the old school where the ball alley now stands. She has never failed to play a leading part in the Community Council, often ploughing a lone furrow in the Tidy Towns Campaign; it was mainly through her endeavours that Newport won the Nationwide Building Society award for the picturesque floral arrangement on the Mulcair's Bank a few years ago.

Harry Ryan, Michael Collins, Mrs. Nora Humphrey's, Fr. O'Keeffe, P.P. Margaret Ryan, and Bill Marnane. Postmaster Limerick Newport News Publications.

Now as she sits back and enjoys a well-deserved rest, she can cast an occasional eye across the Street on the new Post Office. We hope Mrs. Humphrey's will still enjoy many years of contentment and happiness and will continue her involvement in community affairs.

Jack the Postman

My father John (Jack) O'Neill was born in Newport in July 1920 and lived in the cottage down Church Road where the day care centre now stands. He was the only son of the late Mick and Katie, and brother to Bridie, Mary and Joan. He enlisted in the army in Cork in October 1940, where he met his bride to be, Kathleen Flynn. They married in Cork in 1943. When my father left the army in 1945 both of them moved back to the cottage. Times were hard for them but they managed. Their first son Michael was born, followed 12 months later by Ann. They then moved, and ran a small shop down the lane in the Main Street, during the war. Many more children followed. In all my mother had 21 pregnancies, sixteen of us are still living to-day.

In May 1946 my father joined the Post-Office, delivering mail in Killoscully, Rearcross, Tour, Ballyard and Birdhill, and for years he achieved all this on a bicycle. He became well known on his rounds and spoke highly of all the people with whom he came into contact. During his spare time you would find him sitting by the banks of the Mulcair River with a fishing-rod in his hands, enjoying the chat with other fishermen. His favourite place for a quiet drink was Madge Creagh's in Main Street whom he used to say was a proper lady. He often spoke of the many enjoyable evenings he spent there. Eventually my father and mother, with 6 children moved to a house in Black Road in September 1951. In the years 1962-64 their eldest daughters emigrated to America, but both of them had the pleasure of visiting them all in their homes in July 1977. The years flew by and. times got easier for them. We were like two separate families. When we, the youngest, were growing up, the eldest ones were gone out into the world. I will never understand, even to day, how my parents reared so many of us.

Sadly, my father died after a minor road accident in March 1981, but anyone who knew him, has nothing but good stories and memories to relate back to us. He was a man of value and many talents. He will never be forgotten and I hope that, we (his family) can live up to his name.

By Mrs. Teresa Daly (Daughter)

Newport News Publications 1998.

Killaloe Post Office

Post Master, Mr. Thomas Kelly.

The mail from Dublin arrives every morning at twenty-five minutes past ten and is despatched every afternoon at three. The mail from Limerick arrives every evening at a quarter past five and leaves every morning at eight.

Bassett's Directory 1875-6

Killaloe, Ballina and Birdhill Post-Office, Stamp Office

Post-Office

Post Mistress-Thompson, Ann

Letters arrive at 6.00 a.m. and 4.45 p.m.

Letters are despatched at 7.45 a.m. and 7.30 p.m.

Money Order Office and Savings' Bank

Stamp Office

Distributor-Thompson, Ann

Bassett's Directory 1880-1

Killaloe, Ballina and Birdhill Post-Office, Stamp Office

Post-Office

Postmistress - M. Hill

Letters arrive at 6.00 a.m., and 4.45 p.m.

Letters are despatched at 7.45 a.m., and 7.30 p.m.

Money Order Office and Savings' Bank

Stamp Office

Distributor - M. Hill

Bassett's Directory 1880-1

Cars

To Limerick - The mail car at a quarter before seven every evening form the Post-office

O'Briensbridge Postmaster

Walker, James; O'Brien's Bridge

Pigot's Directory, 1824

Birdhill Post Office

The Post Office in Birdhill was first operated by Martin Hassett. When he was granted a vintner's licence in 1890 he was obliged to give up the Post Office, which was handed over to his wife's niece, Mary Healy, Ballinteeno. She later went to Newport, leaving the business to her sister Maggie, in 1903, Maggie married Matt Hayes (coole) who built a fine house which served as the P.O. for almost 40 years (now Kelly's residence). They also bought a site opposite, from Gleeson, on which was built the store, which is now owned by the County Council. At the rear of this store was a well laid out garden where strawberries and apples were an irresistible temptation to a couple of generations. Hayes's also ran a shop with the Post Office, selling sweets, cigarettes, groceries and newspapers. For many years the only daily paper was bought by Charlie Going. The Guardian was more widely bought for 1d, the remaining $^1/_2$ would be held for your next visit. With the death of the Hayes's, Maura Herbert became Post Mistress and Kelly's bought the old Post Office as a residence in 1967.

Kevin Griffin Ballina/Boher 1988.

Killaloe Post Office

In June 1921, two Ballina men were before a Field General Court-martial at Limerick.

Michael Fenton, Roolagh, an assistant in Killaloe Post Office, Ballina, was charged with communicating, without lawful authority, information which might be directly useful to hostile persons, by making a copy of a telegram dated May 23rd, which purported to be sent from the Auxiliaries in Killaloe, preparatory to communicating it to unknown persons. John Kent of Ballymalone was charged with being unlawfully in possession of a telegram purporting to be sent from the Auxiliaries, Killaloe, and which might be useful to hostile persons.

Both men were found guilty of these offences. Michael Fenton received seven years, Penal servitude. John Kent was sentenced to one year in jail with hard labour.

Kevin Griffin Snr. Kevin Griffin Jnr.

Ballina / Boher 2000.

Nenagh Guardian.

The Christmas Box

A couple of months before I was born, my father got the position of postman in our village. The year was 1944; the weekly wages were thirty five shillings. As I was the youngest of ten children, it would amaze the present generation how we survived on a lowly wage. We were very lucky back in 1944 when we had no worries about large bills, as we had no car insurance, car tax, phone bills, ESB bills or a mortgage. We had all our own organic food, our own hens and chickens, eggs our own meat and we even got to sell a pig to buy shoes for the winter, as we went barefoot for the summer. In the early years my older brothers assisted my father with the Christmas rush. They would have to borrow my mother's "High Nelly" which was equipped with a fine basket in the front and a strong spring loaded carrier at the back. As years went by the older boys either emigrated to America or went in to service with the dreaded farmer. When I was about twelve years old it was my turn to take on the mantle of assistant postman at Christmas time. By then we were the proud owners of a lovely pony and trap.

Christmas week was the toughest week of the year in our house. Our day started at half past six. On a cold, dark December morning we had to be at the post office by seven o'clock. Normally the sorting of the mail was over by half past eight but at Christmas it could go on until noon or even one o'clock. At that time there were three postmen in the village. The Postmaster sorted the mail for the different areas and then the individual postmen would sort their own mail for their own routes. So you can imagine, it was nearly getting dusk before delivery would begin My father was a man who would only partake in a half pint of stout maybe after Mass on a Sunday or on a social occasion such as a funeral or wedding. So it was a big worry for my mother that he would get through Christmas week without any mishaps. For the first couple of days I used the "High Nelly" when I had to deliver to outlying places, like the Hill and the Bog and Ragamus or Fitz's of the Island. My father kept to the main route and hoped to catch the farmers or their servant boys at the creamery in order to offload a good deal of the mail to them. Later on in the week we changed our method of transport. I progressed to the post bike which had a large flat carrier in the front to carry the parcels and my father resorted to the pony and trap which carried the bulk of the letters and all the parcels Every now and then I met up with him to get more letters and parcels for outlying parts, as the route was 22 miles long. It was very important to get finished before dark as at that time the Guards were very strict on vehicles without flash lamps.

The second last day before Christmas the mail was the heaviest and it might be nine or ten pm. before we would finish. That was also the day when people began dishing out the "Christmas Boxes" in cash and liquid form, such as throws of whiskey. According to my father, the poor person living in the cottage came up with a half crown, the small farmer gave five shillings and the big farmer ten shillings if he felt generous. There was a big Stud Farm in the village and being the owner, an ex Captain of the British Army, and I suppose the local squire, always gave two pounds. More than a week's wages! So as you can imagine' the Christmas Box" was not just a tip for the postman at Christmas time. To our family it was the annual bonus which would go to pay off bills in the local shops and stores, buy our clothes and maybe a new boarded chair or put two new bonhams in the sty for the coming year.

On Christmas Eve we returned to the bicycles, but I was often sorry that my father stayed with the pony and trap because by Christmas Eve he was top heavy from all the glasses of whiskey and bottles of stout handed out by the people. I remember one night coming around Coughlan's bend. The bike went front under my father and it skidded along the icy road with my father after it. I tried my best to get him back on the bike but all to no avail. We were about half mile from home so all I could do was to prop my father up against the bike and stagger the rest of the way home, where my mother was out of her mind at this stage with worry, as at six 'clock of a Christmas Eve, she had not yet begun her Christmas shopping. There was no such thing as early shopping for Christmas in our house. After my father had handed over the days "takings" he would eat his dinner and retire to bed exhausted. I then had to don the oil coat and accompany my mother to do her late Christmas shopping. I will never forget those long Christmas Eve days and the burden a child of twelve had to endure.

So while you are relaxing this Christmas, please spare a thought for our brave postmen and women.

After Christmas our lives returned to normal. My father had his round completed by twelve thirty or one o'clock. He spent the rest of the day tilling his garden or helping neighbouring farmers.

Philip Lavery.
Carrowkeale Newport.,
Newport News Publications.

A Man from Bruff

J. D. Bourchier. 31st December 1921

Bourchier in Bulgarian costume31st December1921

A man from Bruff, Co. Limerick, holds a particular distinction—that of being the first Irishman to have been featured on a foreign stamp.

Born in 1850, James David Bourchier took a classical degree in Trinity College, Dublin, another at King's College, Cambridge and went on to teach at Eton.

However, increasing deafness forced him to give up his chosen career and almost by accident, he took a job with *The Times* in the Balkans.

His sympathies lay with the local movements towards freedom from 500 years of Turkish rule, and he became the confidant of, and counsellor to all the political leaders in the area.

He was particularly supportive of the Bulgarians in their 1903 rising against the Turks, and wrote of their plight and sufferings with great insistence.

The Bulgarians signified their debt to Bourchier by marking the first anniversary of his death in 1920, with a seven stamp set, a unique honour at a time when it was virtually unknown for a country to so honour a foreigner.

The Dawn. Issue No. 7.

The Closing of
Clarina Post Office

Clarina Post Office closed last December when Mrs. Muriel Bradfield retired as Postmistress.

Muriel's retirement brought to an end 113 years of her family's involvement in Clarina Post Office. Muriel's grandmother, Margaret Walsh opened a sub Post Office in Clarina in 1889. Prior to this, Michael Cusack was Postmaster in Clarina in 1886. He was also the local grocer and the Post Office was situated at Clarina cross, where McCarthy's house now stands.

William Hartigan was the next Postmaster in the same Post Office. He came from Croom and his brother was living at the Brick Lodge where Bill Davoren now lives. This William Hartigan was a great granduncle of Maurice Hartigan and Bill Davoren.

While the Post Office was run by Mr. Cusack and Mr. Hartigan, there was very little employment in the area and the local people were living in very poor conditions. The country was slowly recovering from the great famine, which ended just a few years previously, when one million people were forced to emigrate and another million died of starvation.

At first we had the Walsh family. Muriel's grandmother was Margaret O'Brien from Knockfearnea and she married George Walsh, who was born in Tuogh in Adare. Mrs. Walsh kept the Post Office going until her death in 1928. Her husband George died on Christmas morning 1926. Around the turn of the twentieth century the mail was delivered by pony and trap to Clarina. The driver pulled in beside the house and threw the bag of mail in through a specially designed window that would spring shut.

George and Margaret Walsh had four children. Bill worked in the shipping department of Ranks: Dick operated a garage in Thomas St, Limerick (he was Bob's father): Ruth worked as a clerk in the GPO in Limerick and at that time there were only three in total working in the exchange. Ruth later became Mrs. Hazelbeck. Finally, Louise, who married George Ruttle from Askeaton in 1905.

Louise 'the eldest, took over the Post Office on the death of her mother in 1928. So now the name changed to Ruttle. Louise or Lui as she was known, ran the Post Office until her death in 1956. Her husband, George, died in his 90th 'year in 1964.

George and Lui had four children. The eldest was Violet. She married Lionel Watts, who lived alongside the old schoolhouse across the road from the Post Office where Baz Miller now lives. Then there was Edith, who married Eddie Hartigan from Castleconnell. Ivan was their third child and he worked for many years with Western Electric Sound. Muriel was the youngest and she makes no secret of the fact that she was born in 1918. Muriel took over the Post Office in 1956 on the death of her mother. Muriel commenced working in the Post Office in 1934 and continued on for another 67 years until 2001.

Muriel went to St. Michael's Primary school, beside St. Michael's Church in Pery Square. Pupils are still going to this school today. She received her secondary education at Villier's School, N.C.Rd., Limerick. In 1962 Muriel married Frank Bradfield from Kildorrery in Cork. So now the name changes to Bradfield.

Frank Bradfield had no time for the shop or Post Office. He preferred the outdoor life of farming and loved caring for the animals. He also liked a pint and was very interested in sport. Way back in 1968 we here in Ballybrown were collecting money from house to house to pay for the G.A.A. field and clubhouse, but nobody called to Frank as they thought he would not be interested. One night I was watching a match at the hurling field gate when Frank walked up to me and gave his donation. He said "Ye must have plenty of money when ye don't go and collect it from the people'. Frank Bradfield died suddenly in 1973.

From 1973 until last December, Muriel carried on the business mainly on her own. Her first cousin, Bob Walsh assisted her from time to time. Bob was retired, having worked earlier in his life at Boyd's and later at Todd's in Limerick.

As well as running the Post Office. the Walsh's, later the Ruttles and finally Muriel carried out a general merchant's business, selling groceries, petrol, paraffin oil, coal, turf and animal feed. They had a horse and car and later a lorry that was driven by the late Jim McDonnell.

In the early years there were two postmen working in Clarina Post Office. There was a Murphy man from Tervoe who was one of the earliest postmen. Another combination was that of Mrs. May Nan Hartigan and Paddy Fitzgerald. May Nan took the job on the death of her husband. Jimmy Hartigan, Ballybrown, Secretary of Limerick County G.A.A. Board, is a grandson of Nan's. He also works for An Post, carrying on the family tradition.

Paddy Fitzgerald. Johnny's brother, was uncle to Frank and Gerry Fitzgerald. Later on then we had Jimmy O'Neill and Sean O'Shaughnessy. Sean was a noted

Irish dancer. He immigrated to Boston in 1956 and presently lives in New York. Sean is a brother of Seamus O'Shaughnessy.

In Muriel's tenure at the Post Office it was robbed on six occasions. It was also attacked in 1921 during the troubles. It is interesting that down the years the Post Office at all times was run by the ladies. This is just a short description of the Post Office during Muriel's family covering a period of 113 years,

which saw the Post Office change from a British - establishment prior to 1922, to what we call An Post today.

I know that each and every parishioner will join with me in wishing Muriel a very long and happy retirement. Clarina Post Office will be sadly missed as a focal point and a great meeting place, which it was down through the years.
Ballybrown Parish Journal 2002.

Muriel Bradfield Postmistress

Clarina Post Office 1930

Clarina Post Office 2001

May Nan Hartigan former Postwoman Clarina

Liam Hayes Ballybrown Postman since 1982

Jimmy O'Neill, Clarina 1969

EXTRACTS FROM REPORTS AND MINUTES IN ROYAL MAIL ARCHIVE

DRUMGEELY SHANNON

1965   SUB POST OFFICE OPENED MONDAY 5 APRIL 1965

1965
to   SUB POSTMASTER: JAMES PASCAL CLANCY APRIL 1965.
1967   13 JUNE 1967. RESIGNED.

1967   SUB POST OFFICE CLOSED TUESDAY 13 JUNE 1967 AND RE-OPENED THE NEXT DAY IN A CHEMIST'S SHOP IN FERGUS DRIVE SHANNON UNDER MRS KATHLEEN CASSIDY.

1969   FIRST ENTRY IN EOLAI AN PHOIST 1969 AS DROIM GAIBHLE / DRUMGEELY.

1986   REQUEST FOR THE RE-ESTABLISHMENT OF A SUB POST OFFICE AT DRUMGEELY, AS THE NEW SHANNON POST OFFICE WAS WAS REFUSED BY AN POST IN DECEMBER 1986.

NO POSTMARKS SHOWING 'DROIM GAIBHLE' OR 'DRUMGEELY' HAVE BEEN RECORDED. POSSIBLY THE MAIL WAS CANCELLED AT SHANNON AIRPORT.

FERGUS DRIVE, SHANNON

1967   SUB POST OFFICE OPENED 14 JUNE 1967 IN A CHEMIST'S SHOP IN FERGUS DRIVE, SHANNON.

1967   MRS KATHLEEN CASSIDY (d/b 26 March 1930) APPOINTED SUB POSTMISTRESS 14 JUNE 1967. [Occupation: Chemist] Fergus Drive.

1967
to   SUB POSTMISTRESS: MRS KATHLEEN CASSIDY
1972

1971	FIRST ENTRY IN EOLAI AN PHOIST.
1972	SUB POST OFFICE CLOSED ON 11 MARCH 1972 TO CO-INCIDE WITH REMOVAL OF SUB POST OFFICE TO SHANNON SHOPPING CENTRE, APPROXIMATELY _ MILE AWAY, STILL UNDER MRS KATHLEEN CASSIDY.

| 1972 | MRS KATHLEEN CASSIDY CEASED TO BE POSTMISTRESS SATURDAY 11 MARCH 1972. REASON: OFFICE CLOSED AND REMOVED TO SHANNON TOWN (CENTRE). MRS CASSIDY MOVED   WITH THE OFFICE. |

| 1973 | SUPPLEMENT NUMBER DATED NOVEMBER 1973 TO EOLAI AN PHOIST 1971 CEIDE AN FHORGHAIS / FERGUS DRIVE". |

1975	CEIDE AN FHORGHAIS HANDSTAMP (C'AN FHORGHAIS AN TSIONNA)
1978	IN USE 27 V 75
	6 V 76
	12 VIII 76
	6 V 77
	21 V1 78
	4 VIII 78

ADDITIONALLY, A REGISTRATION LABEL WITH HANDSTAMPED FERGUS DRIVE SHANNON IS RECORDED:

      12 August 76

SHANNON

| 1984 | SHANNON TOWN POST OFFICE COMBINED WITH SHANNON AIRPORT (ARRIVALS) POST OFFICE, WHICH CLOSED DOWN AT THE SAME TIME, TO BECOME SHANNON / SIONAINN, A NEW DISTRICT, DEPARTMENTAL COMPANY POST OFFICE IN NEW PREMISES, ON MONDAY 16 APRIL 1984. THE NEW OFFICE LOCATED SOME 50 METRES FROM THE PREVIOUS, INCORPORATED A LARGE SORTING OFFICE AND WAS ONLY THE SECOND NEW P&T DEPARTMENTAL POST OFFICE SINCE 1922. |

1984   NEW DEPARTMENTAL COMPANY OFFICE OPENED MONDAY 16
        APRIL 1984.

1984   BRENDAN SULLIVAN APPOINTED DISTRICT POSTMASTER 16
        APRIL1984. A native of Co Clare
        JOINED POST OFFICE 1946
            SKIBBEREEN
            CAHIRCIVEEN
            MACROOM
            SHANNON

1984
to   DISTRICT POSTMASTER: P J (BRENDAN) SULLIVAN
1989

1984   ANGELA HORKAN AND EDDIE BANVILLE WERE POST OFFICE
        CLERKS AT THE TIME OF THE OPENING.
1984   EOLAI AN PHOIST 1984 VOL.1 READS, "INSERT SIONAINN
        CO.AN CHLAIR - SHANNON CO.CLARE"

1986   SHANNON POST OFFICE ROBBED OF CASH AT 10.30 HOURS ON
        SATURDAY 16 AUGUST 1986.   £420 TAKEN.
        POSTMASTER: BRENDAN SULLIVAN

1989   P J (BRENDAN) SULLIVAN CEASED TO BE DISTRICT
        POSTMASTER MAY 1989.
        RETIRED. BECAME ASSISTANT TO HIS WIFE EILEEN, WHO WAS
        SUB POSTMISTRESS OF O'CONNELL STREET TOWN SUB OFFICE,
        ENNIS.

1989
to   DISTRICT POSTMASTER: MICHAEL REILLY
1992

1992   MICHAEL REILLY CEASED TO BE DISTRICT POSTMASTER... 1992.
        APPOINTED POSTMASTER OF CASTLEBAR. TOOK UP NEW
        DUTIES ON 8 SEPTEMBER 1992.

1992 to 1993	ACTING DISTRICT POSTMASTER: BRENDAN MALONE
1993 1993	THE DISTRICT POST OFFICE WAS LOCATED AS IN 1984. BRENDAN MALONE CEASED TO BE ACTING DISTRICT POSTMASTER in 1993.
1993 to 1995	DISTRICT MANAGER: CON KENNEDY
1995	CON KENNEDY CEASED TO BE DISTRICT MANAGER BEFORE JULY 1995.
1995 to 1997	MANAGER: TONY LOONEY
1997	TONY LOONEY CEASED TO BE MANAGER 1997.
1997	BRENDAN MALONE APPOINTED ACTING MANAGER 1997. PREVIOUSLY ACTING DISTRICT POSTMASTER SHANNON POST OFFICE 1992 TO 1993.
1997 to 2000	ACTING MANAGER: BRENDAN MALONE

1997   THE CLARE CHAMPION
LAST POST FOR MAIL ORDER
SHANNON MAIL ORDER.
THE COMPANY, WHICH HAS BEEN STRUGGLING FOR
SURVIVAL THROUGHOUT THE 1990s, IS TO BE SHUT DOWN BY
AER RIANTA SHANNON WITH THE LOSS OF 14 JOBS.
28 November 1997

1998   THE CLARE CHAMPION
ANY ATTEMPT TO DOWNGRADE THE POSITION OF
POSTMASTER AT SHANNON TOWN CENTRE POST OFFICE WILL
BE STRONGLY RESISTED. THAT WAS THE MESSAGE FROM
MEMBERS OF SHANNON TOWN COMMISSIONERS THIS WEEK
AMID SPECULATION THAT THE RECENTLY RETIRED
POSTMASTER IS TO BE REPLACED BY AN INSPECTOR. 10 April
1998

1998   THE CLARE CHAMPION
.... THE COMMISSIONERS WROTE TO THE HEAD POST
OFFICE IN LIMERICK LAST MONTH TO EXPRESS CONCERN
ABOUT ANY POSSIBLE DOWNGRADING OF THE SHANNON
TOWN CENTRE POST OFFICE. RESPONDING TO THE LETTER,
ACTING HEAD POSTMASTER PAT CARROLL SAID THE ISSUE
HAD BEEN REMITTED TO CORK. ... 8 May 1998

1998   TONY LOONEY MANAGER IN DECEMBER 1998

1999   "PADDY CARROLL ACTING HEAD POSTMASTER FOR THE
DISTRICT ..... " [The Clare Champion 5 November 1999]
Note: Incorrect - he was HPM Limerick not Shannon.

1999   "PAT O'CARROLL HEAD POSTMASTER..... "
[The Clare Champion 10 December 1999]
Note: Incorrect – Pat Carroll was HPM Limerick not Shannon.

2000 TIM O'CONNOR APPOINTED "DISTRICT POSTMASTER"
    JULY 2000.
    PREVIOUSLY AT:
    TRALEE
    GALWAY
    NAAS
    LIMERICK GPO (27 YEARS)
    The Clare Champion 28 July 2000

2000
 to MANAGER: TIM (TIMMY) O'CONNOR
2007 at least

2004 TIM O'CONNOR MANAGER IN OCTOBER 2004.

2004 SHANNON SORTING OFFICE MOVED BY NOVEMBER 2004 TO:
     UNIT 18B
     EAST PARK
     SMITHSTOWN INDUSTRIAL ESTATE
     SHANNON
     SHANNON POST OFFICE

    THE POST OFFICE ITSELF REMAINED IN THE SAME LOCATION
    AS IN 1984

2007 TIM O'CONNOR MANAGER IN MARCH 2007.

2007 THE POST OFFICE WAS LOCATED AS IN 1984.

By Tony Cassidy Ennis

ROYAL MAIL ARCHIVES AND ENNIS NEWSPAPERS

1900   WATERFORD AND LIMERICK RAILWAY. ENNIS TO LIMERICK
        IRREGULAR NIGHT MAIL SERVICE. LIMERICK AND ENNIS
        FORWARD PARCEL BASKETS, ETC., DEALT WITH IN THE
        SORTING TENDER WHILE IT IS STANDING AT THE LIMERICK
        STATION. that's all it says minute 27 July 1900

1903   LIMERICK TO LIMERICK JUNCTION S C (SORTING CARRIAGE).
        PROPOSED EXTENSION TO ENNIS & REVISION OF STAFF AND
        WORK IN SORTING CARRIAGE.   that's all it says
        ENNIS. PROPOSED RELIEF OF STAFF ON EARLY MORNING
        DUTIES. 77753. minute 24 Aug 1903

1919   THE SATURDAY RECORD AND CLARE JOURNAL
        An Ennis Newspaper
        CLARE RAILWAY OUTRAGE
        STONES PLACED ON THE LINE
        THE EARLY MAIL TRAIN FROM LIMERICK TO ENNIS ON
        MONDAY MORNING RAN INTO AN OBSTRUCTION ON THE
        LINE BETWEEN BALLYCAR AND ARDSOLLUS STATION, AND
        THE ENGINE SUSTAINED DAMAGE WITH THE RESULT THAT A
        SECOND ENGINE HAD TO BE OBTAINED. THE MAIL WAS FOUR
        (HOURS) LATE IN ENNIS. IT WAS FOUND ON INVESTIGATION
        THAT THE COPING STONES ON THE BRIDGE CLOSE BY HAD
        BEEN REMOVED AND PLACED ON THE PERMANENT WAY. THE
        EARLY MAIL WAS NOT CARRYING PASSENGERS AND NO
        INJURY WAS SUSTAINED BY THE DRIVER, GUARD OR FIREMAN.
        Saturday 13 December 1919

1920   THE SATURDAY RECORD
        An Ennis Newspaper
        ON FRIDAY NIGHT (17 December) THE GOODS TRAIN, WHICH
        WAS CARRYING THE MAILS FROM ENNIS TO LIMERICK, WAS
        RAIDED AT CRATLOE BY A PARTY OF ARMED AND MASKED
        MEN WHO EXAMINED THE MAIL BAG AND CARRIED OFF
        SOME LETTERS.

Saturday 18 December 1920
[an item appeared in the David McDonnell auction of Nov 1998 that had been posted and cancelled at Quin, Co Clare, stolen and opened, and subsequently sealed and labelled at Limerick on 22 December 1920]

1921   THE CLARE CHAMPION
An Ennis Newspaper
MAILS RAIDED. THE MAIL TRAIN FROM LIMERICK, DUE AT ENNIS AT ABOUT 4.30 am, WAS HELD UP BY A LARGE PARTY AT CRATLOE ON FRIDAY AND THE MAILS, INCLUDING ALL THOSE FOR WEST CLARE, WERE TAKEN. 26 March 1921
(This actually occurred on the 11 March 1921).

NOTICES TO POSTMASTER & SUB POSTMASTERS

CIVIL WAR PERIOD

1922   Parcels for Ireland
The following instruction is issued at the request of the Postmaster General of the Irish Free State:-
Parcels for places in the following counties should not be accepted until further notice:-

Clare.	King's Co.	Sligo.
Cork.	Limerick.	Tipperary.
Galway.	Mayo.	Waterford.
Kerry.	Roscommon.	

p299 British Post Office Circular 19 July 1922

1922   Mails for LIMERICK, ENNIS and CO.CLARE, are going today per SS "Edern" to Clarecastle. The G.S & W. Railway Company are sending a letter to their Stationmaster in Ennis asking him to provide a train service to convey bags of mail to Ennis, and, if possible, to some of the stations between Ennis and Limerick. The West Clare Railway is not working but the Postmaster, Ennis, is being told to arrange road services instead.

From (Irish) Postmaster General's Mail Report for 21 July 1922 detailed on P79 of Ireland: The Postal History of the Transitional Period by Dr Cyril I Dulin published by MacDonnell Whyte Ltd, Dublin, 1992

1922   On Sunday morning July 22 (1922), there was rejoicing in Ennis and district when it became known that the SS Edern had arrived in Clarecastle with a cargo of provisions. The boat had been chartered by John D Moloney MCC, P J McNamara UDC, Patrick Hogan and John Bredin of the Ennis Public Safety Committee and on board were 170 tons of provisions, 100 tons of beer and 378 bags of mail for Ennis and Limerick. When the boat left Clarecastle on the following Wednesday, it had on board 4 tons of butter, five tons of hide and skins, one ton of eggs, 738 empty beer barrels and 178 bags of mail. The SS Edern was, however, to pay another visit to the port at Clarecastle within a few weeks, and this time it had on board 1,000 barrels of stout and 30 tons of foodstuffs for Messrs Bredin of Ennis, who distributed the stout throughout the county.
Eamon de Valera & The Banner County by Kevin J Browne, Glendale Press 1982.

1922   Parcels for Ireland
The Postmaster General is informed by the Postmaster General, Irish Provisional Government, that non-perishable parcels for the City of Cork and for all places in the counties of Galway, Mayo, Tipperary and Waterford will now be accepted for transmission, but may be subject to delay in delivery. There is still no Parcel Post service to places in the County of Cork (other than Cork City) or to places in the counties of Clare, Kerry and Limerick.
British Post Office Circular 30 August 1922

1922   Parcels for Ireland
The Postmaster General is informed by the Postmaster General, Irish Provisional Government, that non-perishable parcels for the counties of Clare and Limerick may now be accepted for transmission. The notice in the Post Office Circular of the 30th of August is modified

accordingly.
British Post Office Circular 6 September 1922

POSTMASTERS ENNIS

1934   THOMAS A DALY APPOINTED POSTMASTER approx.. .
1934 (i.e. 18 Months prior to March 1936)
Previously:
included: Chief Superintendent Limerick 1922-1934

1934
to   POSTMASTER ENNIS: THOMAS A (TOM) DALY
1936

1936   THE CLARE CHAMPION An Ennis Newspaper
MR THOMAS A DALY, POSTMASTER ENNIS, HAS BEEN
APPOINTED POSTMASTER LIMERICK IN SUCCESSION TO MR
NORMILE (WHO) TRANSFERRED TO CORK SOME MONTHS
AGO. PRIOR TO HIS TRANSLATION TO ENNIS EIGHTEEN
MONTHS AGO, MR DALY HELD THE POSITION OF CHIEF
SUPERINTENDENT LIMERICK SINCE 1922.
Saturday 21 March 1936

1936   THOMAS (TOM) A DALY CEASED TO BE POSTMASTER .. ..1936.
TRANSFERRED BACK TO LIMERICK AS POSTMASTER OF
LIMERICK.

1936   THE CLARE CHAMPION   An Ennis Newspaper
SEAN O'CONNOR, POSTMASTER AT DONEGAL, HAS BEEN
APPOINTED POSTMASTER AT ENNIS. MR O'CONNOR, A
NATIVE   OF Co DONEGAL WENT TO DONEGAL TOWN FROM
LIMERICK ALMOST ELEVEN YEARS AGO.
Saturday 9 May 1936

1936   JOHN (SEAN) PATRICK O'CONNOR
        APPOINTED POSTMASTER ENNIS.
        Native of Dungannon, Co Waterford
        Previously: included:
                        .... Dungannon
                        .... Belturbet
                        .... Limerick to 1926
                        .... Donegal 1926-34
        COMMENCED ENNIS WEDNESDAY 15 JULY 1936.

1936
to   POSTMASTER ENNIS: JOHN (SEAN) PATRICK O'CONNOR
1950

1953   J. LAWRENCE (LARRY) O'NEIL APPOINTED POSTMASTER ENNIS.
        Native of Solohead, Co.Tipperary
        Previously:
          (first) Postboy ?   Limerick   1914
                   Postmaster   Ballinasloe   24/4/1942 to 18/5/48
                   Postmaster   Carlow   1948 to 1953
        COMMENCED ENNIS .... 1953.

1953
to   POSTMASTER ENNIS: J. LAWRENCE (LARRY) O'NEIL
1962

1965   SEAN LAVELLE APPOINTED POSTMASTER.
        Previously: Clerk   Longford Town
                         Supervisor   Shannon
                         Postmaster   Castlebar
                         Postmaster   Portlaoise
                         Postmaster   Shannon Airport
        COMMENCED ENNIS THURSDAY 15 APRIL 1965.

1965
to   POSTMASTER ENNIS: SEAN LAVELLE
1980

1980   SEAN LAVELLE CEASED TO BE POSTMASTER WEDNESDAY 7
        MAY 1980. APPOINTED POSTMASTER LIMERICK G.P.O. FROM
        THURSDAY 8 MAY 1980.

1989   JIMMY REAL TRANSFERRED FROM ENNIS TO LIMERICK WHERE
        HE BECAME HEAD POSTMASTER.

1991   FRED HOURIGAN APPOINTED HEAD POSTMASTER ENNIS.
        Previously:
        included: Assistant Head Postmaster Limerick.
        COMMENCED ENNIS .. NOVEMBER 1991.

1991
to   HEAD POSTMASTER ENNIS: FRED HOURIGAN
1992

1992   FRED HOURIGAN CEASED TO BE HEAD POSTMASTER IN ENNIS
        ON FRIDAY 11 SEPTEMBER 1992. APPOINTED HEAD
        POSTMASTER LIMERICK, COMMENCING MONDAY 14
        SEPTEMBER 1992. [Retired from Limerick in Summer 1996]

1996   DES HORGAN APPOINTED DISTRICT MANAGER ENNIS
        Previously:
        included:.   Post Office Clerk   Limerick
                            Postmaster   Donegal
                            Postmaster   Athlone
                COMMENCED ENNIS 1 APRIL 1996.

Tony Kennedy

EXTRACTS FROM REPORTS AND MINUTES IN ROYAL MAIL ARCHIVE

LIMERICK TO KILRUSH AND KILKEE   SUMMER MAIL SERVICE.

1832 VOL3 P308 N693	KILRUSH TO KILKEE EXPERIMENTAL PENNY POST. "SMALL BRANCH POST" APPLICATION FROM DR. MASSY. KILKEE STATED TO BE A THRIVING BATHING PLACE MUCH FREQUENTED BY THE INHABITANTS OF LIMERICK. 8 BRITISH MILES FROM KILRUSH. Minute approved 25 Oct 1832
1833	PENNY POST BETWEEN KILRUSH AND KILKEE 6MILES, 6FURLONGS ESTABLISHED ON 22 JUNE 1833. First Report from the Select Committee on Postage 1838 - Appendix 24 Revenue from Penny Postage, Ireland March 1838
1838	THE MAIL BETWEEN KILRUSH AND KILKEE WAS LISTED AS A FOOT POST. Second Report from the Select Committee on Postage 1838 - Appendix 53 Return, in Detail, showing the present Rates of conveying the Mails. July 1838.
1842 VOL12 P572 N213	KILRUSH & KILKEE HORSE POST DISCONTINUED. BECAME KILRUSH - KILKEE FOOT MESSENGER. (HORSE POST WOULD COST £29) Minute approved 19 Feb 1842
1843 VOL13 P72 N347	KILRUSH & KILKEE. MR. O'DWYER'S OFFER TO CONTINUE HORSE POST (at £20 p.a.) INSTEAD OF FOOT POST . "NOT TO ACCEPT" (i.e. not approved) refused 29 Mar 1843

1844 VOL16 P131 N713	KILRUSH & KILKEE MAIL CAR. AS TO PAYMENT OF GUARANTEE. Minute approved 25 June 1844
1844 VOL16 P282 N930	KILRUSH & KILKEE MAIL CAR. FOOT POST TO BE ESTABLISHED. WITHDRAWAL OF THE GUARANTEE FOR THE ADDITIONAL EXPENSE OF THE KILRUSH + KILKEE MAIL CAR. I SUBMIT THAT THE OLD ARRANGEMENT OF FOOT POST SHOULD BE AT ONCE RESORTED TO. Minute approved 23 Aug 1844
1844 VOL16 P538 N1303	KILRUSH & KILKEE MAIL CAR RESORTED TO. THE PRESENT FOOT RUNNER BETWEEN KILRUSH & KILKEE TO SUBSTITUTE A MAIL CAR FOR THE CONVEYANCE OF THE BAGS FOR THE SAME ALLOWANCE NOW RECEIVED VIZ. £20 A YEAR. Minute approved 2 Dec 1844
1845 VOL17 P196 N...	KILRUSH & KILKEE MAIL CAR. MR. WORRALL'S APPLICATION TO BE RELIEVED FROM PAYMENT OF GUARANTEE FOR. Minute approved 1845
1846 VOL17 P196 N...	KILRUSH & KILKEE MAIL CAR. MR. WORRALL TO PAY GUARANTEE FOR - BY INSTALLMENTS. Minute approved 1846
1848 VOL25 P278 N562	ENNIS & KILRUSH MAIL CAR. MR. WILLIAM'S TENDER ACCEPTED (Michael Williams) Minute approved 1 April 1848
1848	MAIL CAR CONTRACT WITH MICHAEL WILLIAMS FOR MAIL BETWEEN ENNIS A & KILRUSH DATED 12 APRIL 1848. Expenses Book of the Solicitor General's Office

1851 VOL30 P511 N858 KILRUSH & KILKEE. AS TO BEING SERVED BY A
          FOOT RUNNER.
          "IF NO PERSON CAN BE FOUND WILLING TO
          UNDERTAKE THE MAIL CAR SERVICE FOR
          THE SUM NOW PAID £20" ....
          "RESORT TO FOOT RUNNER."
          Minute approved 6 July 1851

1861 VOL4 P295 N931 KILRUSH AND KILKEE. ESTABLISHMENT OF A
          SECOND DELIVERY AND DESPATCH VIA
          LIMERICK & FOYNES RAILWAY.
          Minute approved 2 Aug 1861

1861   THE CLARE JOURNAL
          An Ennis Newspaper
          THE DAY MAIL FROM LIMERICK TO KILRUSH +
          KILKEE VIA FOYNES RAILWAY AND KELPIE
          STEAMER WILL BE DISPATCHED FOR THE
          FIRST TIME ON THIS MONDAY.
          THE MAIL WILL BE MADE UP EACH DAY AT
          ONE O'CLOCK. LETTERS FROM DUBLIN FOR
          KILRUSH & KILKEE, ARRIVING BY MIDDAY
          TRAIN, ARE ALSO FORWARDED. August 1861

1861   WE ARE GLAD TO ANNOUNCE ON RELIABLE
          AUTHORITY THAT A MAIL BAG FOR THE
          CONVEYANCE OF LETTERS AND NEWSPAPERS
          TO AND FROM KILKEE TO LIMERICK DAILY
          WILL BE CARRIED DIRECTLY TO THE 'KELPIE'
          STEAMER AND FOYNES RAILWAY,
          SUNDAYS EXCEPTED.
          From "125 Years Ago" in the Clare Champion
          newspaper of ... August 1986

1863

KILKEE, KILRUSH. A MONEY ORDER OFFICE.
POSTMASTER HUGH HOGAN.
MAIL ARRIVED 10.45 am / DISPATCHED 1.45 pm
"DURING THE SUMMER MONTHS AN EXTRA
MAIL IS DISPATCHED BY STEAMER FROM
KILRUSH, BY FOYNES RAILWAY. ARRIVES 6 pm
LEAVES 9 am. THIS IS A GREAT
ACCOMODATION TO VISITORS TO KILKEE
DURING THE SUMMER MONTHS."
The Clare Almanack
Royal Mail Archives

1867 VOL13 P191 N947

(LIMERICK TO) KILRUSH AND KILKEE. DAY
MAIL SERVICE DISCONTINUED.   AUTHORITY
FOR PAYMENT TO RAILWAY COMPANY
CANCELLED
Minute approved 10 Dec 1867

1893 VOL63   N673

KILRUSH + KILKEE POSTAL SERVICE.
QUESTION OF IMPROVING.
MR MAGUIRE M.P. No.55879
"THE POSTMASTER GENERAL
WITH REFERENCE TO YOUR ANSWER TO MR
McGUIRE'S QUESTION IN THE HOUSE OF
COMMONS ON THE 10th ULTIMO I REGRET TO
SAY THAT IT APPEARS TO BE IMPRACTICABLE
AT PRESENT TO COME TO ANY
ARRANGEMENT WITH THE WEST CLARE
RAILWAY COMPANY FOR IMPROVING THE
POSTAL SERVICE TO KILRUSH AND
KILKEE ON ACCOUNT OF THE
UNREASONABLE TERMS WHICH THEY
DEMAND FOR THE CONVEYANCE OF THE
MAILS. THE DEPARTMENT HAS AN
AGREEMENT WITH THE COMPANY FOR THE
GENERAL USE OF THEIR LINE AS FAR AS

MILTOWN MALBAY, FOR A PAYMENT OF £350 A YEAR, BUT THEY HAVE GIVEN NOTICE TO TERMINATE THE AGREEMENT ON THE 30th SEPTEMBER NEXT AND HAVE DEMANDED A PAYMENT OF £1000 A YEAR FOR THE GENERAL USE OF THE WHOLE LINE AS NOW EXTENDED TO KILRUSH AND   KILKEE. UNDER THE CIRCUMSTANCES IT SEEMS INEXPEDIENT TO MAKE ANY FURTHER USE OF THE LINE THAN IS MADE AT PRESENT UNTIL THE TERMS OF THE NEW AGREEMENT HAVE BEEN FURTHER CONSIDERED.

"IT WAS HOPED THAT SOME ARRANGEMENT MIGHT BE MADE FOR CONVEYING, BY THE NEW LINE, THE DAY MAIL TO & FROM KILRUSH AND KILKEE, WHICH ARE ESTABLISHED DURING THE SUMMER MONTHS ONLY. THE MAILS ARE AT PRESENT SENT BY RAIL FROM LIMERICK TO FOYNES, THENCE TO KILRUSH BY STEAMER, AND THENCE BY CAR TO KILKEE.   BUT THE WEST CLARE RAILWAY COMPANY DEMAND A PAYMENT OF £125 A YEAR FOR THE SERVICE AND THE UNREASONABLENESS OF THIS SUM MAY BE GATHERED FROM THE FACT THAT IF THE MAILS WERE PAID FOR AT THE FULL PARCEL RATES LEVIED BY THE RAILWAY COMPANY, THE ANNUAL EXPENSE WOULD ONLY BE ABOUT £31 A YEAR. THE ALTERATION WOULD INVOLVE AN ADDITIONAL EXPENDITURE OF £117 A YEAR; AND THE CIRCUMSTANCES DO NOT WARRANT SO HIGH A PAYMENT, WHICH WOULD CAUSE THE DAY MAIL SERVICE TO BE CARRIED AT A SERIOUS LOSS TO THE REVENUE. UNDER THE CIRCUMSTANCES, THEREFORE, I SUBMIT THAT

THE USUAL SUMMER DAY MAIL SERVICE TO
KILRUSH AND KILKEE VIA LIMERICK, FOYNES
AND KILRUSH, SHOULD BE CONTINUED THIS
YEAR".
"IF YOU SO APPROVE, MR McGUIRE SHALL BE
INFORMED ACCORDINGLY IN A LETTER
PREPARED FOR YOUR SIGNATURE."
Minute approved A.M. 4 May 1893

Tony Kennedy

SIX ENNIS POSTAL OFFICIALS JOIN THE NEW ARMY

Amongst the number of those who have volunteered for active service are six officers from the Ennis Postal District, two Clerks and four Postmen. Three additional Clerks have, since the war commenced, taken charge of special telegraphic arrangements at distant Coastal Guard Stations.

For the relief of the families and dependants of postal servants now serving in the Army and Navy, a subscription list has been opened, amounts varying from one penny to one shilling being contributed by all grades of the service. The Ennis Postal District contributions amount to £2 weekly. The fund is chiefly controlled by Post Office officials in Dublin.

Ennis Newspaper 26/10/14

ENNIS POST OFFICE CLERK AWARDED MILITARY DISTINCTION

We have learned with pleasure that Mr. J.A. Hayes, Clerk attached to the Ennis G.P.O. who is at present serving in the Royal Engineers, has been awarded the Military Medal for bravery displayed at the battle of the Somme. He has received the congratulations of his Commanding Officer, Captain Gerard W. Williams, Royal Engineer who writes:-

"I congratulate you and feel sure that if you carry on as you have done that other and higher decorations will come to you. We are proud of you."

And so are his old friends in Ennis with whom he was most popular.

Ennis newspaper 14/8/16

Extract from The Last Farwell. by Patrick McNamara.

OIFIG AN PHUIST

UAIRE GNÓTHA
HOURS OF BUSINESS.

Saghas Gnótha	Laethe Seachtmhaine WEEK DAYS	Domhantaí & Laethe Saoire Bainc SUNDAYS AND BANK HOLIDAYS	CLASS OF BUSINESS
Postuíocht	8.0am. TO 7.0pm.	9.0am. TO 10.30am.	POSTAL
Telegraf	-do-	-do-	TELEGRAPH
Telefón	-do-	-do-	TELEPHONE

Postanna Isteach
INWARD MAILS

Postanna Amach
OUTWARD MAILS

Ó FROM	Am Seachada TIME OF DELIVERY	GO TO	Am is Déanaí chun Postála i gCóir LATEST TIME OF POSTING FOR		
			Leitreacha LETTERS	Beartán PARCELS	Clárathachta REGISTRATION
Laethe Seachtmhaine WEEK DAYS		**Laethe Seachtmhaine** WEEK DAYS			
		GENERAL DAY MAILS (ALL PARTS)	ordinary 7.0pm. Late Fee 7.15pm.	3. 0pm.	Parcels 3. 0pm. Letters 3.45pm. Late Fee Letters 4. 0pm.
GENERAL NIGHT MAILS (FROM ALL PARTS)	Letters 7.0am.	GREAT BRITAIN (via Rosslare)	ordinary 5.45. Late Fee 6.0pm.	5.45pm.	5.45pm.
	Parcels 8.30am.	GENERAL NIGHT MAILS (ALL PARTS)	ordinary 6.30pm. Late Fee 6.15pm.	7. 0pm.	7. 0pm.
		SUPPLEMENTARY MAIL (Dublin and North and East of Ireland.	8. 0pm.		
		CROOM	11. 0am.	11. 0am.	11. 0am.
		ATHLONE AND WEST OF IRELAND	3.0pm.	3.0pm.	3.0pm.
GENERAL DAY MAILS (FROM ALL PARTS)	Letters 11.25am.	FOR ENNIS and Limerick Dist.generally " 7.0am. local delivery	3. 0am.	7. 0pm.	7. 0pm.
	Parcels 3. 0pm.	" 6.35am. " 11.25am. local delivery	6.35am. 11. 0am.	11. 0am.	11. 0am.
		∅ Letters may be posted in late fee box at barrier on station platform up to 4.0pm.			
Domhantaí agus **Laethe Saoire Bainc** SUNDAYS AND BANK HOLIDAYS		**Domhantaí** SUNDAYS			
		* Letters may be posted in late fee box at barrier on station platform up to 9.40pm.			
NIL	—	~~NIL~~ ALL PARTS except S of Ireld	12. 40pm	—	10.30 A/n

TÁ EÓLUIDHE AN PHUIST LE FAGHÁIL I N-AON PHOST OIFIG.
EÓLUIDHE AN PHUIST (POST OFFICE GUIDE) MAY BE OBTAINED AT ANY POST OFFICE.

M.P. 543.

(3318).Wt.2683—373.500.10/27.A.T.&Co.,Ltd.

October 1927
Size 41.5x 33.5cm (17.6x13ins)

Symbols used by the Post Office

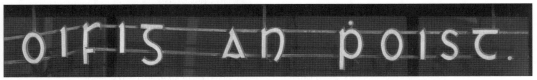

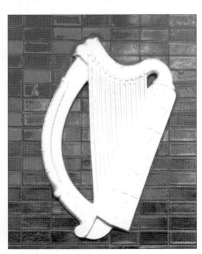

1794 PO Half Penny Coin

Cap Badge

Junior Postman's Belt Buckle

Arm Strap

Tunic Buttons 1920 and 1975

Tunic Badge Numbers

P&T Logo

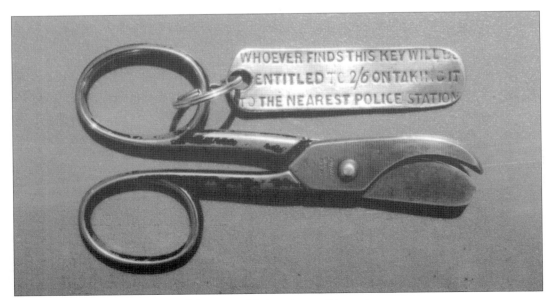

Scissors used for opening mail bags etc

M.P. 320

RABAÒ

ÒO ÒAOINE ATÁ AR FOSTÚ FÉN

Roinn Poirt aʒur Teleʒrafa

aʒ iompair nó aʒ seaċaòaò litreaċa, etc.

CAUTION

to persons employed under the

DEPARTMENT OF POSTS AND TELEGRAPHS

in the Conveyance and Delivery of Letters, etc.

Under the Post Office Act any person employed to convey or deliver a Mail Bag or postal packet in course of transmission by post is liable to a fine not exceeding £20 for any of the following offences, viz:—

For conveying Passengers in any Mail Cart or Mail Van without special authority.

For leaving unprotected any Mail Bag or postal packet.

For drunkenness while employed in conveying or delivering a Mail Bag or postal packet.

For carelessness, negligence, or other misconduct whereby the safety of a Mail Bag or postal packet shall be endangered.

For conveying or delivering any postal packet otherwise than in the ordinary course of Post.

For wilful loss of time when on duty.

7021. O.No. A17926H. 300/4/58. C. & W., Ltd., D.

April 1958 - Size 25x28cm (11.5x8.2ins)

Hand Stamps

SHANNON AIRPORT
TO
DUBLIN

2 D

Inward Foreign Parcel Section
Custom Section C. S. O

DELAY CAUSED BY USE OF
INCORRECT POSTAL ADDRESS

.... P To Pay

Initials:

ATTENDED TO		
In	By	On
Kardex		
Wages		
An Clar		
Capitation		
Insured List		
MP 496		
MP 385		
Cycles		

Franking Machine Logos

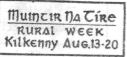

84

85

86

87

88

MAKE THE
ROADS SAFE

89

90

92

93

94

95

96

97

98

99

100

101

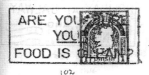

102

```
BIA GLAN-
BIA FOLLÁIN!
```

103

104

WORLD PLOUGHING
WEXFORD OCT 5-6
210

Visit The
CORK
STAMP EXHIBITION
Oct. 13th
211

6
MARCH
1974
NAVAN
212

MENTAL HEALTH
Your concern
213

Council of
Europe
1949 - 1974
214

DON'T MISS
SKIBBEREEN
WELCOME HOME WEEK
26th July to 5th August, 1974
215

VISIT THE
CORK STAMP
EXHIBITION
12TH. OCTOBER
216

KILL SHOW
(Co. KILDARE)
WHIT MONDAY
see you there !
218

18
MAY
25
JUNIOR CHAMBER
COMMUNITY WEEK
219

CONSERVE
ENERGY
220

Let your fingers
do the walking
Use the
GOLDEN PAGES
221

1
MAR
1976
NAVAN
TRADE
FAIR
222

GIVING
FOR
LIVING
223

WEXFORD
FESTIVAL
OPERA
25
224

26
KILTY
CENTRE
WEST CORK
226

Down with
high blood
pressure
Message
from the Irish Heart Foundation
229

COLLECT
POSTAGE
STAMPS
230

BLIAIN
IDIRNÁISIÚNTA
AN LINBH
1979
231

PLEASE SHOW
DISTRICT NUMBERS
IN DUBLIN
ADDRESSES
232

You've got to get
saving.
National Savings Committee
233

ARE YOU ON THE DRAFT
REGISTER OF ELECTORS?
CHECK NOW AT YOUR
POST OFFICE
234

NOTICE.

That there may be no mistake with regard to the Sale of Postage Stamps, I think it right to remind the Letter Receivers that this is the Day fixed by the Post Master General for the Public obtaining STAMPS at every Post Office at the *Fixed Prices,---viz.* One Penny and Twopence for the Labels, and One Penny Farthing and Twopence Farthing for the Covers.

The Post Master General will *require all Letter Receivers to keep a supply of Stamps by them.* They have already been informed, that they may obtain them from the *Post Office or the Stamp Office;* but that if they prefer the latter, they must give Notice to the Post Master General of their intention to do so.

All applications for Stamps to the POST OFFICE must be *made to me in Writing.*

R. SMITH,

Superintending President.

Twopenny Post Office,
July 1st, 1840.

Cruises Royal Hotel

ROYAL MAIL COACH HOTEL

ESTABLISHED 1791.

Hotel from Which Bianconi's Coach Started for Dublin
Courtesy of Patrick McNamara

Frank O'Connor. Copyright 2007